The Best of the Scotsman

The Best of the Scotsman

Edited by Ruth Wishart

Polygon

Edinburgh

Published by
Polygon
22 George Square
Edinburgh

Set in Melior by Bibliocraft, Dundee and
printed and bound in Great Britain by
Hartnolls Ltd, Bodmin, Cornwall

A CIP record is available

ISBN 0 7486 6196 4

Contents

Foreword

RUTH WISHART

For the fully qualified newspaper junkie there can be nothing more satisfying than being presented with a year's supply all at once. And nothing more frustrating than subsequently having to reduce such an enviable feast into publisher sized bites.

The difficulty, as you may well imagine, lay not with the selection of enough good journalism which could confidently stand the test of time but the agonising process of having to omit so many fine articles and interviews. Editing an anthology, I suspect, is a swift path to sobriety given the number of erstwhile jovial colleagues who may never feel constrained to buy me a drink again!

The news desk probably has most cause to complain, much of their work by its very nature having a brief shelf life. An exception to this was the material assembled by chief reporter Alan Hutchison, and Marcello Mega, on the background to the trial of Robert Black, the child molester and killer.

Sometimes, as with the award of this year's Booker prize, editorial demarcation lines would disappear as reporters, columnists, and our own feisty correspondents on the Letters Page worked themselves into assorted degrees of lather over the same story.

The Royals proved a constant source of inspiration throughout the paper with the possible exception of the *Scotsman* sports desk who have never seemed able to take polo terribly seriously.

On other occasions the worst of times could bring out the best of journalism . . . the tributes to the late John Smith, the commitment of relief workers in Rwanda, the inimitable dispatches of Michael Pye from America and James Meek in Eastern Europe.

Similarly, it was a year whose hallmark was the unexpected peace processes in the Middle East and in Ireland and the miracle of an apparently reborn South Africa.

There proved rich seams of humour in 1994 too, and, as you might expect of a paper like the *Scotsman*, immensely entertaining contributions on the arts. Graham High's superb draughtsmanship is well represented as is the wicked wit of pocket cartoonist Ian White.

All that and a clutch of award-winning columnists to boot. I hope you find the mix as irresistible in the reading as I did in the compilation.

Politically astute

The death of a premier in waiting

KEITH AITKEN

13 May 1994

Only in classical drama does tragedy bring resolution. In the real world, it brings confusion, disjuncture and void. The sudden death of John Smith, is, beyond dispute, a tragedy on every level: for his family and friends; for the party he led with such commanding authority; and for a country which has lost a politician of rare depth and vision in an age when such qualities too often come second to presentational slickness. It is in the way of politics, with its synthetic alliances and enmities, to laud the newly dead, but the reaction yesterday was strikingly different from the usual casual warmth. The gasp of dismay from the Scottish Tory conference on hearing the news was as sincere as it was moving: Ian Lang, not the most demonstrative of politicians, was among many of Mr Smith's opponents visibly shaken by the magnitude of the loss.

For Labour, the blow is simply devastating. John Smith towered over his colleagues. He was fortunate to inherit from Neil Kinnock a party which had finally learned the skills of cohesion and discipline, but it was also demoralised and despondent. Mr Smith could not and did not change that overnight, but he did provide Labour from the first with an asset which Mr Kinnock had failed convincingly to confer: a leader who looked unmistakeably like a Prime Minister. As Margaret Thatcher generously and perceptively remarked yesterday, he came into the job fitting it perfectly. Even those who disagreed with him (and he could be stubborn and wounding in an argument) never found room to doubt his integrity or erudition. The union leaders whom he took on and bested over party democracy at last year's conference bore their defeat without the vindictiveness other leaders might have provoked. There are very few contemporary politicians – indeed, it is hard to think of another – who command equal respect in the boardroom and the building site, yet that was John Smith's accomplishment. People who would never have voted for him held him in high regard. The harsh truth that none of his potential successors measure up to him in that respect requires the necessary addendum that neither does anyone else in the Commons. That is one part of the immense void he leaves in his party.

Social justice

Another is the synthesis of ideas that he represented. He was undoubtedly of the party right, yet he was not – in the sense that the term is used pejoratively – a moderate. There was passion beneath the pragmatism, and never far beneath. He saw, and articulated, a distinction between modernising policy and trimming principles. Like Donald Dewar, who is of the same mould, he would have been unimaginable in the Social Democratic Party. It is fitting that his last speech included a powerful advocacy of a policy that was never going to be easy to sell and that was unambiguously socialist – a national minimum wage. Social justice was a fixed theme in his speeches, and a goal which he saw both as being perfectly compatible with economic efficiency and as requiring no apology. It was instinctive in him, as it is in many of Scottish presbyterian background; and yet it also afforded the ideal binding with which to gather and hold the trust of Labour's disparate political elements. His successors may find it hard to bring off the same effect, but they will surely try.

Equally close to his political core, and to his vision for the party, was constitutional reform. He was, in the Callaghan government, a more eloquent defender of Labour's doomed devolution scheme than perhaps the scheme ultimately merited, and yet the scars of that experience made him all the more resolved in his determination to deliver a parliament on the Calton Hill. Instead of avoiding that prickly issue, as was Mr Kinnock's instinct, he built it into a wider programme of constitutional renewal, set within the context of a European Union in which he believed tenaciously. It was a programme that was beginning to shine against the backdrop of a Government grown sloppy and casual of the proprieties after 15 years in office.

Downing Street credentials

That sort of approach to policy will, if they have any sense, be Mr Smith's most enduring legacy to those who follow him.

Oddly, it also gave rise to perhaps the most telling criticism of his leadership. The policy review has lately begun to yield some ideas – for example, on attracting private capital to public investment – that are fresh, imaginative and credible. But it has not been a rapid process. There have been periods when Labour has almost seemed complacently content to win an election by default: to allow the Government's product to decay, rather than to market its own. It is also true that Mr Smith was a less powerful performer at the lectern or in the studio than in Commons debates, where he was formidable. It lent a slightly old-fashioned air to his leadership. He was a parliamentarian rather than a purveyor of stunts and sound-bites, an issues politician rather than a packaged personality.

Neil Kinnock, paying tribute yesterday, spoke of the anger that accompanied his grief. It is a just emotion. In less than two years as leader, Mr Smith had both established his credentials for Downing Street and laid the foundations of a politics that may last the Labour Party for decades. That he should have been denied the rewards is cruel. Others may yet reap them. Mr Kinnock showed the party what it could no longer afford to be. Mr Smith showed it what it could become.

A man of deep passion

EWEN MacASKILL

13 May 1994

John Smith was little understood by the London-based political corps. He was invariably portrayed as a dull, cautious presbyterian who was unable to raise either his own profile or that of his party. The common conclusion was that if he became prime minister it would be by default: it would be a vote against the Conservatives rather than a vote for Labour, portrayed as uninspiring, lacking any clear policy.

The misunderstanding was partly because Smith did not court the press. Most of the political editors barely knew him. He was seldom a metropolitan man. Each weekend he went back to Scotland and his family.

Smith was laid-back but it was not because he was lazy, as one paper said recently, nor was it because he did not know where he was going. His relaxed nature was a reflection not of complacency but of confidence.

From the day he became party leader in 1992, he had a clear strategy for winning the next general election. As far as Smith was concerned, there would not be a general election until 1996 or 97 and there was no point in raising his profile until about a year from the poll. Popping up endlessly on television, giving his views on anything and everything, would simply risk making him appear stale by the time election campaigning began in earnest.

A member of the shadow cabinet, confirming that view, said yesterday: "The media wanted an all-singing, all-dancing leader now. John knew when it would be necessary to provide a few fireworks and it wasn't now."

Smith happily cultivated an image of caution but underneath was a passionate and moral politician. On the Commons Terrace one evening last summer, dining with half-a-dozen journalists, Smith spoke about his plans for constitutional reform. The details were not new but what was new for many was the depth of his passion. For the first time, they saw that the proposals, such as an elected House of Lords, came from a deep anger about inequality in society, about the continuation of the class system.

The moral outrage came from the sense of justice and equality that were very much a product of his childhood in Argyll, education in Glasgow and adult life in Scotland. His speeches, especially at the party conference last year, echoed that and would have been as appropriate coming from a pulpit as from the podium. As the Liberal Democrat, Menzies Campbell, said yesterday he was a presbyterian but with all the virtues and none of the vices.

If Smith had won the general election, that morality, with its inherent radicalism would have ensured he would not have been the safe dull prime minister so many predicted.

Smith inherited the party from Neil Kinnock, whose reputation has been steadily rising as the extent to which he remodelled the party is appreciated. Kinnock himself had ended the in-fighting, at least in public, and pushed through the organisational reforms needed to make the party electable. But Kinnock himself was never able to persuade the public that he himself, as a former left-wing firebrand who moved to the centre, was trustworthy.

It was Smith, consistently on the right of the party throughout his political career, who made the jump, providing Labour with a credibility that put it 20 points or more ahead of the Conservatives in the polls. Even more surprisingly, the same polls put Labour ahead for the first time in almost two decades in two key areas: economic management and law and order, both of which the Conservatives had claimed as their own.

When Smith became leader, the debate within the party was between the modernisers, such as Tony Blair and Gordon Brown, who wanted to loosen the links with the unions, and the traditionalists, such as John Prescott. Smith was sufficiently astute to bridge both camps, though he leant more towards the traditionalists, particularly towards the union bosses such as John Edmonds of the GMB, who had campaigned for him as leader.

And yet, in the biggest test of his two years as leader, he found himself directly taking on Edmonds at last October's party conference over "one member, one vote" in Labour's conference. Until only hours before the vote, the result was uncertain. It was a rare public glimpse of Smith's determination, his readiness to take a risk.

The actual mechanics of "one member, one vote" were not as important as the symbolism of a Labour leader standing up to a union boss and winning. The belief was that it would make it more difficult for the Tory claim that Labour was the lap-dog of the unions. Subsequent polls showing the electorate losing their distrust of Labour suggest that he was successful.

But many of the other difficult issues were postponed, leaving a public perception that Labour had no clear policies. Smith's intention was that the party conference in October 1995 was to be the vital one, when specific policies would be unveiled on which to fight the next election. He believed the Labour Party in the run-up to the 1992 election had committed itself much too early to detailed policies, from defence to social issues.

The issue of proportional representation was thought by Smith to be irrelevant so he had it kicked into the future. He also sidelined debate on the future of the welfare state by setting up a Commission on Social Justice, but that was due to report later this year and the issue was set to dominate October's party conference. Similarly with the economy, the shadow chancellor, Gordon Brown, had an especially difficult brief because he was unable to speak in detail about either taxation or spending.

Smith's biggest political mistake was, when shadow chancellor, he announced an alternative budget in the run-up to the 1992 election setting out how the better off would pay more in taxes and the poorer less. It was disastrous, turning off both middle-class and working class voters, especially in the south of England. Part of the problem was that Smith, as a moral man, believed others would accept the justice of what he was proposing. He was wrong.

As leader, his tendency to take Labour closer to the centre of the political spectrum backfired over the European exchange rate mechanism in September 1992. Labour was unable to take full advantage of the fiasco because its policy had been almost identical to the Government's.

There are other disappointments, though Smith cannot be held to be wholly responsible for those. He did not halt the decline in party membership, for instance.

But as a parliamentarian, Smith was one of the best speakers from the Despatch Box in setpiece debates, using his wit to undermine opponents, not least John Major, who was often left isolated as his own back-benchers struggled to suppress giggles. But, surprisingly, he often failed to replicate such form at Prime Minister's Question Time, where he could find himself wrong-footed by Major.

In private, he had more of an open door than Kinnock. His private office was liberally filled with Scots but they did not set up impenetrable barriers. Any Labour MP was free to visit his office, where he or she would be given a hearing, though weak arguments would be met with short shrift from the intellectually tough Smith. He would sit down to dinner in the Commons with any of his MPs, even those who had recently incurred his wrath. He was well-liked for his banter and wicked humour, full of gossip about Westminster or recalling stories from his days in the Scottish courts.

Another characteristic was that he showed little interest in foreign affairs, making no trips, for instance, to Washington, though with a Democrat at the White House he would have been assured of a better welcome than his predecessor received from the Republican Reagan. For Smith, winning the election was central and foreign affairs were peripheral to that.

Just how important Smith had become to the Labour Party dawned on MPs yesterday as they speculated on who might replace him. There were groans from Labour MPs at some of the potential candidates because of the impact they would have on the electorate and fears over others that they might create damaging splits.

In the run-up to the last general election, Smith was livid over a column in *The Scotsman* predicting a Tory victory. He bet me a case of vintage champagne that Labour would win. I declined on the grounds of cost (and a friend of Smith's said later that he would not have comfortably found the money either if he had lost).

Smith often joked about it later. If he had survived, I would happily have bet on him becoming the next prime minister. It is a testimony to the man that none of those who will seek to replace him looks such a safe bet.

One of the best loved and most admired Scotsmen

RUTH WISHART

13 May 1994

There were those who complained occasionally about John Smith's energy. Shouldn't he be a bit more visible, be seen to be doing more to damage the Government? And then you wondered if maybe they all had a collective case of mistaken identity on their hands. John Smith was never anything other than formidably energetic.

A couple of weeks ago I popped in to see the family when he was bedridden with badly sprained ligaments. Typically, he was surrounded by papers, fulminating about missing the planned launch of Labour's local election campaigns. He hobbled downstairs to chat to Elizabeth and the girls but almost immediately switched on *The World At One* to catch Margaret Beckett. Then, he called his office in London to discuss tactics. If John Smith was idle in pursuit of success for his party it was a strange kind of indolence. He wanted power for all the unfashionable reasons ... to bring back equality of opportunity, to restore some of the virtues which underpinned his own unshakeable morality.

Ironically, it was John Smith, more than any other politician I have known, who knew exactly which basics he wanted his country to come back to.

They mocked his bank managerial mode at times; the overtly presbyterian tone of some of his speeches. But his beliefs were the rock on which he built his life and his home as well as his career. Almost uniquely in his trade he was beyond corruption.

I once asked Elizabeth why, after so many less than lucrative years in opposition, he continued to turn down the offers which came tumbling in from companies and institutions throughout the city. He couldn't possibly risk it, she said. He wouldn't know for sure how they conducted their business. Yesterday, the word integrity was used constantly about John Smith. And it was no accident that it sprang to so many lips.

But the commentators were also unanimous in suggesting that the Labour leadership had brought him no particular airs and graces; no inclination to distance himself from the friendly banter of colleagues, or his usual friends.

There were at least four good reasons why John never got ideas above his station. To Elizabeth and Sarah, Jane and Catherine he wasn't a former minister or a future prime minister. He was the man they teased unmercifully about his waist line; the man round whom they draped ever more outrageous ties to offset the obligatory pinstripe, the man for whom they bought jokey tartan boxer shorts to celebrate his first speech to conference as Labour leader. He wore them, too.

They would post less than flattering pictures on the fridge to remind him that snacking was not to be recommended for a man not ever built to be lean. When John had his first heart attack in 1988 there was a period when he became evangelical about calorie-counted food and even found low-calorie wine.

Happily for those privileged to share his hospitality it was a short lived phase.

He was the most hospitable of men. Several times in the last few years friends and family gathered for summer parties in his home to celebrate important birthdays in the girls' lives. The last was the best: a twin celebration last summer of John's and Elizabeth's silver wedding and Jane's 21st. The sun shone, the champagne flowed and John paid the most touching personal tribute to the family he loved more than anything else in his life.

They had a horrendous day yesterday. Dealing publicly with what for most of us is a private tragedy when we suffer similar loss. Later, they will take comfort from having had, as a husband or father, one of the most talented, but, more importantly, one of the best loved and most admired Scotsmen of his generation.

Taking the John Smith unrest cure

DONALD DEWAR

13 May 1994

All I can do now is remember John. The dispassionate, considered judgments are for other times.

The two of us hitchhiking from Glasgow to Guildford to hear Hugh Gaitskell at a Fabian weekend school. John playing football with a fearsome disregard for life and limb. The Fabians had seen nothing like it and said so. The game was abandoned. We must have been the only delegates gathered there to discuss the future of the party who arrived courtesy of an Ardrishaig fish lorry.

John being interviewed for an apprenticeship by a Glasgow law firm among deed boxes and legal probity was offered a position at a salary of £75. A week? asked John. A year, said the senior partner, and John left.

John charging round East Fife in the 1961 by-election, bringing the word of socialism to country towns that had no intention of listening. Backed by a mob hand of Glasgow students it was an experience that took me into serious politics and had for me incalculable consequences. John from the very beginning influenced others.

He had an enormous capacity for enjoyment. All the talk of the douce bank manager image was a nonsense. He was the most sociable of men. An evening with John Smith could be an unrest cure – a combination of Gaelic songs, gossip, friendship with interludes of intense and unexpected debate about anything and everything. The certainty was the evening would run well into morning. Those who threw in a careless thought were always liable to a brutal challenge with the ground being cut from under their feet.

He was a great friend to have and a man of infinite kindness. No reservations, no holding back. Loyalty was important to him and never one-sided.

John did not become president of Glasgow University Union. He could have done, but saw no point in it. He learned the debating trade because it was of practical use, but he was the last man to be interested in the trappings of power. No-one could ever accuse him of keeping up appearances. Pleasure never got in the way of his degrees or the serious business of learning his political trade.

Some things can be said about the man's politics. I heard a journalist hours after John's death picking on his consistency as though it were a fault. John had staying power. He was a very persistent politician. It was one of his virtues.

For John, a Scottish parliament was unfinished business. He made his reputation in the Commons wrestling the 1978 Act through a reluctant House only to find Scotland itself reluctant when the crunch came. Since then, much has changed. He was proud of the commitment which the party now has. He was strong in his support and, with some help from his friends, convinced the party that devolution was a matter of principle and never expediency. That argument has been well and truly won. The commitment is unbreakable and built in. When the day comes, I will think of him.

On Europe, he was no soft touch. I remember his irritation when, as Trade Secretary he first confronted the Brussels logjams. He knew Britain had to play a constructive part helping to drive and shape Europe's future. He was totally convinced Labour was the natural European party in British politics. For us, the Single Market could never be the be-all and end-all.

There has been a revolution in Labour thinking. It was right that in his last speech he reaffirmed his belief in Britain's European future. He has left the party in good standing with friends and with influence. Look back to the early Seventies, when John, as a young back-bencher, first defied the Whips, and you can see the scale of the achievement. He had courage.

Politicians have to be hard and John would walk through walls if he had to. He was never afraid to risk all if that was the right option. The one-member, one-vote clash at last year's conference was a triumph for his cool judgement and determination. He wanted the party to be electable: that was the essential battle which led to all else and he has made a great contribution to its winning.

John was once accused by a colleague of being the Brezhnev of the party. He was tough, well-organised and he did get his own way. He hated the scarring inequality he found in the country. He despised the politicians who decorated their speeches with reference to opportunity and hope but destroyed these when in power. He loved the Labour Party, which was for him the only vehicle for change. I've been asked if John had ever contemplated joining the SDP. The very asking of the question was proof the questioner did not know the man.

I have a menu, stained and dog-eared, of a Glasgow University Labour Club dinner I chaired many long years ago. It is signed by the two speakers, John Smith and Hugh Gaitskell: the link is too painful. Shortly after Gaitskell's death, the party took power and frittered it away. John has set the priorities and prepared the party for power in a way that suggests that disappointment will not return.

For his friends, the loss will be great. John was a man of worth and weight. A man who told the truth as he saw it and always stood by his friends.

13

Getting a grip at No 10

BERNARD INGHAM

16 February 1994

Since analysis is crucial to the formulation of any public relations programme, let us first examine the legacy which Gus O'Donnell has bequeathed to Chris Meyer who has now moved into 10 Downing Street from the No 2 post in our Washington DC Embassy.

Mr O'Donnell has been popular with the Parliamentary Lobby. He brought a certain calm to the relationship after my 11 increasingly turbulent years with Denis Thatcher's "reptiles". Mr Meyer arrives with an excellent reputation after his stint as the Foreign Secretary's spokesman in the Eighties during which he and I caused much pain to an unduly pious Canada during the 1987 Vancouver Commonwealth conference. Mr Meyer is a robust diplomat who has a lively sense of humour. The least of his worries is his relationship with journalists. It has always been good.

Instead, his problems lie with the Government, the Parliamentary Conservative Party and his Prime Minister in roughly that order. So what's wrong with the Government? I cannot subscribe to the view that it has run out of steam. It is not in the pockets of civil servants. Just ask them in the Department of Education and the Home Office, for example, where respectively John Patten has just reorganised the top echelon and Michael Howard displays considerable independence of mind, even from former Tory home secretaries.

But its 15 years in office *is* a problem. After such a long run, there is always a risk that voters will say it is time for a change. Not much – apart from the economy – has gone right since the speculators forced Britain out of the ERM in September 1992. In other words, the Government gets little credit for the subsequent fall in interest rates and latterly unemployment since its hand was forced.

It is also saddled with the consequences of boosting public spending commitments before the last election and the drastic cut in direct taxation during the 1980s. With the swingeing April tax increases to come, Labour is making a meal of its claim that the Government will take more from the average tax payer than did Denis "Tax until the pips squeak" Healey in the late 1970s. In short, it is harder, if not impossible, for the Tories credibly to claim they are the low tax party.

Labour leader, John Smith, is also trying to paint the Government party as a sleaze bucket into which an alarming spate of junior ministers and backbenchers – not to mention Tory controlled Westminster City Council – were poured by the media over the New Year. His aim – sadly aided and abetted by a procession of Conservative MPs since ex-Heritage minister David Mellor's dalliance with a "resting" actress in 1992 – is to destroy the Government's reputation for managerial competence, fiscal rigour and moral authority. Mr Smith probably cannot believe his luck.

Mr Meyer cannot do anything about the Conservative Parliamentary Party. Nor, as a civil servant, can he make up for the manifest deficiencies of Conservative Central Office which looks like taking a pasting – along with the party as a whole – at the local council and European Parliamentary elections in May and June. The Government's expected dismal showing is already spawning speculation that Mr Major may be challenged as leader of the Conservative Party in November.

Which brings me to Mr Meyer's other problems – the Prime Minister himself. Mr Major's collegiate approach to Government is contrasted unfavourably with the fiercely demanding leadership of the Thatcher years. He has acquired a reputation for never sacking anyone, however deserving. This has reinforced an impression of weakness stemming from a parliamentary majority of 17 – only a third of Lady Thatcher's lowest.

Mr Major is also hypersensitive to media coverage and opinion. This is a weakness because the media believe they can hurt him. Mr Meyer has somehow to persuade his new boss that a much more relaxed approach to the media would bring a double bonus: by appearing less vulnerable he would, in fact, become more powerful.

There is, however, something to be said for Mr Major. He has managed, more or less to hold his party together even though the Maastricht Bill effectively rendered his Government

15
•

a minority administration in the House. Given the movement of Euro-opinion over the last 12 months, British Eurosceptics might also give him the credit for exposing the Foreign Office's contradictions and exploding the pretensions of the ERM.

For whatever reasons, the economy is now growing and inflation is historically low. He has also shown much political courage over Northern Ireland.

So what do Mr Major and his Government require? First, discipline. I suspect that every minister who steps out of line in the future will get no quarter from the Prime Minister. The Earl of Caithness and Alan Duncan, MP for Rutland and Melton and a parliamentary private secretary, disappeared with the speed of light when they embarrassed the Government early this year.

A rougher, tougher cutting edge would help to secure the second requirement, assuming continued growth. This is a sustained period of ministerial competence. The Government cannot afford many more cock-ups.

Third, Mr Major needs to concern himself with recovering his prime ministerial authority. If it's accepted that the Tory Party cannot rid itself of its leader every time it panics without reference to the electorate then the Government's as well as Mr Major's most pressing need is for him to grow into power as distinct from office, with the economy.

Mr Meyer will best be able to serve his boss and Government if he can get a grip over the Government's presentational machine, persuade his prime minister to rise above the mundane, identify where he wants to lead us and then communicate the Government's firmness of purpose. There is already some evidence that he (Mr Meyer) is having an impact – with the Prime Minister seeming more robust. This needs to be sustained. Articulating longer-term goals and convincing people we can achieve them is much more important than worrying about the impression created by today's airwaves or tomorrow's fish and chips paper.

Madame Ecosse célèbre

DOUGLAS FRASER

3 June 1994

Startling yellow posters simply declare "Winnie for Europe". No surname. No party. Just Winnie. Only Churchill and Pooh Bear have managed such recognition. The bills are attached to her agent's Renault, from which a familiar voice booms across Dingwall. "Thish is Sean Connery shpeaking. Winnie Ewing ish an outshtanding MP for the Highlandsh and Islandsh. She's sho effective, the resht of Shcotland thinksh she's Shcotland'sh only MP."

Of course, Connery is still promoting Scottish Nationalism from the Coshta del Shol. Only his taped voice has made it to Ross-shire. Pedestrians look confused by hearing James Bond, while seeing Mrs Ewing wave regally from the car.

And that royal resemblance keeps coming back. At a ceilidh in Ullapool, a performer confesses to an unusual case of nerves: "It's like singing in front of the Queen." And a former opponent remembers his 1989 battle with Ewing for Europe's biggest constituency: "It was a bit like running against the Queen Mother – she occupies non-political space."

A Shetland journalist noted similarities with another female politician who enjoys similar name recognition. It was the withering contempt for one of his questions that brought Maggie to mind. The reporter has a point: there is also the absence of humility and the ability to appear an outsider battling against the system even when on the inside. Both women talk reverentially of their small-time businessmen fathers, and there is the use of the Royal "we". We are not, however, a grandmother, a point to which the Glaswegian mother of three returns with some regret.

This is, she says, her final fling at the hustings, after more than a quarter century of restless campaigning and political vaudeville. But back at Goodwill, their Moray home and HQ, her husband, Stewart, hints uncharitably that this farewell tour may be the first of many.

The campaigning bug will certainly be hard to shake for someone who basks in such a kenspeckle reputation. Fame has not withered Madame Ecosse, a name she was more than happy to adopt from the columns of *Le Monde* in the 1970s. In her eight-page campaign newsletter, Ewing's irrepressible smile and occasionally tousled hair appear no fewer than 27 times – and there are few 64-year-old women who would volunteer to be pictured in jogging gear, even for charity.

Talk of her fame leads back to the Hamilton by-election in 1967. The 37-year old criminal lawyer took on a 17,000 Labour majority in the governing party's Lanarkshire heartland, with the aim of cutting it to around 2,000. But she won, becoming the first SNP MP since 1945.

"Ever since Hamilton, I've been weel kent," she says. "I was thrown into world fame without ever having been in the press before. My life changed completely, and I haven't really had any anonymity in my life since then. I found that hard when I was young, though it's fine when you're my age.

"We've only had three rude signs so far this time. In Hamilton, I got a lot more than that, and in Caithness, I used to get spat at because I was against nuclear reprocessing."

During a "meet and greet" campaign stop in a run-down part of Alness, a transplanted Blantyre man tells her he voted for her back then. "If you meet anyone who voted for you in '67, they always tell you," says Ewing. "I suppose it's the feeling of having played a part in an exciting moment in history."

Her friends also remember the thrill. Jean Urquhart was a teenager who got to know Ewing before her election success, and now runs the Ceilidh Place in Ullapool.

"I don't remember anything more exciting than the Hamilton by-election," she recalls. "It was an extraordinary thing that this Scottish and glamorous woman was going into the House of Commons. It had all the atmosphere of risk about it. She was in shock, and when she went into Westminster, it was horrendous."

No-one, says Ewing, has ever been treated that badly in the Commons. "A chill ran along the Labour back-benches looking for a spine to run up," she quotes from an account of her arrival.

She still refers to her foes as "the Labourites," as if they were an ungodly Biblical tribe. The *Sunday Express* from the pre-political correctness era of 1967 describes the hostility: "She turned up in the chamber in a long, brightly-coloured pink, green and blue skullcap – bringing cries of 'Here comes Gypsy Rose' and 'Tell us our fortune, Winnie'."

The extravagant style has extended into pensionable age. Ewing usually drives a two-seat, open-top roadster, she is an enthusiastic singer at ceilidhs, and brightens up the douce environs of Easter Ross with a striking navy and white striped jacket, yellow rosette, navy slacks and slightly grubby training shoes.

How does this Glaswegian flamboyance combine with the High-lands and Islands reserve? Isn't she, well, one might almost say, a bit gallus?

Madame Ecosse flinches and responds sharply: "I genuinely like people. I'm an extrovert."

She recovers quickly. "My father was a great entertainer. I played piano for him in a concert party. He was the kind that had everyone cheering up when he came into a room.

"I don't remember being shy. When other people were shy, I used to ask why."

Her lone stance in the Commons continued until 1970, when she lost Hamilton. But she was back in 1974 with another stunning upset. This time, she was in Moray and Nairn, unseating Gordon Campbell, the Conservatives' Scottish Secretary. "This is the millennium," she declared with customary extravagance.

Having taken on the party's European portfolio, "which nobody else wanted," prime minister Harold Wilson the following year appointed her the SNP's unelected representative in the European Parliament. Direct elections were not until 1979, when she won the Highlands and Islands seat against the odds.

Yet still she was written off. When she stood again in 1984, Russell Johnston, the local Liberal MP, was a dead cert to beat her. But Ewing increased her share of the vote to 42 per cent, and went on to boost it to a thumping 52 per cent in 1989. That provoked a victory speech in pidgin Gaelic (she came last in the Mod's adult learners section in 1981, but is characteristically undaunted) and a march with her supporters into the Inverness sunlight led by a piper.

The secret of her success, according to one analysis, is that she splits her opponents' votes. In Moray and Nairn, she is up against the Tories. In the Western Isles, it is Labour. The other constituencies have personal votes for Liberal Democrat MPs. Only the SNP is a contender in all the areas.

Her other great asset is her hard work. Travelling 50,000 miles each year, she still finds the energy to harangue anybody who will listen on her pet hates and campaigns; Spanish fishermen, nuclear dumpers, Palestinian terrorism, timeshare operators, the arms trade, Gaelic, third world aid, a Highland University, a Dornoch rail bridge, endless battles for Euro-funding, and so it goes on.

Her style is to make waves, to huff and puff, stabbing the air, denouncing all-comers as absurd and ludicrous, firing off broadsides of outrage by letter and press release. There are still signs of the the indignant young woman of the 1960s, made both weary and impatient when the finer points of detail cloud the broad sweep of lyrically-waxed Ewing vision.

"Everyone has some reserve of affection for her," says one media commentator. "But she always does her best to obliterate that by harping on and on."

Yet the style appears to get results, or at least attention. Even Douglas Hurd thinks so. In an unwitting endorsement on the Ewing campaign video, he salutes Britain's only MEP to belong to neither Conservative nor Labour as a prize beater of the system. "Any system which is devised, Mrs Ewing will certainly beat it," says the Foreign Secretary.

All this is to forget that she is a nationalist. It is as if Madame Ecosse has become a one-woman political phenomenon, whose representation of the Highlands and Islands is barely linked to her political creed.

Yet she speaks passionately about the cause she has supported since, she once claimed, she was ten years-old and cruising down the Clyde: "The band started playing *Road to the Isles* and I think I knew then I was a Scottish Nationalist."

People have been educated into the meaning of Scottish independence, she adds. "They don't think we're daft any more."

So her final ambition is to be brought out of retirement to become the first speaker of Scotland's parliament: "I think I could keep them in order."

A dose of the old salt

EWEN MACASKILL

11 June 1994

John Prescott reached into the bookcase of his Westminster office, a turret that looks out over the Commons, and pulled out a copy of a toughly-worded pamphlet he had written in 1966 in support of the seamen's strike, *Not Wanted On Voyage*. It is a title that could be applied to his own life, in which he has so often been the outsider, the troublemaker they wanted to leave behind.

Proudly handing over the pamphlet, he laughs: "That could almost be my epitaph. Not wanted on voyage. This voyage. Any voyage."

It can be applied literally to his eight years as a lowly waiter on Cunard liners, when his union activities outraged captains and employers, at one point leading to him being threatened with mutiny.

And it can be applied to much of his time at Westminster. He had a poor relationship with the former Labour leader, Neil Kinnock. Prescott was seen as a relic from the old-style Labour Party; and Kinnock and the coterie of image-makers and advisers that surrounded him kept Prescott on the outside.

Prescott, brought up in the hard world of the seamen's union in the ports of Hull and Grimsby in the 1950s and 1960s, has kept battling on. Yesterday, he put his name forward for the Labour leadership contest. He will not beat Tony Blair for the leadership but he should give Margaret Beckett a close run for the deputy leadership. However, he would only take the post if it were combined with one of the senior economic portfolios, for example his present post of shadow employment secretary.

His most attractive quality is his straight-talking, refreshing in a Westminster world where even many off-the-record conversations are guarded. MPs who know him well describe him as warm, with verbal explosions usually short-lived. A friendly MP said: "Sometimes he is gruff but there is a hell of a human being there."

His weaknesses are identified as having "an unattractive chip on his shoulder about his working-class background" – he is one of the few remaining Labour MPs who left school at 15. He is seen as vain, susceptible to praise. And his outspokenness might be a liability in the middle of a sensitive general election campaign.

In spite of his image as Labour's *Incredible Hulk*, he is extremely bright, searching for new ideas and good at choosing talented advisers and bringing promising young MPs into his team – people like Brian Wilson, MP for Cunninghame North, who speaks highly of him. He has written pamphlets on a range of issues, from regional government to full employment. One of the key ideas of the last year was his, that public ownership of bodies such as British Rail could be coupled with infusions of private finance.

So, is the image as a bluff northerner something he keeps as a useful front? "No, I don't. It is my style, that I'm direct, aggressive. I think it comes from your trade union background, for God's sake. Even your style of delivery. I used to speak fast to stop anyone else getting in. If you were at a strike meeting, if you stopped for a second, like, they'd be in."

He added: "If *Spitting Image* develops that line of your personality, it sort of comes with you. If *Spitting Image* is to deal with you one way or another, I think I'd rather be the one belting someone than somebody belting me."

Prescott is portrayed in the leadership contest as a "traditionalist" standing against the "modernisers" represented by Blair, backed by close friend and shadow Chancellor, Gordon Brown. Prescott and Brown, both part of an economics team which includes Robin Cook, have a prickly relationship. However, Prescott has managed to reach an understanding with Blair.

Soon after the 1992 general election defeat, Prescott made clear his opposition to the red rose image-makers and the Blair-Brown camp which he characterised as the beautiful people. He went "ape", according to one MP, over Blair's apparent move towards the Clintonisation of the Labour Party.

This would suggest a poor relationship between the two. But a little known incident suggests otherwise and says much about Prescott. In the middle of the row about Clintonisation, the two drove to Hull to address a meeting and in the course of the drive, worked through their differences.

The risk in the contest for Prescott is that he receives a humiliating vote, one that will see him become an outsider again, though he is probably too valuable to Labour for that to happen.

Prescott, 56, went from school at the age of 15 to be a trainee chef in a hotel for two years, followed by eight as a steward on liners, serving drinks and meals. On one run, he waited on the former Tory Prime Minister, Anthony Eden, on a trip to New Zealand after Eden had been forced out over the Suez crisis. Prescott had joined the ship after being suspended by Cunard for "indifferent discipline" – union activity.

He went on to Ruskin College, Oxford, home of many union-sponsored students, and then Hull University before becoming an MP.

Norman Godman, Labour MP for Greenock and Port Glasgow, is a close friend and recalls many incidents from their days together in the ports of the north of England, some illustrating Prescott's toughness, others his humour. On one occasion the two squared up to each other after a row over a float for a May Day parade. Godman had gone to a lot of trouble to have a huge replica built of the Silver Cod Trophy, an annual award for fishermen. The two fell out when Prescott told him it did not look like "a ******* fish".

Godman said that after various exchanges: "I told him to come outside. He is not slow in coming forward. We were not bosom friends for a while."

Godman also recalls that Prescott once took direct action after a ship's air-conditioning failed in the crew's quarters. Prescott wandered round the first-class area with a thermometer, ostentatiously making the case that the air-conditioning was working everywhere else. Godman said: "The captain went apoplectic about this lowly steward." Prescott was threatened with a charge of mutiny.

As a politician, Prescott's high point came last October when he made a speech in support of John Smith and "one member, one vote" for party elections. The speech was a ramble but it came from the heart and every one knew what he meant. Even in interviews, he speaks quickly, skipping key words. But the sense is clear.

He was not close to the late John Smith but the two got on well enough, especially after that speech, in contrast to the way he was sidelined by Kinnock.

The differences between him and Blair are not clear. The left-wing label does not readily attach itself to Prescott. He is too much of a pragmatist to become trapped in ideological positions. He is happier with the term "traditionalist".

"Modernisers have a favourable ring about them, suggesting that you should be for the present rather than the past," Prescott said. "I would emphasise that traditional values in a modern setting are still relevant to a Labour government. I would emphasise what a Labour government did in 1945, bringing in full employment and a welfare system. I think those values of full employment and social justice will be my cry in this election."

The modernisers see Labour's links with the unions as an electoral liability. Prescott sees the Labour Party as a movement that includes the unions, but concedes there is a public perception about union power. He counters that the pendulum has swung too far away from collective rights. "Try getting a mortgage with a three-month contract. Unions can be a force for good. Sometimes they can be a bit daft," he said.

Both Kinnock and Smith promised legislation to set up a Scottish parliament in the first year of a Labour government. Can Prescott make a similar pledge? He points out that his pamphlet on regional government in 1982, subsequently adopted by the party, was the result of a request to him by the then leader, Michael Foot, to try to find a way of ending the competing interests of the Scots in favour of devolution and the north of England Labour MPs who were opposed. The pamphlet proposed regional economic agencies throughout England, with local government reform to follow, while the Scots went ahead with devolution.

"To be honest, whoever is prime minister, it is a commitment given to Scotland and, given the chance, we will carry it out immediately."

Prescott's room at Westminster is among the best of any MP, whitewashed and bright, windows all round the turret. On a shelf are Russian babushka dolls, each with the features of a senior member of the shadow Cabinet, with the leader being the biggest, the deputy the second biggest, and so on. If Prescott is successful in his quest, he will need to have a new set made.

Echoes of the past in moment of truce

SEVERIN CARRELL

5 September 1994

"New rules, different game," the RUC commander told the Sinn Fein man. The officer had been ordered to allow the Republicans their ritualistic demonstration outside the fortified police station.

A week ago, heavily armoured Royal Ulster Constabulary Land-Rovers, their engines furiously gunning, would have slewed across the front of Antrim Road Police station as soon as the Sinn Fein activists tried to set foot in their direction.

But last Friday, on the second day of the Republican ceasefire, about 100 men and women from across north Belfast were allowed to spread themselves in a line down the centre of the Antrim Road. Ten women pushed prams with them, a crude symbol of community resistance.

They had appeared suddenly in a series of cars, bang on 2pm, in a carefully orchestrated action designed to maintain the political momentum, carrying placards deploring RUC collusion with Loyalist terrorists.

The area, the Sinn Fein councillor Joe Austin told reporters, was the old hunting ground of Brian Nelson, the British Army agent in the Ulster Defence Association who was convicted in 1992 for conspiring to murder five Roman Catholics.

Nelson's case is seen by Republicans as proof positive that the British Government happily uses a variety of tools to quell their revolt, including using their agents to feed intelligence information to Loyalist gunmen.

But the demonstration was also a tribute to the unemployed Roman Catholic labourer shot dead 22 hours into the ceasefire, in a nearby quiet and wooded residential suburb, by the Ulster Freedom Fighters, a cover name for the UDA.

John O'Hanlon, 32, died from five gunshot wounds as he helped a friend of ten years to fix a car wheel, crouched on his mate's driveway late one evening, the car bathed in yellow light from the open garage doors and the last moments of dusk.

A quiet innocent with a three-year-old son, he was murdered simply to prove that the Loyalist were also big players in the guerrilla warfare game. The UFF was shoving a V-sign in the faces of the world, using Mr O'Hanlon's life.

On Tuesday, the Sinn Fein demonstration would not have been tolerated, but by Friday the IRA truce had changed all that – although it appeared at first that the army had yet to read the memo. They acted out the hardened responses of 25 years of violent confrontation.

Army Land-Rovers had screeched up immediately the crowd gathered. Soldiers and police spewed out across the front of the station, provoking a blunt expletive from a shocked watching journalist from Australian radio.

The soldiers, the RUC and their armoured vehicles just as suddenly melted away, leaving the demonstrators to carry on their curiously emotionless and mechanical ritual for the television cameras. This now, it seems, is the propaganda war.

In a neatly tied loop, Sinn Fein had brought together a man's violent death with state/terrorist collusion. Coming so quickly after its declaration of a complete ceasefire, this smacks of an opportunism, which diverted attention from one aspect of the story that the cameras failed to capture.

Outside the closed and neatly boxed world of the television screen and the politics of the paramilitary, life in Northern Ireland carries on, despite the scripted triumphalism of Gerry Adams's rally outside Sinn Fein's Andersontown Road headquarters on Wednesday.

Yes, we did remark on a noticeable lightness of step as people walked. Belfast was bathed in glorious sunshine, soldiers patrolled with a looser gait and faces did seem to be smiling a little more readily. Yet there were no street parties or celebrations anywhere in the city.

This was no Northern Irish version of VE Day. There was instead an extended pause, which hung in the air like a question mark.

An opinion poll of 1,000 people from across the province, published in Friday's *Belfast Telegraph*, illustrated in some detail how little the IRA and Sinn Fein are trusted, despite the masterful sophistication of their political coup on Wednesday.

Cynicism and doubt lay behind the lack of spontaneous celebration. Where London and Dublin demanded three months of peace before Sinn Fein could sit at their table, the people of Northern Ireland generally looked for 12 months or more.

Although the published statistics failed to distinguish in enough detail the different responses of Protestant and Roman Catholic, 46 per cent of Catholics believed the IRA should have to turn in its arsenal before Sinn Fein is even invited to negotiate.

This scepticism runs deep. Only small groups of militants from either side are taking to the streets. In a profound irony, not lost on the force nor many Catholics, the RUC is now under attack, from working-class Loyalists in the Protestant heartlands of Belfast, for oppressive policing.

On Thursday and Friday night, several hundred Loyalist women and children marched through Protestant streets just north of the Shankill Road. In a series of ugly and tense confrontations, police came under attack from a hail of firecrackers and the occasional missile.

Here were uncanny echoes with the Republican rallies. Exchange the location and the players, and the language, allegations and targets appear to be the same.

The police stood and took it all. As the man said, new rules, different game.

They became targets for a hail of firecrackers at Tennent Street police station. They danced away to the cackles of the crowd when the bangers landed at their feet, and refrained from charging down the crowd of women and kids who broke through their cordons.

Protestant politicians repeatedly complained last week that security force patrols had doubled since the ceasefire.

The RUC denies such accusations, but they underline a crucial point: working-class Unionists believe they have been secretly sold down the river by John Major.

As for many Catholics, before and now, the security forces represent the state on their streets.

"What are they doing here?" one woman furiously asked. "We're not the ones killing and maiming innocent people. They should be chasing those f***ing bastards in the IRA over there. What are they going to do now? Let them go?"

There remains another vignette barely reported outside Northern Ireland.

On Thursday evening, the day of the ceasefire, the Unionist

parties succeeded in postponing for 21 days a full meeting of Belfast Council.

In the council chamber, the full intensity of the mutual hatred between Unionist and Republican seemed to have spilled over when the Protestant councillors Fred Cobain and Nigel Dodds said the Sinn Fein's links with the IRA fatally undermined its democratic credentials.

That the mutual hostility exists is undoubted, but this posturing is also part of the game. The Unionist parties found themselves comprehensively outmanoeuvred by Sinn Fein last week. They had, and still have, no real response to the ceasefire.

That vote for an adjournment, one senior Protestant councillor told Joe Austin from Sinn Fein immediately afterwards, was an opportunity for the Unionists to grab a little publicity. Mr Austin and he spent 20 minutes discussing local football that evening.

Muffled mutterings mean reshuffle is as 'unclear' as mud

FORDYCE MAXWELL

25 July 1994

Extensive attempts to offer huge sums of money for information on what really happened in the Prime Minister's reshuffle have failed. The best we can offer is a secretly-taped conversation between his official driver and the Rt Hon William Arthur Waldegrave on his way to his first Cabinet meeting in his new job as Minister of Agriculture, Fisheries and Food:

"I don't want to (unclear) . . . well get off on the wrong foot, but is this going to be my regular car?"

"(unclear) . . . have you got against ladas then, sir?"

"Absolutely . . . (unclear) all, but (unclear) . . . it all, it's a bit, you know?"

"Better than the Trabant, 'innit – as Mrs S used to say."

"Mrs S?'

"Mrs Shephard, her wot's gorn to education. Blimey, strike a light, she was a little darlin'. Let me say this, she'd say, and orf she'd . . . (unclear) well go . . ."

"Excuse me, we can drop the cheeky cheery Cockney bit. I have been a minister before. Just get me to the meeting."

"Sorry, sir, some of the minsters like a bit of the old patois. Reminds them of being in a taxi, gives my advice on how to run your department, or the country come to that, an authentic ring."

'I'm quite . . . (unclear) capable of running my own department, thank you. Just get me there in . . . (unclear) . . . piece. God, what do I . . . (unclear) . . . know about farming and fishing and . . . (unclear whimpering noise) . . . food?"

"Is that a rhetorical question, sir?"

'Of course it's a . . . (unclear) question. Don't tell me you know all about . . . (unclear) farming. Only farmers know anything about farming and not even them half the time. And they tend to know . . . (unclear) about anything else."

"Ah well, sir, if you don't mind me saying so, I've picked up a wrinkle here and there in the course of my duties with several of your predecessors. Now Fred Peart . . ."

"Several? Don't drivers get promotion? What did you do to get stuck with the Ministry of Agriculture?"

"It's the war wounds, sir. That and a tendency to run over old ladies . . . Whoops . . . (unclear) me, close one there, never mind the hand signals sir."

"(muffled) . . . actually, I think she meant that particular hand signal for you."

"Not at all, sir, that's the all-purpose signal the locals have for Government ministers. But, bless me sir, old Fred Peart never let it worry him."

"Fred who?"

"A Labour man, sir."

"That explains why I . . . (unclear) . . . heard of him I suppose. Good, was he? Pressed the right buttons for the yeomen?"

"Very popular, sir. Of course, that was in the days when we set our own farm prices with an annual review. Then Jim Prior, Lord Prior as is of course . . ."

"Jim? Well, I'm . . . (unclear) Jim, Min of Ag."

"Oh yes, sir, very fiery chap he was too. Quite choleric at times. Used to worry me sick if he'd had one of those price review arguments with the farmers, he'd have a fit right there on the pavement."

"Price review?"

"We don't have them now, sir. No worries. It's all done in Brussels. Why wee MacGregor, I mean John MacGregor . . ."

"That's all right. He's gone completely. Call him what you like . . . (unclear) me, you have to laugh. I'd forgotten he'd been in the salt mines as well."

"Quite, sir. Most of them have. Take Mr Gummer . . ."

"No chance. How did the little . . . (unclear) get on?"

"Quite well for a little . . . (unclear) really. Give him a platform and he'd talk the hind leg off a donkey – or even a European commissioner. On and on and on he'd go, farmers begging for mercy. But he wouldn't stop."

"But did he know what he was talking about? That's what worries me."

"It doesn't usually worry Government ministers, sir, if you don't mind me saying so, of course."

"Well, it's worrying me now. Any tips?"

30
•

"Learn a few key phrases, sir. That's my advice. Baffle them with brains . . . (unclear) . . . liberty of taking a photocopy of Mrs Shephard's list. Here, try a few."

"Let's see . . . (long pause) . . . does every one start with: Let me say this?"

"She found it very effective, sir. Look earnest and soulful when you say it, then, wham, hit them with something like: Sheep quota allocation to producers in category 3c for the 1993 sheep annual premium is being dealt with as a matter of priority by my department . . ."

"You're very good. But . . . (unclear) . . . it mean?"

"Who knows, sir? But it seems to keep them happy."

". . . (unclear) . . . German demands will not be tolerated . . . we have the best beef in the world . . . scientific evidence supports everything my department has done . . ."

"There you are, sir. You're getting the hand of it in no time. Try a few more."

"The potato marketing scheme is a subject which we have considered at great length in enormous detail . . . (unclear) . . . got to laugh haven't you?"

"As little as possible is my advice, sir. These farming types like to think that you're taking their problems seriously. Particularly the Welsh, sir. Not a lot of laughs in the hills and valleys apparently. No jokes about praying in church on Sundays and on their neighbours the rest of the week. Watch out for the Scots too. Very touchy, pick a fight in an empty room as Mr Gummer used to say."

"I see. Well, we seem to . . . (unclear moaning sound) . . . here. Any last words of wisdom?"

"Don't do photocalls with animals. Very messy. All you have to do is make soothing noises and say that you're keeping matters under full and careful review. That should tide you over until the election . . ."

"Election! . . . (unclear for several seconds) . . . election!?"

"Sorry, sir, I forgot that Cabinet hasn't been told yet . . . but a few of the drivers were talking about it just before I left . . ."

". . . (unclear moaning) . . . election . . ."

"There, there, sir. Don't worry. It'll soon be that nice Gavin Strang's problem. Oh, and don't forget your camp stool, sir. The agricultural minister doesn't actually get a seat at the Cabinet table."

". . . (unclear sobbing) . . . election! With my . . . (unclear) . . . majority. Camp stool! (unclear fading groan and sound of door)."

"Goodbye, sir. Have a nice day."

Cultural Divisions

PRESUMABLY IT'S A FRINGE MEETING...

Returned to sender

MARCELLO MEGA

20 January 1994

Take three titles valued at anything up to about £25 for £1 each. Marcello Mega could not resist the offer but his book club membership has become a spine-chiller.

Ever wanted to terminate a membership when the club or its terms no longer suited you and found that it just would not let you go?

I'd heard of such things – people caught up with terrorist or other criminal organisations who "knew too much"; poor souls who had found themselves ensnared in some dodgy religious sect; a marriage gone wrong even.

Trying to walk away from all those can no doubt seriously damage your health. But a book club shouldn't be too complicated, I thought. More fool me.

Most will have seen the extremely tempting introductory offer for The Softback Preview in the national press. Take three books valued at anything up to about £25 each from a varied selection for only £1 each, throw in £1.99 for postage and packing, and receive membership with no obligation ever to purchase another title.

I eagerly filled in the form, received my selection and gleefully sent off the £4.99. That was almost two years ago. For the next 18 months I enjoyed an on-off relationship with TSP, receiving a catalogue every two months, declining some obscure Books of the Month but occasionally purchasing some work or other.

Then I received an unsolicited book. The postman apparently had failed to negotiate entry for a few days as a result of a failure with the security system at my flat and, not knowing that, I had dallied in refusing the latest "editor's choice". I wrote explaining that and was promptly sent a postage-paid package to return the book.

Then I went on holiday . . . and returned to find two unwanted books of the month. I had to concede it was my own fault. In preparing for the holiday, I'd forgotten to decline the editor's choice. The day after I left, a second catalogue arrived. With my return still 13 days away, I was doomed to receive another book.

It cost me about £2.50 to return them. I questioned the wisdom of automatically sending out unordered books. In those days the club was based in Wiltshire and it was possible to reach it by telephone. TSP said it would not consider changing the system. Not wanting a repetition whenever I went on holiday, I cancelled my membership.

So I was somewhat surprised to receive another catalogue offering more books and demanding payment of £38.12. Apparently, I had a "seriously overdue account". I wrote explaining that I had resigned from the club, returned some books I had not wished to receive in the first place and owed nothing.

Another book arrived. As I no longer considered myself a member, I had failed to inform them I did not want the editor's choice.

By this time, November, the club had moved to Middlesex and I obtained a new telephone number. I tried to phone on countless occasions at all times of the day. I was always met with the engaged tone.

So I started phoning outside office hours. I would get an answer phone telling me the offices were open from 8am to 6pm daily, thanking me for calling but not asking me to leave a message. I tried anyway. "Please phone me," I urged.

There was no return call, no acknowledgement of my letter, but a few weeks later another catalogue dropped on my mat with a statement telling me I now owed £28.13, £9.99 less than before for some reason. There was also a red letter bearing the legend "final notice".

This was from Nigel Holland, "chief accountant". It warned: "Unless payment in full is received . . . within seven days your account will be passed to a debt collection agency with instructions to take whatever action is necessary to settle the matter."

I wrote to Nigel explaining for what seemed the umpteenth time that I had resigned, had returned some books and owed nothing.

Three weeks later, another red letter and, somehow more annoyingly, another catalogue offering books from a club I no longer belonged to. That was late December. Hardly a day has gone by since then when I have not spent a few minutes trying to get through to TSP on the phone. It should not bother me as much as it has. I have done nothing wrong. But it has got to me and I have even begun to fantasise about beating to a pulp anyone who dares to call at my door to collect my "debt". It won't solve anything, but in my increasingly frequent less rational moments I convince myself that someone has to pay for all this. And it won't be me.

Top of the morning

SARAH CHALMERS

22 January 1994

In its first months, GMTV entertained the nation more with off-camera farce than on-camera programming. The show was in trouble, and everyone knew it. But then a strangely familiar figure came bubbling to the rescue. Just who was the saviour on the sofa? Stand in the corner if you said Roland Rat.

The Tory Government was on the verge of a political crisis, bush fires raged through Sydney and the leaders of the western world were about to begin a two-day NATO summit in Brussels. And it was not all plain sailing at Britain's youngest breakfast television station, either. John McIlvride, producer of GMTV's fitness slots, leapt from the seat in the green room, where he had been following the exploits of wacky Mr M on a monitor and let out a cry of anguish. "Oh no! You can't see his suit properly because of that background."

As if that was not catastrophic enough, the temporary presenter of the after-nine slot – Amanda Reddington – was relaying hairdressing horrors to anyone in the green room who could tear themselves away from their cigarettes or the pressing debate over whether or not gold lycra clashed with a scenic blind.

And that was just behind the scenes. In front of the cameras in the tiny South Bank studio the gripping issues of the day were being tackled with equal aplomb. When the nation left for a gruelling day's work on Monday, 10 January, it could do so armed with the knowledge that Racquel wore her own hat to the *Coronation Street* wedding of Reg Holdsworth, those born under Cancer could expect a sudden windfall and presenter Lorraine Kelly thinks the actor Liam Neeson is a "bit of a lad".

A bias toward hard news was not something GMTV was accused of during its first year of transmission. It did, however, come under fire for just about everything else it did.

Even before the debut programme was broadcast on New Year's Day, 1993, sceptics were having a field day. The announcement, 15 months before, that Sunrise Television was to take over the commercial breakfast franchise from outbid TV-am, was met with scorn in many corners.

First the fledgling station had to drop the name Sunrise after discovering Sky had a programme of the same name. This was quickly followed by accusations that their winning bid of £34.6 million was an impossible goal. And the on-air announcement by TV-am chairman Bruce Gyngell that he had received a personal letter of condolence from Margaret Thatcher – under whose premiership the initiative had been instigated – brought yet more predictions of doom.

The whole franchise distribution was being hailed as a fiasco. How, many asked, could TV-am, hour for hour the most profitable station in the world, be cast aside like burnt toast to make way for an unknown?

Not to be outdone, GMTV began to score some own goals. Its pre-show publicity consisted of endless rants about the F (for fanciability) factor of its staff. Even before presenters Fiona Armstrong and Michael Wilson had signed off from the New Year's Day programme, press reviews centred on their wooden presentation and the obvious dearth of sexual chemistry between them.

Things hit an all-time low when advertisers had to be partially refunded because audience figures fell so short of the predicted mark. In total, the station made a loss of £10 million in its first six months, while on Channel 4 Bob Geldof's *The Big Breakfast* had cornered the youth market.

But that was in the early days. Now the producers contend,

things are on the up. *The Big Breakfast* allowed its own ridiculous jingle to become a prophecy and counted its chickens before audience figures had settled.

Current ratings show GMTV, although nowhere near the three million mark regularly pulled by TV-am, leading the present bunch. The latest figures available from the Broadcasting Audience Research Board show weekday viewing figures peaking at 1.5 million for GMTV compared to 0.9 and 0.8 million viewers for the BBC's *Breakfast News* and *The Big Breakfast* respectively.

The official line is that it takes time for presenters to settle in, some fine tuning was needed, and it is the enthusiasm of the team which has saved the day. Unofficially it looks as though the L-factor replaced the F-factor.

Just as the unlikely figure of Roland Rat reversed the fortunes of the ailing TV-am after the famous five left it in need of something stronger than lashings and lashings of home-made lemonade, so it was the reappearance in April of bubbly Scotswoman Lorraine Kelly that seemed to signify the start of brighter mornings for all at GMTV.

To be fair, she had not disappeared completely, as she had been fronting the magazine slot *Top of the Morning* from 8.50–9.25am. Furthermore, hers was not the only job shuffle: Eammon Holmes quickly moved over from the weekend show to warm the space on the sofa beside her and it was goodbye to programme director Lis Howell and Fiona Armstrong, see you around to Michael Wilson (who was demoted to the 6–7 am start), and good morning again to old TV-am favourites Mike Morris (who took over the weekend presenting) and Jimmy Greaves.

The housewives' favourite Dr Hilary Jones was already there and the sofa was not far behind him. Rumour has it that a clandestine trip was made to a television museum to measure the old TV-am bench for a replica to seat the new – or should that be the old – team. GMTV was beginning to look more like TV-am than TV-am did.

Nevertheless it was the return of Queen Lorraine in particular to the prime 7–9am slot which began to woo the viewers back. L is also for loyalty, and although TV-am fans had first cringed at her sing-song brogue, that was at a time when the only other choice of early-morning TV was the news-based *Breakfast Time* on BBC or the even more serious *Channel 4 Daily*.

They stuck with her and grew to love her inane babblings, the way she prefixed everything with "Och ah think" and added "so it does" to the end of most of her sentences.

In her own words: "All of a sudden, TV-am, there it is and viewers of breakfast television are very loyal, fiercely loyal and all of a sudden they see this decision has been made by whoever. They think wait a minute, our pals have been taken off the telly and there's new people. It wouldn't have mattered who they were."

She refuses to be drawn any further on the subject of her predecessors. Crossing her arms and laughing, she says: "I really wouldn't like to say" and repeats the well-worn argument that GMTV would have had an uphill struggle no matter who its first presenters were.

Maybe it is her Scottish heritage rising to the familiar challenge of the underdog. She said: "At the end of the day I couldn't not do it. It was a risk. You were being asked to come in and help resurrect it – along with everybody else," she quickly adds, "I just had to do it. I didn't really have a choice. Eammon and I talked about it and it just had to be done. It was a challenge."

Ms Kelly, 34, entered journalism straight from school. She spent five years on the *East Kilbride News* before joining the BBC as a researcher and then moving to TV-am where she was a reporter for four years before becoming a presenter.

Colleagues from her early days remember her as a determined and enthusiastic operator. Eric Barr has edited the *East Kilbride News* since 1965, and gave the young schoolgirl her first job. He was so impressed by her that he made her a senior reporter when her experience was only that of a junior.

Mike Barr was a senior reporter on the local paper at the time and took Lorraine on one of her first jobs. "She was very good – had a lot of personality. I could see she was going to make it. She worked hard. We were under a lot of pressure through illness for a while and it was really just her and I running the newsroom for a month and we had to get the paper out."

Ms Kelly is not, of course, the first Scotswoman to make her name in current affairs broadcasting. But with neither the glamour of Selina Scott, nor the sharp analytical mind of Kirsty Wark, she is an unusual choice.

Her style is similar to the tabloid TV approach of mid-morning presenters Richard and Judy. She flits from impotence and bereavement to talented pets with hardly a change of facial expression. Guests are never likely to feel intellectually challenged by her.

But she is certainly not two cornflakes short of a packet. Although she says she has never planned her career, it has all worked out rather well so far. When TV-am lost the franchise, she did not enter into the petty jibe-throwing of sofa chum Mike Morris and was duly rewarded with a contract for the new station.

Sitting in the presenters' office after last Monday's show, she professed to being very happy in her job, with no intentions of becoming a full-time mum when her expected first child is born. And who would, with a press officer present during the whole interview?

However, she is brushing up on her driving skills and says she would one day like to go into radio. The L factor will not last forever, and GMTV producers cannot afford to get complacent.

Bruce Gyngell predicted the station would be bankrupt by 1994 and the scars of the first 12 tumultuous months have yet to heal. Ratings may have risen, but morale is yet to follow suit. Nick Skeens was news editor until December 1993 and he lambasted the atmosphere and team spirit at the station in a recent newspaper article.

Having observed a morning's transmission from in-between the television wires of the compact studio, the only apparent function of the continually giggling on-set presence of weathergirl Sally Meen is to manufacture an air of jollity and camaraderie.

Press officers never leave the side of visiting journalists, and unlike the happier days of TV-am, anyone wishing to write an article on the station is excluded from the after show post-mortem.

Channel 4's *Big Breakfast* does not have egg on its face yet, and the team at the South Bank knows it. Any question directed to Ms Kelly about "the competition" was answered as though it was referring solely to Channel 4's offering. She referred to it as being "daft" and "for kids". And if I had a bacon roll for every time the press officer asked me if I knew GMTV's ratings were up, I would not have had to eat lunch or dinner for a week, never mind breakfast.

Northern highlights

TOM MORTON

24 June 1994

*High art called Tom Morton away from his football to mingle
with the elite at the St Magnus Festival on Orkney. But there were
distractions.*

They call it the Flying Shed: the Shorts 360 is not so much a
workhorse of the skies as an airborne Luton van, one with red
leather seats to match its Loganair livery. The only aeroplane
with enough headroom to permit in-flight trampolining flopped
on to Kirkwall airport's tarmac and trundled to an ungainly halt;
I walked into the terminal building, awash with memories and
Orcadian rain.

Inside, the tiny concourse was packed; the British Airways
flight from Glasgow had just landed, and festival artists abounded:
there was Seamus Heaney, looking more like he'd flown in for a
cattle sale than to read poetry; musical instrument cases rattled
along the luggage conveyor, people embraced, and the fleshless
kiss, the spoor of the MacLovey, echoed out along with cries of
"darling!" and "the handle's come off my French horn". The St
Magnus Festival was about to begin, Orkney's annual extravaganza of art, music, poetry and incredibly bad post-gig dancing by
bassoonists. But first, the whisky.

Some invitations are easy to turn down; one to an opening
reception at Highland Park Distillery is not. I launched myself into
the new Highland Park visitors centre at a discreetly high speed
and was relieved to note that few, if any, musicians had arrived.
You can't be too careful where free drink and trombonists are set
to be united.

The instantly-recognisable profile of George Mackay Brown
appeared, in tandem with Seamus Heaney's equally-inimitable
outline; a million-dollar literary front two, ready to perform

wonders on the field, or rather the page . . . but no, football, even as metaphor, had to be put aside for higher things. I was, after all, only there for the culture. Replenishing a glass, I approached the minister of St Magnus Cathedral, and asked him about . . . Cowdenbeath Football Club. Rev Ron Ferguson, author of the quite brilliant book, *Black Diamonds and the Blue Brazil*, told me how he'd once had to give an encouraging, spiritually-uplifting dressing-room talk to the not entirely devout team. Watch out for Ross County next season, I warned.

But enough of football; culture was my beat, art my brief, immersion in important, serious, modern plinky-plonky-crash-bang music my aim. Sir Peter Maxwell Davies, Rackwick composer and festival founder, was pointed out, an elfin figure in grey curls who appeared far younger than his 60-this-week years. I was introduced to the beggar from *The Beggar's Opera*. Wait a minute . . . it was Alistair Bruce, Kirkwall lawyer and well-known from his involvement in the early stages of the Orkney child care case.

Bruce, a stalwart of local amateur dramatics, was just leaving to prepare for his debut later that evening, and gave me a lift to St Magnus Cathedral where something called *Draumkvedet* was billed. I entered my favourite building in the entire world somewhat conscious of previous hospitality. I had, indeed, been hospitalitised. *Draumkvedet* – Dream Song – is a 14th-century Norwegian ballad described in the programme as "a significant Norwegian work of art". Well, it beats shooting whales, I suppose. The ancient red stone of the cathedral glowed, an epic setting for Torvald Moseid's enormously long tapestry, inspired by *Draumkvedet* itself. Bass notes which sounded like underground trains earthquaked from the organ, and a voice to match, that of Geoff Capes lookalike Halvar Hakanes, filled the great building. It was all hugely impressive and quite moving, until after 15 minutes I began thinking about football again. My notes, written on a Loganair "comfort bag", are cryptic but specific: "Organ . . . 1978, Ally McLeod . . . everything ended . . . Scotland, politics, football, opened way for Thatcherism . . . need fish supper."

Hakanes, dressed oddly in T-shirt and dinner suit, sang what was beginning to resemble unplugged Pink Floyd in translation. I left to seek the sizzle of a deep-fat fryer.

Having consumed a sustaining haddock, I trawled through some of my old Kirkwall haunts in search of gossip. A notice on the now-infamous Mumataz Indian Restaurant promised it would reopen on Saturday. The appalling murder there, I was told in the Royal Hotel and the back bar at the St Ola, had shocked everyone deeply, severely. And had I heard any of the jokes? Black humour reaches new levels in the bars of Kirkwall. Everywhere, Orcadians murmured the same growing suspicion that it just might, after all, have been an islander who fired the gun. And in corners, imported policemen sat and listened.

Soon it was time to head for the Phoenix Cinema, a cavernous monoplex of the old moviedrome school. There I met Camera How, the Gaelic photographer, newly arrived from Glasgow and muttering about the lack of light. Through the gloom, details of a superb, very complex stage-set emerged, and as Alistair Bruce made his entrance, light and music trickled forth and *The Beggar's Opera* began. So here it was at last, then: modern classical music played on classical instruments, not an amplifier or Fender Stratocaster in sight. Was it plinky-plonk-crash-bang? Well, not really; perhaps in places. Six Maxwell Davies proteges under the direction of Alasdair Nicolson had provided the music "devised from the original airs", so it wasn't really modern at all; it was performed, impeccably, by the Scottish Chamber Orchestra Ensemble, casually dressed and placed, aptly enough, in their own on-stage drinking den. The acting and singing by the local St Magnus Players was, inevitably, uneven, and perhaps the production was attempting to play a little out of its league; as Cowdenbeath will find in their first game of the season, Ron, when they meet the mighty Ross County at Victoria Park, Dingwall, in front of the kind of crowd the Blue Brazil can only dream about. But no more about football.

Next morning Stromness beckons, that wonderful clutter of twisted streets and houses, waterfalling down Brinkie's Brae. Inside the modern Academy, which has that school odour of wet wool, used socks, textbooks and stale sweat, Seamus Heaney is reading to a packed lecture theatre. I find myself sitting next to George Mackay Brown, who appears to know everybody in the room except me. I take out a notebook. So does he. "I'm doing a write up for the *Orcadian*," says the man who may well be our greatest living author, yet still contributes a weekly column to his local newspaper. "Maybe we can compare notes afterwards." I nod, weakly. It's one of those terrible moments when you at last meet someone you've admired for decades, and have all these things you want to ask and share, but comment casually on the weather and settle down to listen. In the spellbinding hour that follows, Heaney's warm, Bushmills Malt of a personality infuses some of his most famous work – *Blackberry Picking*, *The Railway Children* – and introduces stunning newer material like *Keeping Going* dedicated to his farmer brother in Northern Ireland: "You keep old roads open/By driving on the new ones." Next to me GMB gives little grunts of satisfaction at particularly powerful moments. "That was excellent," he says afterwards. I nod.

All Heaney's books, which are being sold downstairs, disappear like lightning; the salesman is another author, Duncan Maclean, whose collection of stories, *Bucket of Tongues* is soon to be followed by two novels and a book about Texan country swing star Bob Wills, of Texas Playboys fame. Duncan has settled in Stromness and seems set to follow Irvine Welsh into the literary firmament of young'n'visceral Scottish writers. Deservedly so, as there is not enough country and western music in Scottish literature. "I'm going to Texas for two months," he reveals, "to research the Bob Wills book." Now that's what I call research. Camera How and I spend the rest of the day researching the 75th anniversary of the Imperial German Fleet's scuttling in Scapa Flow, tracking down two eye witnesses of the event, doing interviews and setting up arrangements for pictures the next day.

Back in Kirkwall, Shetland's very own Bongshang have arrived, ready to take the Festival Club by storm with their brand of jazz-rock-folk bluegrass. They blow up the PA speakers while soundchecking, and it becomes clear that Orkney's sound engineers are having a little trouble coping with the polite demands of Shetland's top band. The BBC Philharmonic are playing at the cathedral, but there's the little matter of Ireland's opening World Cup match . . . the Shetland contingent, including Lerwick-educated Camera How, take over control of the Bothy Bar's television, force the cessation of all music, and encourage the now-legendary Irish victory. Bongshang take the stage of a packed Festival Club only to find that the sound engineer does not know how to engineer sound out of his hastily-repaired PA system. He goes to telephone someone, while the band grows increasingly annoyed. I press a few buttons haphazardly, and somehow the amplifiers burst into life, much to the chagrin of the embarrassed knob-twiddler. I spend the rest of the evening shouting at him to turn the fiddle up, but he ignores me. He is, after all, an expert.

Next day, I decamp from Kirkwall's West End Hotel to Thira,

a Stromness guest house which features probably the best home cooking in Orkney. Alison Shearer's clootie dumpling is to die for, you can carry-in your own wine, the views of Hoy Sound are stunning, and it's cheap. I trundle to the Festival Club, where Boogalusa, one of ten million ersatz cajun bands currently on the folk circuit, bring viola players and bassoonists and MacLoveys onto the dancefloor in their Travoltaesque droves. On mineral water, it's all very peculiar, especially when the disco's video monitors begin showing Bunuel's collaboration with Dali, *Un Chien Anadalou*.

I spend Monday engaged in the serious business of business journalism, interviewing cheesemakers and jewellery manufacturers. No free samples. Camera How is ready to depart for the south, so we have lunch at the reopened Mumataz. Mushroom bhaji? It's off. So are the king prawns. The restaurant shows no sign of the recent horror which afflicted it, save a certain nervousness from the staff. We discreetly cover the day's horrific news pictures of the Ulster pub shooting, and settle for chicken, which is mild but excellent.

Later, there is *The Rainbow*, a musical entertainment by Sir Peter Maxwell Davies himself, performed by the pupils of Stromness Primary School. It is wonderful plinky-plonk without the crash-bang, beautifully acted and atrociously sung in the best traditions of primary school productions everywhere. Back in Stromness, I discover that while everyday Orcadians consider what they tend to sarcastically drawl as "the festivaaaal" something for the gentry, the arty bourgeoisie and tourists, Sir Peter himself is regarded with universal affection and respect. Nobody local has a bad word to say about him, which in an island community is a truly impressive accolade. Even though one Stromnessian dismisses the Maxwell Davies ouevre memorably as "sounding like a canteen of cutlery falling down a stair".

Tuesday, the Flying Shed arrived to take me home. Enjoy yourself? asked a solicitous stewardess. Well, I replied, put it this way. It was a game of two halves. But generally, I'm over the moon with it. We got a result. And the football was quite good too.

Editorial

MARY MILLER

28 October 1994

Mary Miller re-visits Gian Carlo Menotti's Festival at Spoleto.

Up the Via della Spagno, there is a cat who thinks she is a geranium. Over the railings, draped around in scarlet and pink petals, she drips fur and languid paws, watching with wide lemon eyes as we blink in the strong sunlight, and clatter over the cobbles to the Teatro Caio Mellisa, where Spoleto Festival's heart beats, at the lunchtime concerts. The theatre, as ever, is jammed with brown limbs and vivid dresses. Few theatres can be so Italian, so vivacious, all gilt and plush, with tiny decorated boxes like jewel pouches climbing to a gallery where straining fingers can trace the vine leaves and painted prettiness across the ceiling.

Today is Menotti's birthday, and the Colla family have brought a puppet to dance for him. After a somewhat louche display – this monkey's tricks are Italianate and languid – it jumps into his arms, bearing a posy of marigolds. But, as ever, Gian Carlo Menotti has discoveries to show us. Today, an astonishing young pianist, Orli Shaham plays Prokofiev – later, Kyoko Takezawa will play the violin with tiger-like strength and grace. We hear Menotti songs – these about longing and distance – ("don't mention the singer, she's *all wrong* says Menotti), accompanied by Jean-Yves Thibaudet, resplendent in Versace, with remarkable scarlet socks. Thibaudet, a Spoleto regular, is a marvel, the playboy of the wunderkind world, the man for whom the mobile phone was invented. A natural virtuoso, he showed us, in four days, some of the most sensitive and exciting pianism heard this decade. He showed us, too, a wardrobe less subtle, but quite incandescent with flair. With Carter Brey and Takezawa, he played the Brahms B major piano trio more beautifully and with more sense of revelation than ever heard. Before it, breathing charm and encouragement, he accompanied a young, nervous singer who had arrived, without pianist, to beg an audition for the opera chorus. Later, at the Torricella pool, 'phone in hand, he entertains the Spoleto Festival Orchestra, enjoying a rare afternoon off, with tales of terrible tours.

During days of dazzling light, fresh figs, dusty noon hush, and bells, deep and clonking, in counterpoint with bells distant and contralto, we heard Steven Isserlis play Menotti, Takezawa play Prokofiev, and the irrespressible American flautist Paula Robinson play 20 operas in three minutes, arranged by William Schumann. Real opera is at the Teatro Nuovo, in a brilliant Gunter Kramer production of Berg's *Wozzeck*, set by Graziano Gregori in chilling monochrome, with a huge, shuddering clock hanging over the scene. Kramer's conception is highly individual. He explores beyond the plot, to the darkness beyond the relationships. Wozzeck, sick and bleary, confronts the horrors of his imagination, Marie sings to the child about abduction by a gipsy, and the idiot – Kramer has him drift into various roles throughout the opera – takes the little boy into his arms, away, a dreaming captive. Blood dominates the tale, but we see none, until Marie's death. Then, down the clockface, streams shocking scarlet. At the end, the children play, and Wozzeck's child sings his shaky little hop-hop from the idiot's arms. He steps away, and is tripped by his own toy sword. We are left with minds naked – excited, unsure, amazed.

In the pit, the orchestra is sensational. Conductor Steven Mercurio has such a profound understanding of this swirling, fractured score that the black and white of the notes on the page seem physically part of the onstage drama. The musical pacing is wonderful – the sounds stumble then rush, to erupt in a last act apotheosis of such beauty that one wept. William Stone and Kristine Ciensinski are Wozzeck and Marie, both fabulously imaginative artists, Norman Bailey is truly horrid as the Doctor. Several dismembered frogs lie in a neat row, frontstage. The cast, quite frequently, lie beside them, as we and Berg dissect their minds.

By contrast, Poulenc's *les Mamelles de Tiresias*, to Apollinaire's story is a balloon-bursting, red-white-and very blue explosion of nonsensical extravagence, full of grown babies, men in frocks, nurses uniforms, wicked angular melody and smart rhythmn. This production, by Alfredo Arias, and set amidst the metal-veined legs of the Eiffel Tower by Robert Plate, should be seen, as true therapy, whenever the blight of British political correctness looms, unsmiling. Men having babies may embrace one gritty issue: real joy, spectacle and stunning musical sophistication in the theatre sweeps all the dust of pretention before it.

In the great, golden Duomo, the Festival Chorus, with Donald Nally are keening through weird, atonal Huber, as Fra Lippo's Madonna gazes, indulgent from the walls. The pews are packed – the cast of *Wozzeck* are sitting on each other's knees, Spoletini grandparents have toddlers, silent, in their arms – as they begin Part Two of Bach's B minor Mass, the *Cruxificus*'s weaving suspensions hanging like a silk floss in the air. Later, the Eton College Chamber Orchestra play creditably at the Teatro Nuovo, with Simon Crawford-Philips a formidable, musicianly soloist in Beethoven's G major piano concerto. Later still, there's jazz: Bernstein, Anteil and Gershwin from the Festival Orchestra and Steven Mercurio. "Very sharp-edged, very nasty, very New York" says Mercurio, as introduction. Very good, too, we agreed, heading for the Tric-Trac, to sit up too late listening to Menotti tell tales of Marilyn Monroe and movie machinations.

We drift from American theatre to French ballet, past Spoletoscienza at San Nicolo, down past Spoletocinema at the Corso, pausing to pay lip service to Berlucchi, the spumante Festival sponsor. The bubbles of excitement are rising, the seats are laid in the Piazza, and as the sun sets to peach, we sit amidst thousands, to hear the Orchestra dell' Accademia di S. Cecilia play Beethoven's 9th symphony. Doves settle, crooning, during the first movement, and night swallows sing the Ode to Joy. After all the radiance, the music and the magic, we sit a-while in silence. Palazzo Campella has fireworks later. A deep peace comes first.

Lighting up Kelman

CATHERINE LOCKERBIE

19 March 1994

Everybody knows all about Kelman. "Kelmanesque" has already become insouciant shorthand: Glasgow mean streets, bad language by the bucket-load, a cast-list of alkies and no-hopers. Nothing ever happens. People just chunter on. Not exactly a laugh a minute.

The new novel, *How Late It Was, How Late*, will not disappoint the stereotype-spreaders. Is it about an inadequate with criminal associations? Check. Is it set among Glasgow boozers and schemes and rainswept streets? Check. Is it full of f***s? Check.

It is possible to argue that in no other country except Britain would such a major author be subject to such reductive labelling. It's only a little over a decade since his first book, *Not, Not While The Giro* was published in Britain, by Polygon (he was published in the States as long ago as 1973). Since that time, he has published stories, plays and novels; and his new mode of working-class writing (*inside* the heads of the characters, instead of *outside* pulling their strings) and his unapologetic use of the vernacular (which is the language of his characters – how could he do otherwise, if he is to represent them with integrity?) has had a real impact on Scottish letters and thought. A whole generation of younger writers has directly imitated or indirectly been influenced by him. He's there, staring with his blue eyes, in the country's consciousness.

Yet still people get stuck on the surface; still a combination of laziness, snootiness and political squeamishness conspire to distort the image of an author of immensely sophisticated narratives and philosophical insight. One *History of Scottish Literature* delivers itself of this stunningly patrician judgement: "James Kelman gives voice to the socially deprived. Unfortunately, what they have to say ... is not always very interesting." It goes on to discuss his Booker-shortlisted last novel, *A Disaffection*: "The novel's main strength lies in its unadulterated and unvarnished replication of

Glasgow dialogue, as used among the educationally disadvantaged: dialogue of a sort that appears completely to accept its own purility *(sic)*."

Such bizarrely wrong-headed and *unliterary* comments are all too commonplace. Offended by a few f***s, they fail totally to see that James Kelman's work is not about swearing; it is, if anything, about the *soul*. Perhaps this would sit better in the European tradition, unafraid of a bit of existential delving, regardless of the social class of the delver, than in the collection of cosy domestic superficialities which pass for modern literature in much of Britain.

How Late It was, How Late, to be published later this month, could be, should be, called a masterpiece. The brilliantly sustained voice of one Sammy Samuels who finds himself blind after a beating by the police, it has profound levels of irony, compassion and humour (yes folks, Kelman is *funny*). It's a work of intuition transformed by art, with Kelman's typical hypnotic inner narrative – there's no omniscient mover of pawns on the chess-board here, no "three days later", no skipping bits. The blindness, of course, is an obvious device for the individual adrift in a hostile world, but it was never planned as such. "The blindness came as a surprise to me," says Kelman. "Sometimes you just feel this leap into the unknown coming, and you think "good god, this is going to happen", you cover your face with your hands, but then the leap is made. Once you're into it, there's no turning back. You have to go with it, you have to pay laborious attention to detail – there's no escape route for the character, so there can be none for us. You need to follow through that concreteness of operating with one sense less."

Questioned about terrorism he disclaims all knowledge of, not knowing where his girlfriend has disappeared to, confronted by sinister and tortuous state procedures, Sammy swaggers through with a constant stream of self-galvanising patter, keeping the darkness at bay with a balance of despairing wit and Beckettian resignation, battering on. It's a paradigm and perfect crowning of Kelman's work to date: the distinctive, deliberately repetitive cadences of his sentences have never been so insistent, the uncanny entering into another man's consciousness never so complete. It requires to be *read*, not reduced by snickering and simplistic tags.

Of course, it will, surely, get its share of ecstatic reviews; but even these seem sometimes to backfire. When one notice of *A*

Disaffection appeared in *The Independent*, comparing him (quite correctly, incidentally) to Zola, Beckett and Camus, guffaws of derision gurgles up across the land. In England, people mutter with pursed lips about reviewers being over-excited by all that macho grittiness. In Scotland, the old who-the-hell-does-he-think-he-is routine swings into action ("they seem to think *I* said these things," says Kelman in resigned bewilderment, "they blame *me* for the hype.") The last edition of the magazine *Cencrastus*, the self-styled "magazine for Scottish and international literature, arts and affairs" devoted three densely printed pages to a clever-clever parody of and attack on Kelman with the offending comparison featuring strongly. For a short while, James Kelman was the shining saviour of Scottish letters; now it seems the right-on thing to do is to remind him of his plebbish place.

Even obviously good reviews, neither breathlessly overstating nor blinkingly uncomprehending, are not guaranteed to please the author: details which reveal the gulf between himself and his middle-class commentators do not escape that preternaturally bright eye of his. The first review of *How Late It Was, How Late* has in fact already appeared. It is a glowing one and it is in Auberon Waugh's *Literary Review* (a nice irony – Kelman despises the Waughs and their ilk.) Despite the reviewer's delighted response to "this astounding novel", Kelman has written on a copy of it, kept in a box file in his study: "First review; first inability to perceive reality."

In the book, the character Sammy, blind, persecuted by questioning from the police, batters against a Kafkaesque wall of bureaucracy in order to register his sightloss". The reviewer comments that he is entrapped in a "paranoid's dystopia". The author notes that "dystopia" is defined as an imaginary place of misery.

"Look at this," he says. *"Imaginary.* The trouble with a lot of the critics is that they have no experience of the world as much of the population experiences it. Okay, Sammy is unable to get himself diagnosed as blind; but the *reality* in the DSS is much worse than that. Thinking this is some sort of fantasy is a perfect example of what Noam Chomsky calls 'intellectual myopia'."

James Kelman is, to get this out of the way, that most quintessential of Scottish figures, the working-class autodidact – like his friend and colleague, Whitbread-winner Jeff Torrington. Born in Govan in 1946, one of five brothers, he left school at 15 and drifted through various spells of unemployment and menial jobs, factory, building site, bus conductor, later becoming a mature student of philosophy and English at Strathclyde University (he disliked the English). In 1972 he enrolled at an evening class run by the poet and remarkable catalyst, Philip Hobsbaum, through whom he met Tom Leonard, Alasdair Gray, Liz Lochhead – the writers who have made West-coast literature such a vigorous force.

His self-education is immense: the walls of his crammed study in his sunny Denniston tenement flat, which he shares with his wife and two grown-up daughters, groan with classics, philosophy, modern fiction, Marx, and you can be sure he's read them. He distils them into a complete independence of mind and a complete, fierce integrity. (In conversation, it's expressed in thoughtful, soft-spoken articulacy: he's friendly, accommodating, patient.)

It's the combination of this integrity, this powerfully fed intelligence and the circumstances of his life and community that fuel his fiction and his life. A pertinent example: one of the jobs he had when younger was in an asbestos factory; he has recently been a full-time worker with the campaign for compensation for victims of asbestosis; and this knowledge, of real life, of real suffering, feeds into the book and feeds his anger at those who would deem them "imaginary".

"Critics might talk about Kafka in relation to this novel," he says, "but the point about Kafka was that he was in workers' insurance. His job was actually trying to get people compensation. The situation in Prague then can't be that different from the state here now. Our state won't acknowledge that people are dying of this disease. In a court, it's the criminal that's on trial; but in cases of industrial injury, even if by some blunder the doctor actually diagnoses you, it's up to the victim to prove that a crime has been committed. Outsiders are strangers to this world, they don't believe it exists, and they start talking about a 'paranoid's dystopia'. "What James Kelman doesn't do however is to offer undigested experience up on a plate: he is far, far too accomplished a writer for that. At no point is the book about asbestos, at no point is it documentary, at no point is it sociological survey. He expects some of his friends from the asbestos campaign to be disappointed that he hasn't built their stories more specifically into the narrative, but as a writer that specificity is not what interests him. In the novel, there is no agenda, though that won't stop critics assuming there must be one – I mean, it's about the

53
.

underprivileged, the oppressed, isn't it? The odd middle-class perception is that because a work is set in a working-class arena, it must somehow be *about* that working-class arena, rather than what Kelman calls "the validity of being". It's as if the work itself can't be seen clearly for the muddle of class prejudice which still bedevils this noble nation of ours.

"People have started attacking me for being an "insular" working-class writer," said Kelman, referring to at least one recent essay by a distinguished poet, professor and critic which suggests that he's somehow deliberately excluding the middle-classes with all that aggressive vernacular, "but these are such facile statements. It's just a political reaction against working-class culture, which they don't see as including philosophy, culture, music. They feel threatened by it, so you get this antipathy, uneasiness coming out."

The point is that this author sets his extraordinary narratives where he does because that is where he comes from, not because he has made some devilish decision to frighten the guid folk of the land. "There are quite a lot of fallacies," he says, "and a basic one is that a writer chooses what he or she writes: that you have the choice of writing about, say, Timothy Clifford or Sammy Samuels. Well, you don't. To attack me for what I write about is just so foolish, it's not a literary comment, it's a political one."

Politics loom large in James Kelman's life – but not the dull, incestuous politics of a discredited parliamentary system. He believes – *knows* that oppression and prejudice are built in with the very bricks and mortar of our governmental institutions, built in to the very structures of thought of those who play the prescribed games. His study has stickers, slogans, dotted unobtrusively along the bookshelves: "Defy authority"; "Media: distortion and disinformation"; "Water theft". He's an activist, a radical, well outside, far to the left, of stale party lines.

His integrity blazes down on entrenched and stultifying ideologies: that favourite phrase "intellectual myopia" again. As far as literature goes, he knows that some of the most vibrant work is disregarded simply because it doesn't fit into the approved canon. "People say my use of language is singular, but it isn't. It's part of a tradition, but one that is overlooked. Here, Tom Leonard's poetry had been around for years before I was published. In American poetry, and in the Caribbean, you get that use of breath and rhythm, the way I write. You'll find it's nearly always the language of a colonised people, it's part of the effect of imperialism, where standard English is not the language used in the home and the playground – Chinua Achebe (the great African Nobel prize-winner) writes about this. People look down on this work, they call it "oral rendition" instead of literature."

He clearly feels strongly, and with reason, the force of that looking down. He recalls with quiet amazement well-meaning academics asking him if he ever revises, if he's ever read Joyce, as if he were some miraculous aberration of nature sprung fully-fledged from Govan, rather than someone who thinks and studies at least as hard as they do. He recalls when he started writing and couldn't get published: "Everyone writes from their own experience. But if your experience is of a certain kind from a certain culture, you quickly find there are things you are not allowed to do, such as use your own language."

As far as life outside literature goes, he is incredulous at the lack of clarity, the lack of perception he sees around him. "The humbug and hypocrisy of the state is constant all the way through. Representational democracy is a contradiction in terms – the actual system doesn't allow it. In my work for anti-racism and industrial disease campaigns, I come up head to head with the state, no messing about. They've drunk in so much disinformation, they're unable to see reality. You speak to them of iniquities and their eyes just glaze over. You say to them: the state kills people; here's the medical evidence; this is empirical; and here's a further thesis which demonstrates that your opposition to helping these people is based on money . . . They don't see it."

He shrugs his shoulders helplessly at the scale of the oppressing ignorance which weighs down on and stunts his peers' daily lives. "Would you expect state institutions to have different values from those of the state? They claim our legal, medical, educational electoral systems are objective – how can they be? All this is self-evident, it's not my opinion. How can reality be an opinion?" A shake of the head. "As an individual, you're overwhelmed with irony."

In life, he stays clear of sterile mainstream debates and involves himself instead in alternative culture – groups, meetings, forums, where "you're not forever having to explain the premises, set the right agenda". In literature, he writes another book, politely goes through the publicity hoops, and hopes that someone will see their way clear to what matters.

Part of what matters is that the political activity does not impinge on the books themselves. His characters are far from activists: surviving, not bettering the world, is their chief concern. "Essentially, I'm a story writer," points out Kelman, patiently. "The story comes first. Authorial intrusion is out. I don't thrust my own thoughts down the throats of my characters. Why should that be surprising? Good art is usually free of political dogma."

Thus, in *How Late It Was, How Late*, all the injustices, all the ironies are not flagged up, fiercely brandishing banners, but rather flow silently, filtered through art, into the creation of the bold Sammy Samuels. Kelman speaks of readers and reviewers constantly bringing their own baggage to his fiction: it's that dragging weight which must be cast aside. The author has chosen to place this latest novel in familiar territory, in familiar cadences, not to make points but to make literature. "All I want to do is to write as well as I can from within my own culture and community, always going more deeply into it. It's therefore just logical that I should write a novel like this, becoming more at home with these linguistic rhythms."

We need to listen to those rhythms: they beat from a vital part of the nation's heart.

Battle lines

GILLIAN HARRIS

13 October 1994

Furious debate has erupted over the Booker Prize being awarded to Glaswegian author James Kelman. The fiercest critic of the decision is one of the judges, Rabbi Julia Neuberger, who told Gillian Harris that the novel was a 'non-read'.

Rabbi Julia Neuberger has read James Kelman's Booker Prize-winning novel, *How Late It Was, How Late*, three times. Each time she found herself hating it all over again. "It got more and more boring," she grumbled. "I started thinking: 'Have I got to get through another 100 pages of this?'" When she sat down with her five fellow judges in August to discuss the short list for this year's £20,000 Booker Prize for Fiction, Neuberger, an author and broadcaster, made it clear that as far as she was concerned Kelman's book was not in the running.

However not everyone shared her opinion and the Glaswegian writer's book was confirmed as one of the six novels shortlisted for Britain's most prestigious literary award.

In the beginning Kelman's book was not tipped to win. That honour went to Jill Paton Walsh's novel, *Knowledge of Angels*, which commandeered column inches because it was published by the author after being rejected by 14 publishing houses.

If Kelman's book was mentioned at all, attention was focused on his use of the word "f***" which appears 4,000 times in the 378-page novel. But by the time William Hill had closed the book on the Booker, Kelman was joint favourite alongside Alan Hollinghurst's gay love story, *The Folding Star*.

Neuberger's objections to Kelman's novel do not stem from the strong language but what she describes as the dreary and monotonous tone.

"It was the only one of the six that I definitely did not want to see win," she said.

"Everyone assumes that I opposed it because of the bad language. I could not give a damn about the language. What I objected to was the monotony.

"I thought it would have been a brilliant exercise to get inside the head of a blind, Glaswegian ex-convict if it had been a short story. But, for me, it did not work as a novel. It could not be sustained as a novel. And for many people it will be completely inaccessible.

"I did not find it in any way engaging. In many ways it was a non-read and certainly not to my taste."

Shortly after Kelman was presented with his prize at the Guildhall in London on Tuesday, Neuberger was asked about the winning novel's plot.

"It's just a drunken Scotsman railing against bureaucracy," she exclaimed.

"My eyes are stretched in disbelief, Kelman was the least favourite of the three front-runners." Until she was presented with her copy of *How Late It Was. How Late*, Ms Neuberger was unfamiliar with Kelman's work. "I once started one of his books – I can't remember what it was called – but I gave up on it. I thought, this is not for me," she said.

Having spurned Kelman's gritty realism, Neuberger was seduced by the lyrical prose of Scotland's second Booker finalist, George Mackay Brown, who wrote *Beside the Ocean of Time*.

"I found his book absolutely gripping," she said. "I have become a great admirer of his although I had not come across him before. Mackay Brown was a real revelation." On Tuesday afternoon, when the judges gathered for the last time to decide the winner, Neuberger was resolute in her determination to see off Kelman.

In what disintegrated into a fractious two-and-a-half hour discussion among the five judges, Neuberger said that two judges strongly favoured Paton Walsh's book, two favoured Hollinghurst and one voted for Kelman.

"It seems to me ridiculous that Kelman should have ended up winning when only one of the judges started off voting for him," she said. "I found the whole thing incredible." Yesterday she announced that the system was "completely barmy" and wrote to the chairman of the Booker prize committee suggesting that a change in the voting rules would make the selection fairer.

"I do not think we had a totally unflawed book among the six," she said.

"But for Kelman's to win just does not make sense. I'm really unhappy. It was my least favourite book."

———————————

There's no dispute: the best book won

ALAN TAYLOR

13 October 1994

Controversy? What controversy? From a personal point of view I cannot see what all the fuss is about. Five judges were asked to read 130 books, whittle them down to a shortlist of six and choose a winner. In such circumstances the likelihood of a unanimous choice seems to me improbable, at least if the past experience of the Booker is anything to go by.

In 1983, according to Booker guru, Martyn Goff, the judges were split between *Shame* by Salman Rushdie and J. M. Coetzee's *The Life and Times of Michael K.* The casting vote fell to the chairman of the judges, Fay Weldon. After much humming and hawing, she finally plumped for Rushdie and the Booker publicity machine whirred into action. But just as Mr Goff was dialling the Press Association he heard a plaintive cry: "Hang on a second, Martyn, I've had a second thought." It was Ms Weldon. Ten minutes later Coetzee's name was engraved on the prize.

People on committees do and say strange things. They can be adamant one moment and open to persuasion the next. As the judging of the Booker on Tuesday demonstrated, anything can happen when you lock five people in a room.

Having already gone ten minutes past the deadline, we had reached an impasse and the prospect of a winner seemed as remote as it had two hours earlier when the meeting began. There were only three books still in the running – Alan Hollinghurst's *The Folding Star, Knowledge of Angels* by Jill Paton Walsh, and James Kelman's *How Late It Was, How Late* – but every attempt to find an outright winner ended in stalemate.

To test the temperature we decided to vote on which one we would like to win. Two judges voted for Hollinghurst and two for Paton Walsh. I voted for Kelman. Though the vote was not binding, the chairman, Prof John Bayley, asked if I would now be prepared to vote either for Paton Walsh or the Hollinghurst. Neither option appealed, but I said that if I had to make a choice I would go for Paton Walsh. This did not please James Wood of the *Guardian*, or Prof Bayley. I suggested an alternative scenario.

Would they not consider voting for Kelman instead of Hollinghurst? With the clock ticking remorselessly, both agreed: Kelman was the winner of the 1994 Booker Prize by three votes to two over Paton Walsh.

It is a narrow margin but let there be no mistake; four of the judges hold *How Late It Was, How Late* in the highest esteem. In all our deliberations Kelman was praised for his integrity, honesty, the bleak beauty of his writing, the blackness of his humour, the stiletto sharpness of his satire. In the opinion of Prof Bayley, Sammy, the novel's protagonist, a Glasgow ex-con who goes blind and has to cope with the consequences, from crossing the road to dealing with the DSS, was the most memorable character in all the books we read.

There is a vision and philosophy behind Kelman's work that is without compare in contemporary fiction. His is a unique and unmistakable voice.

Too much is made of his use of the F-word but it seems to me entirely appropriate and authentic, not a by-word for an inarticulate working class but for particular individuals within it. Some, such as my Booker colleague, Rabbi Julia Neuberger, find Kelman incomprehensible. Others, including myself, think there's no dispute: the best book won.

Memories are made of these

I HAVE BEEN INSTRUCTED TO OFFER YOU A LARGE SUM OF MONEY IF YOU DON'T ASK QUESTIONS ABOUT ROSYTH......

Children first and foremost

BOB CAMPBELL

18 January 1994

Down the stone steps to the basement. Along the corridors to a glass panel in the wall. This was Barts – St Bartholomew's Hospital, in the City of London, just across the way from Smithfield meat market. A tap on the glass, a moment's wait wondering if this really was the right part of this rambling establishment, then the panel slid open and the display of an appointment card brought forth a specimen jar.

"There's a place just round the corner." The "place" was a WC with naked light bulb, an unprepossessing venue to start the investigation into the potential for procreation. Being in a generally diminished state, it felt like attending Franz Kafka's Fertility Problems Clinic. However, given the lack of priority and research awarded male infertility, I was fortunate to have the possibility of treatment. A sperm specimen eventually produced and captured in the jar, it was back to the window and back up the stone steps. Off for a wander in a blur.

The process had begun in the late Seventies when after three years without offspring my wife and I had decided to consult the medics, hence the referral to Barts. Wife went first in those days because it was considered by both medical and folkloric opinion to be largely "a woman's problem". She returned from the hospital with results that showed her to be highly fertile. "They think it may be you who has the problem," she said.

By the time I walked into the consulting room to meet The Man, he who would pronounce on the possibilities, I was an unsteady complex of conflicting emotions: hostility, self-pity, defiance and sheer funk. A friend later informed me of an aphorism applied to senior staff at this hospital: you can always tell a man from Barts . . . but you can't tell him very much. My consultant probably wasn't like that, it was probably more to do with my mental state. Whatever the reason the chemistry was wrong.

What do you do? Journalist. Drink? Yes. Smoke? Yes. Wear tight underpants? Yes. Better examine you . . .

That is the memory of that exchange. It felt like appearing before an examining magistrate . . . Manhood demeaned by unforgiving scientific analysis. In this frame of mind it is a short step from "Why me?" to "Not me, surely". Rationalisation was followed swiftly by self-deception. They probably got it wrong . . . let's keep trying.

We did, to no avail. Infertility is not synonymous with impotence, though the shock of the former may lead to the latter. But a part of my psyche had gone walkabout. A common male trait. Deny this problem and it will cease to exist, in spite of all the evidence to the contrary – particularly an anguished spouse who is left to dash herself against the force field of non-communication.

By the end of 1982 matters had reached crisis point. Adoption was being placed on the agenda. I could not cope . . . again. The family GP, knowing our situation, recommended a different consultant, at the Hackney Hospital this time. The clinic was not a basement, more a kind of prefab, but the consultant it housed held out the last hope for this humbled supplicant.

The same questions evinced the same answers. Examining my undercarriage he said: "Ah, a varicocele" (a varicose condition that affects the quality of the sperm) and more specimens were analysed. The diagnosis was that significant number of my sperm suffered from a condition known as "low motility". Basically this meant that the lazy blighters were incapable of sufficient movement to negotiate the 20 cm journey required to fuse with an egg and begin a baby. Possibly, just possibly, this condition was the result of the varicocele, whose principle effect was to cause overheating down there.

The consultant proceeded to map out my future: stop drinking, stop smoking, throw away the briefs and buy some boxer shorts, and bathe the undercarriage in the coldest bearable water morning and night. Do that for six months and he would operate to remove the varicocele.

Ouch! He had just made me an offer I could not refuse. During the summer of that half-year test of will I only fell off the wagon – almost literally – once, partaking of a particularly inviting cold white rum punch I was concocting for guests before supper.

After an eternity it was November and back in the Hackney recovering from something like a scar from an appendix operation.

It only hurt when trying not to laugh at scabrous jokes made at my expense by visiting newspaper colleagues. Then off to a comfortable, converted gun-emplacement on the cliffs outside Dover to recuperate and reflect upon an uncertain future.

Returning to London a week later we discovered that a best friend was expecting, she and her husband having had to endure a clinical obstacle course as exacting as the one we had experienced. Token congratulations were over-whelmed by despairing jealousy and depression.

Gloomily we went into 1983 childless. The worst two months of the year trudged past. Then March stole up on us and ... yesss. Pregnant. She was pregnant. I never thought it would be possible to experience the suspension of disbelief in so prodigious a fashion.

Never say never. Some weeks later when the pregnancy was nine weeks alive, my wife had her first ante-natal appointment at University College Hospital. We've just had a new super-duper ultra-sound scanner delivered, they said, and could we use it on you, they asked her. She phoned me at work afterwards.

"Are you sitting down?"

"Yes".

"It's triplets."

Collapse of this party.

At the end of September three healthy boys were delivered five weeks early. There are no words to describe that event. Celebration does not do it justice.

We got the boys back home from the neo-natal unit at UCH almost precisely one year after the consultant had wielded the knife. My letter of copious thanks to him was answered in a tone of astonishment and concluded that this was, as far as he knew, an unprecedented outcome following this type of operation.

What was the clincher? Abstinence? Boxer shorts? Bathing till blue in the ... Who cares now? Men who can't have children. Fortunately for them the treatment of male fertility is being given – ever so gradually – a greater priority and some extremely hi-tech IVF-style techniques are being refined and appear to have real potential.

They may not get the treble, but just one would feel like it.

Thou shalt not grass

JOAN McALPINE

12 February 1994

Judas Iscariot broke no commandments. But he remains the Bible's biggest villain. The men who murdered Jesus Christ, the thieves who hung beside him on Golgotha, Pontius Pilot himself, are but scriptural bit-players, compared to him.

Killers and thieves merely broke the law as handed down to Moses. Judas violated the unwritten rule of the street: Don't snitch on your mates. He is history's foremost grass.

Judas earned 30 pieces of silver for his trouble. We never learn whether he could later walk the streets of Jerusalem without fear. Two thousand years on, he would need the equivalent of a couple of gladiators for protections and enough shekels to start a new life in Samaria.

The Judas figure is a regular player in western culture. Look at the honour code enshrined in American gangster movies – like Brian De Palma's *Carlito's Way*. Al Pacino plays Carlito Brigante, a former smack dealer and legend in his own *barrio*, now going straight. His efforts to reform are undermined by crooked lawyer David Kleinfeld, played by Sean Penn. Brigante discovers Kleinfeld tried to set him up. The coke-head lawyer tells the district attorney that Brigante is dealing again – a false accusation. The DA plays Carlito a tape of the telephone conversation containing his friend's betrayal.

He is offered immunity from prosecution and a new life if he testifies against Kleinfeld in the latter's trial for murder. But in spite of the betrayal, Brigante cannot bring himself to squeal.

For all Kleinfeld's education and platinum-bottomed lifestyle, he had no understanding of honour and obligation. "F*** your codes of the street," he sneers. "There's only one rule and that's to save your own ass." When he utters these incriminating lines the audience feels vindicated: we always knew he was a snivelling little sneak.

It is not just gangsters who respect the code. If "Don't get caught" is the unwritten 11th commandment "Thou shalt not grass" must be the 12th.

* * * * *

It's Govan, Glasgow, in the early hours of a chilly Sunday morning in January. Kenny has just left a party to discover track-suit bottoms sticking out of the smashed window of his friend's car. He yanks the waistband and hauls the thief out. "What do you think you're doing, pal?" he yells into the panicking face. Tapes rain down on the icy pavement. "Get out of here!" he shouts, and the guy disappears down a side street.

More party-goers appear in the close mouth. "You mean you let him away without giving him a doing?" someone says. But no-one suggests a citizen's arrest, or even holding onto the thief until the police appear a couple of minutes later.

"What did he look like?" said the constable. Kenny was vague. "Didn't really get a good look at him . . ."

Was it jeans or track-suit trousers?"

"Well, it all happened so quick . . ."

Given a good description and a willingness on Kenny's part to identify the culprit, a squad car might have scooped up the thief as he sprinted through the empty streets. But that's not how things work in Govan.

Why not? Why preserve the 12th commandment above all else? After all, the poor are the real victims of crime. House-breaking is so much more damaging if you are not insured. Vandals who demolish phone boxes hurt the people who cannot afford a telephone at home. If you do not own a car, you have greater need of safe streets on which to walk and wait for the bus.

The playwright Peter McDougall is currently working on a project around this theme. Never one to sentimentalise his up-bringing, he remembers: "I walked into a pub in Greenock many years ago and there was this guy standing at the end of the bar. There was a big circle of space around him. Someone explained that he was the guy who turned your electricity off. To be a grass is to be a social pariah. If someone is grassing people for, say, working while they're on the social, it can send a whole street into turmoil."

McDougall remembers being instilled with the honour code. "You go to school and are warned 'Don't tell tales in class!' Then you are warned you must tell the truth. It's a really contradictory thing."

But who does the law of the street protect? It's not always the good guys. Take the case of Glasgow teenager Paddy Healy, who received seven years last December for taking part in an attack on a man called Patrick White. Mr White nearly bled to death in the street. His suffering was witnessed by Karen Beemer, a young mother who happened to be staying in a house nearby while on holiday from America. Mrs Beemer saw baseball bats crash down on White's body – along with what seemed to be a machete. It was a scythe. Surgeons said the flesh on his back, arms and legs was sliced to the bone.

Mrs Beemer acted swiftly. As soon as it was light, she gathered up her nine-year-old daughter and headed for Heathrow Airport and the next flight home. She testified against Healy after police managed to stop and interview her in the airport.

In another trial last December, four people were sentenced to life imprisonment for the murder of Suzanne Caper. The 16-year-old was held captive in a house on Manchester's run-down East Side. The four, abetted by two others, injected Suzanne with drugs, and tortured her before she was doused with petrol and burned alive.

David Hill, 18, lived next door to the house which became Suzanne's prison. He heard the girl's screams for help – perhaps while she was having her teeth extracted with pliers. Her "gaoler" Jeffrey Leigh, 27 later took Hill to the room where Suzanne was tied to the upturned bed. Asked why he did not report what he saw, Hill replied: "I thought they'd have battered me. If I'd said owt, they'd all have got me, wouldn't they? I didn't know what to do."

Yet he was shocked by what he saw. By this time Suzanne had been severely beaten and her body scrubbed raw with undiluted disinfectant. "She had no hair and did not say anything." Nor did Hill, until the trial. By then it was too late.

The people who murdered Suzanne were drug dealers who caused as much misery in the grim terraces of Moston as their counterparts do in Wester Hailes or Easterhouse.

Scotland has the highest number of drug injectors per head of population in Europe. Everyone knows the dealers. Their BMWs sit outside tenement flats guarded by bull mastiffs. The neighbours on either side are likely to be feeding children on benefits which, according to this month's report from the National Children's Home charity, can no longer purchase the level of nutrition offered by the 19th century workhouse.

On the cusp of maturity, these children may inject their undernourished bodies with poison ultimately supplied by big shot next door. He doesn't need to keep it on the premises. Some minion does that.

Why does no-one tell? Is the old-fashioned honour code used as a shield by criminals to protect themselves from the people whose lives they destroy?

DCI John McKelvie is head of Strathclyde Police's drug's squad. The first thing he does on reaching his office each morning is play the answering machine. Then he listens intently as disembodied voices reveal details of people and places.

Callers are mainly female. Some are concerned mothers who don't want to see it happen to someone else's wean. There are a few vindictive wives who have watched their partner dealing drugs for years without comment until the relationship ends badly. Occasionally one street dealer will grass another to get him off his patch. The cops are wise to that trick.

One thing binds all the callers together – their anonymity.

This makes life hard for McKelvie. He appreciates the calls and says they can provide leads. But he cannot get a sheriff's search warrant on the basis of an anonymous phone call. He must first gather more information through observation. By then the drugs could be distributed.

The people in possession of the hard facts seldom talk. "We might pick up a courier at Glasgow Central Station carrying £25,000 worth of heroin," says McKelvie. "But he'd rather serve his six-year sentence than admit who he was picking them up for."

Det Insp Henry Harper is a blue-jeaned, sweatshirted member of the squad. Sometimes he gives talks about his work to interested groups in the suburbs. "They ask why we don't get couriers to pass on the names. They don't understand that we don't use thumbscrews any more," says Harper, who has 18 years in the force and is realistic about the pressures on people not to grass.

"If we bring someone in for questioning, we are in his life for two hours. He has to live all the other hours of every other day in his scheme. If he co-operates with us, he could get a Mars Bar (scar)."

The widespread use of drugs like cannabis and ecstasy, he

points out, puts huge numbers of young people on the wrong side of the law. "A lot of these kids don't look on smoking cannabis as a crime, just like they don't see underage drinking as a crime. That makes it very difficult to get co-operation," explains Harper.

He gets frustrated that society expects the police to solve problems of its own making. "To someone on social security, working for a dealer, either as a courier or by selling, can be relatively well paid. You get closes of people competing for it."

Harper sees things getting worse. He notices more people trying to escape jury duty. The prosecution needs several witnesses because the chances are one will be struck dumb when the case comes to court. "We need to be able to offer protection to the people who help us," he says. "What can we do for them just now?" He suggests informants should be offered housing elsewhere in Strathclyde. The trouble with this proposal is that desperation to get out of a run-down estate could lead to all sorts of people claiming victimisation, such is the state of Glasgow's council housing.

America has an expensive witness protection programme – particularly designed for those involved in organised crime, the real-life Carlito Brigantes.

Strathclyde Police appointed a senior detective to report on whether such a scheme was needed here. DCI Eric Pile, of the serious crime squad, travelled to America and Manchester, where a scaled-down version of witness protection is offered.

Pile concluded it was not needed here. "Our police divisions quickly stamp on any cases of witness intimidation. Glasgow Sheriff Court is the busiest in Europe. That surely tells you it is not a big problem."

But what about blanket intimidation? Fear does not necessarily come in the form of a direct threat from a hardened criminal. Fear can keep people quiet on all sorts of issues less clearly damaging than drug dealing.

Take the case of Bob and Dot Dunderdale, who were run out of their corner shop on the St Giles estate in Lincoln last summer. The couple ran the shop for five years, getting on well with the locals.

But the smiles gave way to suspicion after an incident when someone was injured at a wedding reception nearby. One of the guests asked to use the shop's telephone to call an ambulance. The ambulance crew arrived with the police – standard practice in 999 calls. But Bob Dunderdale thinks people believe he called the police.

In the following weeks, the windows were broken several times. Dunderdale was summoned to the shop by the police one night to find a big crowd of adults and children just standing around looking menacing. This culminated in a riot in which the shop was ransacked and looted.

Dunderdale was dismayed. "I wouldn't know how to grass someone up," he told the press. The only time he had ever been in court was for his wines and spirits licence. When he caught shop-lifters, he made them put the item back on the shelf. He never involved the law. He obeyed the 12th commandment.

The rioting and looting appears inexplicable to anyone living in comfortable suburbs with Neighbourhood Watch initiatives. By demolishing the shop, the community had deprived itself of a much-needed facility.

Why this apparent self-laceration? In the past, the code of silence made some kind of sense because the community dealt severely with its own law-breakers. But what is its purpose now that street society is so fractured it cannot mete out its own rough justice? The code of silence merely protects the predators. It leaves the victims defenceless.

In that case, why do they persist in not turning to the police for help? Perhaps they feel the law does not protect the marginalised and unemployed, never has and never will. When people are powerless they become insecure, confused and frightened, and blame "the system" for their predicament.

71

Can we expect them to respect the rules of a system which they think has stuffed them? Is it surprising that they also refuse to help the police when their scorn for society's figures of authority extends not only to the police but, sometimes, even to fire-fighters and ambulance crews.

Blantyre is much smaller than Lincoln and less socially divided. The English city boasts rich suburbs as well as poor estates. Blantyre is mainly poor estates. Visitors come to Blantyre to view the birthplace of David Livingstone. Missionaries, mills and mines. The very name evokes images of Presbyterian obligation – the Victorian values of hard work and knowing your place.

I came here to speak to local teenagers about the 12th commandment. Paul, 17, immediately tells the typical story of a young car thief who passed on information about other joy riders to get himself off some charges. "His house was petrol-bombed and his windows were smashed."

Lyndsay, from Springwells, says even talking to the police would arouse suspicion. A small 17-year-old with shiny bobbed hair and freckles, she tells me about her scheme. "It's not so bad now, but gangs there used to barricade the roads with old tyres and pallets," says Lyndsay.

"I was working on an ice cream van at the time," says Jim, 23. "They'd wait until a squad car came behind the barricade and then throw stuff at the polis. It was wild. I'd be serving weans in the middle of all this. But we were never touched, just the polis."

All the young people, apart from Jim, are aged 17. Those not attending school have no income and no place on an official training scheme. They were all decent and bright, having reached adulthood without becoming delinquent. But of the nine I spoke to, eight had been stopped by the police on at least one occasion. It seems that hostility is a two-way process. Being young and working class is enough, in itself, to arouse suspicion of wrong-doing.

Jim first encountered the police at the age of 15. "A guy was stabbed outside my house. The polis said I knew who did it and hauled me in. I hadn't a clue who it was. But they were putting me under a lot of pressure, pointing the finger saying: "You dae know! You dae know!" Later my auntie got me out by calling them for everything, saying I'd done nothing wrong.

"Another time my wee brother and two of his mates were coming home from a party in Motherwell. They were just walking along the street, but the polis hauled them in for nothing. They spent the night in the cells and were let out at six in the morning without being charged."

Gillian, 17 and still at school, remembers when a 19-year-old friend parked his car badly. If the driver had been a businessman, he might have had an irritating journey to the vehicle pound. But it is unlikely he would have been searched in the back of the police "meat wagon".

"We only got out the car to go to the ice cream van. But the polis were pulling up seats and everything. Then they took the boys into the back of the van. They never found anything."

Is there any wonder, that young people regard the police with the same suspicion as the police view them?

The nine also expressed a lack of confidence in the force's

ability to protect them. All say they would have no hesitation in grassing a "beast" – sex offender. Roseanne, a slim 17-year-old with long blonde hair and thin gold chains, once witnessed such an attack. "I was about ten and this wee lassie was raped on the spare ground where we played. The polis took me and my mum round the streets in a car to see if I could spot the man, but I couldn't. Ages later, I saw him. I knew it was him. I told the police who he was but they said the case was closed. I know where he lives. He's still a beast. But the polis won't do anything."

Did the parents and grandparents of the Jims and the Lyndsays of this world also regard authority with such suspicion? As Peter McDougall says, it was always an unwritten rule that you didn't grass, you stuck together.

Were such communities riddled by sporadic, violent crime in the 1950s? How often did a neighbour's children steal your purse? Did old ladies have to stand shop dummies in their hall, like one Blantyre pensioner today, hoping to frighten away intruders?

"You sorted things out yourself in those days," said the taxi driver taking me from scheme to scheme.

He grew up in Partick and can clearly remember the day their flat was broken into. "My father took a look at the damage. Daft stuff had gone, but valuables like jewellery were left behind. He got the neighbour upstairs to have a look. Then he fetched in the neighbour across the landing. They all drew the conclusion that it was kids. Through a process of elimination, they figured out who had done it. My dad went to his dad, who then sorted out his boy. There was never any question of calling the police."

73

Knocking heads together was the way of dealing with petty crime in the old days. Keeping to the 12th commandment these days is a messier business. With violence more endemic, knocking heads together might not be enough.

John is a former house-breaker who stays in a run-down Glasgow housing scheme. Since giving up drugs and the burglary which financed his habit, he has been trying to put something back, particularly through youth work.

Right now he is settling down to watch *Karachi Cops* on telly – we laugh that it puts our conversation into perspective. John's flat is small and softly furnished – like a fortified womb.

"I have to be careful even talking to a journalist," he says. "I could get called a 'fly grass'. That's somebody who doesn't go to the police directly. Someone who tells other people and talk gets about. I'd lose all credibility if I got stuck with that."

John sticks to the street rules. He consciously identifies police as symbols of a hostile system and believes communities should come together to tackle crime.

Andy, a friend of John's, came home recently to find his door smashed down and several CDs stolen. A few days later, a mutual acquaintance revealed he had bought the missing CDs off a boy in the scheme. Having identified the thief, John and Andy tracked him down in the street.

"There were about 40 people coming out houses and looking out windows when we confronted him. When we explained what had happened they accepted it. Andy had a square go at the boy. But I was angry also at my other mate, the one who bought the CDs. He should have known they were stolen."

He knows the Queensberry Rules don't always apply where he lives. There was panic when someone suggested the thief might knife Andy. But John can see no other way: "If it's left to the state then we're no better off. The boy will go inside with older criminals and when he comes out he'll only have learned how not to get caught the next time."

There is also an understanding that the car thief could himself be a victim. John's friend Ken recently caught a young boy making off with his next door neighbour's ghetto-blaster. Ken knew the kid's mother was a drug addict "Grassing him up is not going to help anyone."

John explains: "I'd like a different psychology among kids in places like this. It's not just about taking revenge on an individual who steals from you. It's about making sure he doesn't steal from anyone else. It's all very well to say: 'He'll not come near my place again', while he's tanning the wee woman's house down the road.

"I want a situation where people know they'll get dealt with no matter who they steal from. If that sounds like a vigilante, well I can justify it to my conscience."

John knows that an eye for an eye can lead to a cycle of violence which blinds the already disadvantaged. He would prefer to see a society which protects the weak from the strong. Our laws, with their emphasis on property and vested interest, seem to do the opposite. So the weak turn to codes which further disempower them. And the 12th commandment stays unbroken.

The secret past

MARCELLO MEGA

20 May 1994

No-one ever wanted Robert Black – not even his mother. When Jessie Hunter Black realised she was pregnant, she made two decisions: she would keep the birth a secret, and she would give her baby up as soon as possible.

Details of baby Robert's father were not recorded on the birth certificate and his identity remains unknown to this day. Even the fact of his birth was kept secret from most of Jessie's family until they learned about it many years later. His reception into an unwelcoming world could scarcely have been colder.

Central Scotland in the years that followed the end of the Second World War was a busy place. During the war, Jessie Black, who lived in Dock House, Grangemouth, had worked in a munitions factory in the town. The end of the war brought changes for her and for the rest of the workforce in the area as industry adapted to the rebuilding process.

The British Aluminium Company, established in Falkirk in 1943, was expanding in 1946, and BP and ICI were developing at Grangemouth. Jessie Black moved from one factory to another.

She was from a large family, which had itself been affected by unhappiness. Her mother had died when Jessie was still a young girl. Her father, a railway furnaceman, had later remarried and abandoned the family home, leaving the older children to care for the others.

Despite this, when her baby was born on 21 April, 1947, she named him Robert after her absent father. She was 24 and unmarried. As soon as possible after the birth, Robert was placed in the care of the local fostering and adoption agency.

When she was able to work again, Jessie moved to Falkirk where she lived on a council estate and worked as a bus conductor. Soon afterwards, she married a colliery boilerman from Alloa, Francis Hall. They had five children, Jessie never told her husband or children of her first son.

Jessie and Francis Hall followed one of their sons, who by this time was married, and emigrated to Sydney, Australia in 1971. Eventually, the whole family settled around Sydney. It was there, aged about 64, that Jessie died in 1987. She had never made any effort to contact Robert.

Even Jessie's closest family members knew little about him. Her sister, Minnie, who lives in Manchester, was pregnant with her daughter, Sheena, at the same time as Jessie was pregnant, but never saw her nephew. "To this day I don't know who the father was. It was still a secret on the day she died." She learned from the media that Black was her sister's son: "I just couldn't believe it and I still find it hard to accept."

Jessie's brother, Billy Robertson, and his wife, Lilly, only learned about the child years later. They were in England at the time of the birth. Billy was a professional footballer who had started his career with Third Lanark and then moved to Ayr United before going south to play for Manchester United, Stoke City and Reading in the Thirties.

Lily, however, remembers her sister-in-law, Jessie, as "a lovely girl".

The baby Robert was fostered out at the age of six months to Jack Tulip, an aluminium smelter worker from County Durham, and his wife Margaret, who was from Motherwell. They lived in the West Highland village of Kinlochleven and had no children of their own.

Enclosed by mountains, and set between Mamore forest and the River Leven, the village enjoys breath-taking surroundings. But a beautiful landscape is no guarantee of easy living conditions.

Why an illegitimate baby from Falkirk should end up so far from his birthplace remains unclear. However, there was a widespread view at the time that fostered children were better off in rural communities. There was also a connection between Falkirk and Kinlochleven since both had a strong British Aluminium Company presence.

Equally puzzling was the choice of foster-parents. The Tulips were already in their fifties, and people who saw Margaret Tulip with the baby thought that she was Robert's grandmother. Within months of the child's arrival, Jack Tulip died, leaving Margaret to raise Robert on her own. She was to do so for 11 years, until she too died.

Robert Black's first home, in Garbhein Terrace, was a wooden bungalow, effectively a hut with a corrugated iron roof. The huts had been condemned long before, but still provided accommodation for Kinlochleven's poorer residents.

Few villagers can remember much about the young Robert Black, but what is clear from our investigation is that he suffered appalling neglect. An elderly resident, who was a close neighbour of Mrs Tulip in Garbhein Terrace, has told us that he was often left alone overnight. She said: "Many were the times I washed and fed Bobby Black. Mrs Tulip often spent her nights in the home of her neighbours, a married couple she had been friends with for years. He was left in a cot in his bedroom. It had bare floorboards and no heating.

"Even when she did stay at home, she often slept into the afternoon. We didn't lock our doors in those days and were in and out of each other's houses. I knew little Bobby was in his room alone and started going in to him and taking him to my place. The first time I went in he was crying hard, he was wet through and stiff with the cold. He just had one sheet and no blanket.

"I took him away, washed him, changed his nappy and vest and fed him. Then I would slip him into my bed to settle him down before taking him back to his cot. After a while, when I went in he would hold out his arms to me to be picked up. But sometimes I found his bedroom door locked and had to listen to him cry and not be able to go in.

"I know that as a baby, Bobby had a very very rough life. He was neglected. Nothing can excuse what he has done, but he had a tough start. He was very skinny. Sometimes it would be tea-time before Mrs Tulip woke up and if I couldn't go to him he would be hungry for hours. You just don't know what effect that had on him."

By the time Black's schooling began in Kinlochleven, he and his foster mother had been rehoused at Foyers Road. There is now a public car park on the ground where their home once stood. Colin MacDougall, a life-long resident of Kinlochleven with a strong interest in the history of the village, remembers the young Black well.

"Me and my pals knocked about with him back then. We went to school together. He was pretty much like all of us, except that he didn't seem to mix very well. I don't know how people can say they remember he was evil when he was five. He was just a little lad like the rest of us."

In fact Black, who needed thick, strong glasses from an early age, was often locked in his home by Mrs Tulip who had trouble controlling him. He was once severely belted for escaping through his bedroom window, and was similarly treated on many other occasions. His trousers and pants were removed when he was to be punished, and his legs were frequently disfigured by bruises.

As a child, he had a fear of something hiding beneath his bed and wet the bed on at least one occasion. This prompted another belting.

He was a rather isolated child, never taking the Tulip name and therefore easily identified as an orphan. He cried on his first day at school.

Mr MacDougall recalls that Black often played on the nearby Garbhein mountain and that he had a dog called Sheila that he appeared to be strongly attached to. "He didn't always play with the crowd. When we got older, we used to play commandoes up on Garbhein. He played with us sometimes, but usually he would get a younger crowd round him so that he could be the gang leader."

Thus far, Black's childhood sounds normal – while far from being an outgoing lad, he was growing up in a healthy environment. But even at a very early stage, there was another side to him. It remains a mystery whether anything of a sexual nature happened to the young Robert Black as he grew up with his middle-aged foster mother. He recalls that she was strict with him, but he felt enough affection for her to have wept at her funeral in 1958.

It may be significant that Black remembers nothing of what happened to him before the age of five. Unlike most children who retain some vivid memories of their early years, Black's memory is blank – it is almost as if it has been wiped clean.

Nevertheless something caused him to become pre-occupied by sex at an unusually early age. Many years later, following his arrest, Black told a psychiatrist: "I've always had a weakness for little girls. I've grown up, but it stayed with me."

He recalls at the age of five going behind a shed with a little girl to undress. "We stripped each other off," he said. Then, at the age of about eight, he assaulted a baby girl in Kinlochleven.

He was pushing the child in a pushchair for a neighbour when he decided to take the little girl into his house. He removed her nappy and touched her vagina. He was then about eight.

By the same age he had also started to abuse himself by putting different objects into his anus.

While other children of his age were playing with toys, he was increasingly being drawn towards a life of sexual depravity.

The families who lost everything

ALAN HUTCHISON

20 May 1994

79

The raw, uncontrollable grief has faded but there is still deep pain etched on the faces of Liz and Fordyce Maxwell. They can talk about it now without tears in their eyes, one starting a sentence and the other finishing it, but nearly 12 years later their hearts are still broken.

It will always be this way for Liz and Fordyce Maxwell, for Annette and John Hogg and for Jacki Harper. They have been to hell on earth. There can be no greater pain for parents than to have their child snatched away, abused and murdered. And for long agonising days and nights to pass without knowing what has happened.

"You have them from little babies. You nurture them and protect them. They are the centre of your life. You think they are always going to be there . . ." The words flow slowly from Liz in a haunting, almost spiritual way. Her language is poetic; her pain only too real.

Fordyce sits beside her, supporting her at every turn. This a difficult interview for them to give: and a difficult one for me to conduct. We are not only fellow journalists but long-standing friends.

"There was this cheery cheerio. 'I'm away to play tennis', and that was it. There was never even a kiss good-bye, a casual thing and she was gone and we were never ever to see her again. It was just too sudden."

It was 30 July, 1982. Susan Maxwell, a happy 11-year-old schoolgirl on her summer holidays had met up with a friend in the morning and had arranged to play tennis in the afternoon. It was a blazing hot day and Susan wanted to cycle the two miles from her home at Cramond Hill Farm, Cornhill on Tweed, Northumberland to the tennis courts at Coldstream, just across the Scottish border.

But Liz, at home with her two other children, Jacqueline, then aged four and Tom, three, was concerned about the traffic on the busy A697 road. Susan had never before made any journey on her own. A compromise was reached: a situation any parent will be familiar with as children start to show their need for independence. A farm mechanic gave Susan a lift to the courts and it was agreed she could walk home.

Liz, however, worried about her doing so. About the time Susan's tennis match was expected to finish, she set off to drive over the Coldstream bridge in the expectation of meeting her daughter. It was shortly after 4 pm, the last time Susan was seen alive. Liz had missed her by a matter of minutes.

The agony of a missing child turned to horror two weeks later when the body of a badly decomposed young girl was discovered in a wooded area, 25 yards from a main road in Staffordshire. It was Susan. She could only be identified from her dental records. The police strongly advised Liz and Fordyce not to look at the body.

In the long days, weeks and months that followed, Liz and Fordyce tried to cope with a life that had been shattered. Liz has no doubts that had she not had two young children to look after she too would, by now, be dead. "At the beginning you just try to put one foot in front of the other," she said. "I would tell myself: 'Just try and get through the next hour'. I would hang out washing or make some soup and try to keep it at bay for a little longer."

Fordyce would find himself thinking that if he drove that road often enough, one of these times Susan would be there. And for months Liz would look out the window of their farm cottage at the time the school bus arrived and tell herself: "This time she will be there." The happy home had become a place of despair.

The happy home down on the farm at Cornhill had been a long time coming for Liz and Fordyce. In the months before the horrific death of Susan they had found contentment after a number of troubled years. Both had had unhappy first marriages and little Susie had already experienced tragedy with the death of her father, Liz's first husband.

Liz, now 46, and Fordyce, 48, met working for *The Scotsman*. Liz had arrived as a reporter in 1973, separated from her husband and struggling to bring up her two-year-old daughter on her own. Fordyce had joined the newspaper four years earlier and was working on the agriculture desk. They married in March 1976 and set up home in Edinburgh but one year later they moved to the family farm at Cornhill. "I had always wanted to go full time at farming," said Fordyce. Liz was excited at the prospect. She told me at the time that it would be such a safe environment in which to bring up Susie.

Liz suffered a miscarriage and had two difficult births with Jacqueline and Tom. But as summer 1982 beckoned life was becoming almost idyllic for the Maxwells. Susie had been adopted by Fordyce and was loving her new life on the farm. She had a Shetland pony and would help Fordyce to feed the calves.

Liz said: "We had three lovely children, we were happily married, we did not have two pence to rub together but life was perfect. It was almost as if things were too good to be true."

The second last day of July will always be a day that a dark cloud descends on the Maxwell home. That date comes between the birthdays of Liz and Fordyce's two other children. Tom's birthday falls on 26 July and Jacqueline's on 4 August. There can never be a proper celebration for them. Then there are annual reminders: the harvest and the smell of grass and flowers. For Liz and Fordyce each July and August takes them back to the summer of 1982.

There have been other poignant moments. One day Tom asked

his mother: "Will I ever be 12?" "It was almost as if he thought that you get to 11 and then you die," said Liz.

Now the children are young adults: Jacqueline, 16 and Tom, 14, and their parents are proud of the way they have turned out. "To a certain extent we have seen through Jacqueline what Susie would have been like. Her little sister has now become a big sister. We have seen what Susie would have been like as a young woman which has made it even worse because she would have been such a nice girl and a lovely person."

Fordyce, who is now agricultural editor and columnist on *The Scotsman*, continued: "At the same time when we had three children and Tom and Jacqueline were about two and four and Susie was 11 we thought Susie was quite a big girl. It is only now when we look back, and we see 11 year olds that we realise that she was just a wee girl."

Liz took a deep breath and added: "We have lost her but she has lost everything. We don't know what she went through. We just hope she did not suffer too much. She lost her childhood, the fun of growing up, school, university, boy-friends, her own family. You realise how precious life is. Nothing else really matters."

Susie lies at rest in a sloping graveyard within sight of the farm. The inscription on her headstone tells of a precious daughter and a beloved sister and in her small coffin is a letter from her parents.

Their message to their daughter, so cruelly plucked from their grasp, says: "Sorry we did not have a chance to say goodbye properly. We love you very much." Mum and dad also put her teddy bear in beside her.

"In the beginning we used to go every day," said Liz, "and then it became once a week. We go on Christmas Eve and take a holly wreath and on the 30th of July. Nobody wants to be in a churchyard but it is a beautiful spot, surrounded by fields. It is sometimes a comfort to go, sometimes it is not."

Finding the man who caused such pain and seeing him sentenced does not lessen the agony. "What we have always said is that the worst thing that happened was Susie dying," said Fordyce. "People will say justice has been done," continued Liz, "as if that is going to make everything OK. The fact that someone is being punished for it does not make the loss any less."

Liz, who courageously completed an Open University BA course after Susan's death and who has now returned to journalism as chief reporter on the *Berwick Advertiser*, added: "We could have ended up on drink and drugs and become totally bitter. It has destroyed part of us but we feel we owe it to the children and to ourselves that this man is not going to destroy everything.

"That is not to say that we are not heartbroken and don't miss her every day. We would have done everything for this not to have happened."

For the love of Katie

KENNY KEMP

Her soft fingers gently stroked my face as I lay asleep. I opened my eyes to see a little girl lean across. I caught the aroma of her sweet fishy breath as she kissed my balding head and whispered: "Daddy, night-night."

It wasn't night-night though, but early morning and this was the first glimpse of the day of a round face which renewed a belief in the wonder and worth of human life.

This is a personal story about imperfection in an imperfect world. When you push the trolley around Safeway you expect all your shopping to be of the highest quality. It is the same when you buy a brand new car, you don't expect any flaws. It has become a modern expectation of 20th century living; if it isn't perfect throw it back.

And it is the same ethos which is driving doctors and scientists in their extensive search to map out and eradicate genetic abnormality and defects in foetuses. Many of their clinical achievements must be applauded but there is a danger that something special will be squandered in this welter of progress – the appreciation of the value of a human life.

For five years I have had the exquisite delight of loving the girl with the kisses who, by the way, just happens to have a few genetic abnormalities.

Had modern science been advanced enough, I and my wife, Gail, would never have felt a profoundly emotional experience and another tiny human life would have been consigned to the hospital incinerator.

As Katie celebrated her fifth birthday this week I'd like to assert her right to a proper place in our civilised society. Knowing her, and other children like her, has been a humbling lesson in a world which places so much emphasis on power, intellect and glamour. During her small lifespan the abuse of children has gone on relentlessly with the awful death of James Bulger, the slaughter of thousands of babies in Rwanda and, this week, the burial of the Liverpool baby found dead in a dustbin. Katie's story is altogether different.

She was born in Simpson's Maternity Pavilion in Edinburgh after a normal pregnancy. Ante-natal testing suggested nothing untoward except perhaps baby didn't bounce so much in Gail's tummy.

But cradling the purple bundle in my arms for the first time moments after her birth I knew something was different. It was her slanted eyes. Gail said she had a Chinese look and I thought it was Down's Syndrome.

Nellie, the Irish midwife who had shared our ecstasy at the birth, looked anxious as she whisked the baby away. Those few lonely minutes in the labour suite brought a dull ache deep in the pit of my gut. It was the most acute moment of our lives. Gail was exhausted, battered by gas and air, emotionally drained by the punishing agony of childbirth. Her short-lived elation was beginning to evaporate as anxiety crept in.

The swing doors crashed open and Nellie returned with a consultant paediatrician. He was straight to the point and confirmed our baby showed all the classic signs of Down's Syndrome – a general floppiness caused by poor muscle tone, a thickened neck, Chinese eyes – but said it would take a couple of days for tests to confirm any genetic abnormality. With Down's Syndrome you get an extra chromosome, trisomy 21, which is part of the 21st chromosome in the human DNA chain. It shifts, or translocates, itself and fuses with another chomosome, usually the 14th, and this abnormal human blueprint affects every single cell in the body.

We were shocked but knew things could have been far worse. On a warm May evening only 18 months previously our 17-week-old son, Angus, had died suddenly in his cot. Nobody could tell us why and it still remains a medical mystery. But what we understood was that life, the living and breathing variety, the fun and games variety, was fragile and precious.

Without ever discussing it, we both realised Katie would stay with us, through thick or thin. We believed that no-one else could protect her as well as her parents. The hospital suggested quietly that a home could be found if we did not want to take her. It was a kindly get-out for us but we firmly declined.

The nurses and the tea trolley ladies were our emotional crutches in these early hours. We were given a side ward while Katie fought to stay alive in intensive care, dozing under the burning glow of the incubator lights. The hospital cocooned us, wrapped us in protective care which made going home a week later a frightening experience. We would be on our own.

Katie pulled through and so the first months at home became an unknown journey while we worried about Katie's health. Heart problems afflict nearly 50 per cent of children with Down's Syndrome and many die very young because of this. We were lucky: Katie was given an all-clear at the Royal Hospital for Sick Children in Edinburgh. She had an opaque cataract in one eye and as surgery to remedy this was ruled out by the Eye Pavilion experts, we waited to find out if she would lose the sight in the other eye. Thankfully her one good eye held out – and still does. Then hearing difficulties were diagnosed which first required grommets and then her adenoids taken out.

At home in the mornings it was a round of talking, songs and colourful objects rattled in front of Katie's face. The experts' buzz word was "stimulation". For months there was little feedback, just two blank eyes staring up beyond our gaze. We were beginning to lose heart, our energy levels took a dive, then one day she just sat up and a tiny little light seemed to be switched on.

She was christened on Christmas Eve at a mobbed and excited West End church where the children sang carols and held Christingle candles in satsumas. The baby wrapped in swaddling clothes was our Katie, quietly burbling in a silken gown.

With two proud grandmothers, both stoical Scottish women who rose to the occasion, a host of family friends, regular visits from health visitors, a home teacher and a watch kept by

Pat Jackson, the visiting paediatric consultant, she was widely adored.

Then came the wonderful Sue, the speech therapist who began coaxing single words out – and stayed for a cup of tea after her official day was over to give a little extra advice.

We found a sympathetic playgroup in Trinity where Bernadette, her helpers and the children knocked a few edges off Katie before she started normal nursery at St Peter's in Morningside last year.

She now has an auxiliary, Mrs Johnson, helping her get a normal start in an integrated environment, but a special school looks likely to be her future road. The other children have been kind and protective, even when she's grabbed their snacks or pulled their hair. At three and four, other children can sense a difference and can see she is slower and they adapt instinctively.

The headmaster, Mr Clarke, and his staff, have met the challenge head on and they have ensured that it has been a worthwhile experience, but it has been a struggle with Lothian Region education department to get enough hours. I'm still waiting for a meeting with the educational psychologist more than a year after asking and several verbal requests. Where's the early educational assessment here?

Through all of this a wonderful character has gradually developed, slow at first but loving and warm. Naughty and cussed at times too, but Katie has shown us she is taking the world in. Her little freckled face exudes innocence and she needs extra nurturing and a lot more patience than myself or Gail ever expected to muster.

Our other children, Sam and Florrie, are much more easy-going and able to be reasoned with, but they also need a chance to develop and prosper.

They need attention too and that can be difficult to achieve with someone as demanding as Katie. It has been harder for Gail because she has been at home, day-in-day-out, with Katie and that has often been a stress which is difficult to explain to other mothers.

Katie sleeps well, loves her food and would devour biscuits all day unless there was a padlock on the tin. She's nearly potty trained after a relentless campaign of almost three years. She can dance and she loves music. It's a cliché that children with Down's Syndrome love singing but there is something about the innate joy of rhythm and melody which transcends our emotions and touches something deep inside Katie.

The wife of the Formula One racing driver Damon Hill was recently interviewed on television. They have a five-year-old son with Down's Syndrome.

She was superbly eloquent. Why do we want to spend all this money getting rid of them? she asked. What is so bad about a set of people who do no harm, but bring a lot of joy and love? They need a little help, but is this a bad thing these days?

Mrs Hill is an inspirational woman. She has taken up the challenge but has also prompted a more fundamental question: why do we have children and do we seriously think about them until they are with us?

My encounters with people in Scotland suggest that the middle class wear their children like badges. "Wee Johnny potty trained at eight months"; "Suzie can write her name and she is only three"; "My son got five A-grade Highers". It is a lifelong competition.

The instant you have a child with DS you realise you can't compete and this can foster a feeling that somehow you have something unworthy.

Katie has made us consider truthfully why we have children and there is nothing unworthy about her or any other child with DS.

It is an interesting statistical footnote that more middle-class parents give up their DS children for adoption than lower income groups. Social stigma is an insidious creature if you want your children to be achievers at all costs.

Last Sunday I cuddled a three-month-old baby with DS in Edinburgh who is still waiting for new parents and an adopted home; her real parents gave up this darling little girl even after going through the trial of IVF treatment.

How they must have suffered.

What Katie has brought into two cynical adult lives is a care, love and compassion which many of us yearn for but never attain. The love of a human being unquantifiable, without barriers or conditions. It is a life to unashamedly nurture, cherish and share.

It would be completely foolish to suggest that ante-natal foetal testing should be halted. Parents must have a right to decide, given their own circumstances, if they are capable of looking after a child diagnosed with severe genetic problems. Life is purgatory for anyone who is forced to look after a severely disabled child.

But the proposition of Down's Syndrome is entirely different. It is not such a horrific prospect and does not deserve to be eradicated by genetic testing.

If a fraction of these resources had been spent on presenting a positive message about DS to trembling mothers-to-be that it is an acceptable part of life, then anxiety and fear could be overcome.

By all means let pregnant mothers have amniocentesis and chronic villus biopsy tests which throw up genetic problems, but we should also have informed choice. Future mothers and fathers should know that having a Down's Syndrome child can be a joy and does not equate with a life of misery. It might not be convenient but there are rich rewards for child and parent.

My crystal ball will not reveal the future for our family and Katie. But at her fifth milestone she is an integral part of a loving family and, given time, she will develop into an adult who must be given a worth-while place in our society.

One last anecdote sums her up. For Katie's third birthday, we tried to teach her *Happy Birthday.* In mid-August we began teaching her the song. When the big day arrived, with family and friends crowded around the cake and candles in a darkened room, she watched in awe as we all sang. We repeated the performance several times but still there was no reply from a bemused birthday girl.

Several hours later, the cake was sliced and parcelled into the party bags, the guests were long gone. Katie was splashing luxuriously in her Radox bubble bath, a Brigitte Bardot in miniature, when the bathroom light bulb fused. We were in darkness, I fetched some candles, lit them and placed them on the window ledge. Katie fixed the flickering light with her good eye and began to sing, in a lovely recognisable voice: "Happy Birthday to You." As she finished she blew in the direction of the sill. This year, when everyone gathered to celebrate her five happy years, she was leading the singing.

Cancer treatment: a case for concern

BRYAN CHRISTIE

22 June 1994

Increasing evidence shows that cancer is best treated by specialists, yet less than 40 per cent of sufferers in Britain are ever given such an opportunity.

The reason is simple – Britain has one of the lowest rates of cancer specialists in Europe.

There is one specialist for every 224,000 people in Britain. Norway has more than three times as many (one for 69,000 people), France has one for every 110,000 and the Netherlands one for every 148,000. Only Portugal is worse off than Britain with one cancer specialist per 225,000 people.

The result is that the majority of patients are seen in their local hospitals by a range of different specialists who share in the treatment of cancer. Few will have been given any formal training in the non-surgical management of cancer.

The treatment in some local hospitals will be very good, especially where a doctor has taken a special interest in a particular cancer and sees a substantial number of cases. That system is developing but not as fast as some people would like.

Earlier this year, a report from the Association of Cancer Physicians highlighted problems that could arise in chemotherapy being administered by doctors with no special training.

"Chemotherapy," it said "is one of the most specialised forms of medical treatment with a potential for great benefit and for great harm. This current state of affairs in the supervision of its delivery is entirely unacceptable and inappropriate."

It has now been established that what is known as stage two breast cancer, where the disease has started to spread, is best treated by a combination of surgery and chemotherapy in premenopausal women but some specialists fear there may be many in Scotland who are not getting that combined form or treatment.

Steps have already been taken in Glasgow to concentrate the treatment of some rarer forms of cancer in specialist centres. A report last year showed that the Western Infirmary's Beatson Oncology Centre was more successful than the other main hospitals in Glasgow in treating testicular cancer with death rates in the other hospitals two and a half times higher than the Beatson.

Although nationally agreed protocols have been established to show how this cancer should be treated, they were followed for only two-thirds of patients treated outwith the Beatson. At the Beatson, the protocol was followed for 97 per cent of patients.

Glasgow's director of public health, Dr Harry Burns, is exercising his role as a purchaser of health care to concentrate services where the evidence shows they can best be provided. The Beatson has the only contract for treating testicular cancer and cases of skin cancer are similarly being directed to Prof Rona McKie's department at the Western Infirmary.

Dr Burns said the aim is to develop a network of cancer care in Glasgow with expertise spreading out from recognised specialists. "We want to create a climate where we have an expert in each hospital who is in touch with his or her colleagues," he said.

Cancer in children provides a model for the kind of progress that could be made. In the 1970's, only one child in five could expect to live beyond five years for most types of cancer; today the figure is closer to four out of every five.

This dramatic improvement has owed much to the improved organisation of services which has seen 80 per cent of children treated by specialists – double the rate for adults.

Cancer services throughout Britain are moving in this type of direction. Last month, the Government announced that cancer treatment would become increasingly specialised and a Scottish Cancer Network has been established for some time with the aim of ensuring that high standards of treatment are getting to the greatest number of patients.

But there are concerns that these good intentions are not being backed up with adequate resources. At the moment, there are only around a dozen medical oncologists working in Scotland, with some of these posts provided with charitable money.

The Association of Cancer Physicians recommends there should be 1.5 oncologists for every 300,000 people and on that basis Scotland would need around 25 – double the present number.

The fame of the former England football captain Bobby Moore, helped him to find his way through the cancer treatment maze in Britain and he ended up at one of the country's best centres, at Edinburgh's Western General hospital.

For two years he was given the best help available but, sadly, it failed to control his colon cancer and he died last year.

Even then, he was still more fortunate than many cancer sufferers. He was able to make the most of the chances offered to him.

Mary is one of those who have not been so lucky. She agreed to talk to *The Scotsman* about her case on condition that we did not name her or the hospital in central Scotland where she was treated.

Five years ago, Mary started feeling unwell and various tests were carried out without any definite conclusion. One day she collapsed and was admitted to hospital. She was shocked to be told she had breast cancer and that the doctors advised that the diseased breast be removed.

Her sister, who is a nurse was concerned about what had happened and suggested Mary should inquire about a less radical lumpectomy, which involves removing the tumour but saving the breast. Mary agreed and that operation was performed.

"They sent the tumour to a pathologist and the results came back that it was malignant. I was told I would need a mastectomy (breast removal) but at that time I felt so well and refused.

"They told me the cancer would return in a year. That was five years ago."

Mary was then left on her own. "I got no drugs, no tests, nothing to help me – nothing at all."

Two years later, while still feeling well, she decided to have a mammogram breast screening test but, because she was under 50 (the age at which women are screened in Scotland) she encountered considerable difficulty in arranging the test.

"I was treated as if I was a naughty child but it came up clear. The hospital told me to disregard it. The mammogram said there was no sign of malignancy but they are still insisting that the pathology report is right.

"I am a very positive person. This kind of thing could frighten the life out of another woman."

91
•

Mary's treatment took place in her local hospital and she has no idea if the surgeon who treated her is just a general surgeon or has any special knowledge of breast cancer.

Mary rang the Glasgow helpline organised by the Breast Care and Mastectomy Association to talk about her treatment.

Caroline Faulder, the charity's UK director, said the inequality of treatment across Britain was made apparent by calls which it receives from people like Mary. "Our aim is to arm women with the sort of knowledge they need to get better services."

She said it is wrong that some surgeons operate on just three or four cases of cancer a year. "There are some general surgeons who are very good with breast cancer, but you would hope your surgeon would see at least 50 cases a year.

"I think this is where women have to become much more active and ask their GP to make a referral to an experienced consultant.

"Until women get up and say we want better treatment, we are not going to get very far."

Many people assume that when they are referred to hospital they are getting the best treatment possible. Sadly, that is not always the case.

Cancer treatment in Glasgow Royal Infirmary, for instance, can approach the highest standards in the world. Existing alongside that excellence is a much less publicised problem.

Three years ago, a report which looked at the surgical treatment of colo-rectal cancer at the hospital found worrying differences among the results achieved by the group of 13 surgeons. One, identified only as surgeon H, stood out. A fifth of his patients died after what was supposed to be a curative operation. Another fifth suffered local recurrance of the cancer.

Most of his colleagues had much better results, with death rates following surgery averaging 6 per cent and local recurrence at 11 per cent. Two-thirds of one surgeon's patients given a curative operation were still alive ten years after surgery, compared with just 20 per cent of another's. The surgeons who operated on the largest number of patients had among the best results.

"The conclusions are clear," said the report. "Some surgeons perform less than optimal surgery; some are less competent technically than their colleagues and some fail to supervise surgeons in training adequately. These factors may compromise survival."

Because the study examined survival over a ten-year period, it looked at operations carried out between 1974-79. It may be that the study is now of no more than historical interest as a number of the surgeons involved have retired. Equally, it will need an updated investigation, which is being conducted, to show if there is any continuing problem.

What is clear is that Glasgow Royal Infirmary knows it had, and may still have, a problem; other hospitals will have much less idea of what happens to cancer patients following surgery.

Colo-rectal cancer is the second most common cancer in Scotland, with 3,000 new cases a year. Only half of sufferers can expect to be alive five years after diagnosis. Surgery is the principal treatment yet there is no agreement among British surgeons on the best type of operation to perform.

An English surgeon has developed a particular technique which has been demonstrated to keep the local recurrence rate down to 5 per cent.

However, Ken Fearon, a consultant surgeon at Edinburgh Royal Infirmary, told a conference recently: "There are some surgeons who do not believe these results and are not carrying out the technique. There is no consensus.

"We cannot agree on what the best operation is or how to do it. There is a phenomenal inter-surgeon variation and this is an issue we clearly have to address in the future on a national level.

Such problems have been known for years but there has been a resistance within the medical profession to talk openly about them. Prof Gordon McVie, scientific director of the Cancer Research Campaign, said that is no longer acceptable and the public has a right to know where they can go to get the best treatment.

He said if a member of his family developed cancer, he would use his contacts to find out which hospital offered the best service. "What I have got is clout to find out. What I should be able to know, everyone should be able to know."

How is the public to get that information? The Scottish Cancer Intelligence Unit has been compiling figures for cancer survival throughout Scotland which are expected to be broken down in the next few months to show what is happening in individual hospitals. It will be given to health boards but it is not clear at the moment if it will be published.

Dr Calum Muir, director of cancer registration in Scotland, said at the moment only crude survival data exist across Scotland and he admitted those do show clear differences from one area to the next. While variations in treatment might have an effect, there could be other more significant influences.

It is known, for instance, that poorer people survive less long with certain cancers than their more affluent counterparts and that could explain why big differences exist from one area to another.

Dr Muir said it would be unhelpful if the press were to use the data to compile league tables of "good" and "bad" hospitals. "This data has to be presented in an accurate and as well interpreted form as possible," he added.

Killings which haunt a father

ALISON DANIELS

94

One Saturday night nearly 17 years ago two teenage girls met after work for a drink. Around 11 pm they left Edinburgh's World's End pub on the Royal Mile with two men who had offered them a lift.

The next day the battered bodies of Helen Scott and Christine Eadie, both 17, were found six miles apart in remote locations in East Lothian. They had been sexually assaulted, beaten and strangled and their hands were tied behind their backs.

In spite of a massive police hunt and an overwhelming number of possible leads and clues, detectives have never come any closer to solving the murder.

Out of the blue a man contacted Lothian and Borders police two weeks ago claiming to have fresh evidence about the case. The new witness told police he was in East Lothian at the estimated time of the murder, near to where the bodies were found and saw two men who fitted police descriptions.

For Helen Scott's retired father, Morain Scott, last fortnight's unexpected telephone call raised fresh hopes that his daughter's killers might finally be caught. But it was also an upsetting experience that has stirred up painful memories.

'Why has the person come forward now? You start thinking someone feels some guilt, remorse, or could be terminally ill and decided to clear their conscience. I just don't know but since the call I've been shattered.

You go through it all again, right back to day one, your mind clocks over although really you never forget it anyway. You just hope again. It's bizarre that someone can come forward 16 years later and say they saw something but you just hope and hope. Funnily enough, as time goes on, when it comes up again, it's worse.

I felt really upset this time, more so than before. I think it's because this is the first time a lead has come up since my wife died. I've always said it killed her, I'm convinced in my mind that all her illnesses came from when this happened to Helen. She was never in good health after that and she ended up with lung cancer.

I realise now what she must have gone through because when things were breaking in the past I had my work to go to while she was at home. I worked for British Telecom and once you got on with it, you had to face people. You were away in another world. I can see now what it's like when you're home and you've got to think about it yourself. It preys on your mind.

I know people say time heals but I think time dulls is more like it because it's there at the back of your mind. There's always something that brings it back, anniversaries, birthdays, and every time you see a murder on the telly, especially if it's a girl. You see their parents and you actually know what they're going through.

The family have obviously tried to get on with their lives. It affected my son most, he was younger – we always said he grew up overnight. He was 11 at the time. It put an extra strain on our marriage. A lot of people don't realise that. It's because of the situation and the stress and you've really got to work hard at it.

I am still as bitter now as I was 16 years ago, if bitter is the right word. I think it's the unknown. If Helen had been killed in a car crash it would've been bad enough to lose her, but to lose her in something which is completely unknown is the worst bit, you don't know what's happened or anything at all about it. I think that is the hardest thing.

My wife used to always say that right from the very night. The phone rang that night and we never ever found out why. I mean these things happen, but that night it was a big, big mystery.

Over the years all the leads seem to have gone cold, that's what I can't comprehend. Right from the start, even from that night, there were three different vehicles mentioned – not one of the owners came forward, not one of them was cleared. I just can't understand that because the police were left with different things they were looking for and they were probably on a wild goose chase. I can only assume that these were people that, for one reason or another, were somewhere that they shouldn't have been. It's a complete mystery.

I'm positive that whoever killed Helen and Christine knew East Lothian very well because I don't think a stranger would have gone to the area where Helen was found without knowing the roads at all, they would've gone the Dunbar road.

Helen had gone to work in the morning and had arranged to go straight out that night. She was never late home, usually before midnight. She would come home in a taxi, she would never risk anything.

They had been in the World's End pub but to this day I have never been in the place. Anyone could've been in there, regulars or passers-by, you weren't going to gain anything by going there after her murder. Where would you've started?

96
•

The thing I feel really strongly about is that I'm convinced someone knows something. Also they say there were two males. Initially they thought one of them would crack and that's what I can't understand, how two people could keep dumb on it, without saying anything, without talking about it even if they were out together. Someone must know.

I mean from the point of the clothes, the handbags, there was nothing found. I suppose they could've been stuffed in a bin bag and that's it but things usually turn up. But nothing came to light at all. Helen still had her watch and her ring – I wear it to this day – but where the rest of her clothes went, her shoes, I just don't know.

The police used to get in touch, they used to be very good, but you can't expect them to come to you with every little thing. At one time, before my wife died, they would phone when I was working and they would say there was something breaking in the *Evening News* tonight or whatever, just to forewarn you. I used to nip home so that she didn't get anything just thrown at her.

This time the first I knew about it was when I read it on Sunday in the newspaper. They're supposed to have spoken to this bloke, according to their story anyway. On the Monday a niece of mine phoned me and asked if I'd heard anything because there was something in the Sunday papers so I thought I'd go and have a word with the police.

I went out to Dalkeith, because the case was there at one time, but when I got there I discovered it was all back in Edinburgh and they gave me the names of a couple of detectives who're working on this follow up. When I got home this chief superintendent phoned me, and told me the same as what he'd said on the telly – that they'd been given this name which they'd already had before but they would obviously have to follow it up again.

This time it's a mystery, it's a name they've had before and I wonder if they couldn't pin anything on it then, then how can they now? You feel now that it's going to be an admission. Someone has lived with this on his conscience for 16 and a half years.

I've always had faith in the police. The media's tried to get me to criticise them but I never like to be critical of them. I think the police are right to play everything low key, they don't want you to think they're on to it this time. Through the years they've had different things to go on.

I still have this photo-fit picture in my mind of one of the men. I can see that face though obviously the person will look nothing like that now. I can remember my wife used to carry that photo-fit around with her. In the early years we used to look at people, you'd go out and you felt you were staring at people.

We never thought of moving away. I visit the cemetery where Helen's buried every Sunday and have done for 16 and a half years. I could count on my fingers the time I've not been there, it's either been because I've been ill or away. My wife used to go up as well and I think we would've been concerned about the cemetery because that's all we've got left.

Believe it or not that's another punishment. I'm not saying we definitely would've cremated Helen but we couldn't because it was a murder and we were told it had to be a burial, so that's something else we were deprived of because of these animals.

I just can't understand why anyone would have done it, more so when there were two of them. You can't think that two men could do the same thing to two girls on the same night and that's what churns through your mind. Maybe something happened to

Christine, and Helen had managed to get to a phone and somebody had taken the phone from her. And how did they get them down to East Lothian? This is the whole mystery of the thing. You try and find reasons and wonder how did nobody ever see them even though it was late at night?

As far as I'm concerned I still want them caught. Somebody said to me when they saw it on telly, would I not rather it was all forgotten but my answer is no, definitely. If they were caught tomorrow, were convicted and put in jail – though I know what I would do with them – I think it would give me peace of mind. I want to see them caught for my late wife's sake, that was always her wish, that they would be caught in her lifetime.

I often look up there at Helen's picture and think why? There's no reason to do what they did. Was it a calculated thing, but how could you go out to do something like that and how could you get on with your life after that? How could they do it?

I think after it happened a part of me died, it's hard to explain, you go out and try to carry on. But I can just be sitting here and look up at the wall, at her photograph and something gels in my mind and I wonder where these men are.'

Testing times ahead

GRAEME WILSON

29 June 1994

It used to be such a beautiful relationship, and strong too. Strong enough, indeed, to grind down the undoubted resolve of the Scottish office and force it into a fundamental review of one of its key policies. But recently the ardour between parent and teachers' leaders has waned somewhat.

While it has obviously not reached the stage of complete separation, the two sides have clearly grown apart since the successful campaign against national testing over two years ago. Their unity then ensured that two out of three pupils in primary four and seven were never tested.

Eventually the Scottish Office gave in by removing their regulations which made testing compulsory, allowing the unions and local authorities to work out systems which gave teachers discretion over when, and in some regions whether, a child should be tested.

Ironically, it is that same issue of national tests which has recently exposed the differences between the two sides.

Earlier this month the biggest teaching union, the Educational Institute of Scotland, voted at its annual conference to renew the boycott of national tests for children between the ages of five and 14. Scotland's two main parent groups – the Scottish School Board Association (SSBA) and the Scottish Parent Teacher Council (SPTC) – quickly signalled their lack of enthusiasm for such a step.

The parents argue that the current system of testing contains the features they fought for during the last boycott. Maybe so, replied the EIS, but the experience of teachers who have now carried out tests is very negative. As a result the EIS is left branding as "educationally unsound" a system of testing supported by parents' leaders.

While differences of opinion on specific issues are not uncommon or unhealthy among allies, the boycott issue has revealed deeper differences between the two leaderships. On the parents' side there is a feeling that the EIS is assuming their support without really arguing its case. The union view, on the other hand, is that the parents' leaders have not fully understood EIS tactics.

The workload issue encapsulates the problems. Since last year the EIS campaign on the amount of work teachers have to do has picked up momentum and has most recently lead to its members voting to withdraw cooperation from all new reforms, including plans to reshape the Highers.

Ann Hill, president of the SSBA, bemoans a lack of communication from the EIS on teachers' problems. "We have said tell us what you want and we will back you all the way but they have never actually told us what needs to be done."

At the SPTC, Judith Gillespie identifies another weakness with the EIS approach on workload. Parents would have been more sympathetic if the workload campaign had concentrated on how their children were suffering because teachers were swamped in an endless stream of reforms. She argued. "The campaign is being sold as teachers have too much to do – that's a tough line to sell when a lot of the parents work hard as well."

The EIS protests that it is being misunderstood. It has held meetings with parents' leaders on workload but its main tactic has been to hold talks with the 12 regional and islands authorities to solve the issue. Union officials say they are nearing agreements with all 12 to control the amount of work flowing into the classroom.

That resolution is in sight, the EIS contends, because the union dealt directly with those who could resolve workload difficulties – the local authorities. On that issue, therefore, there was no need to mobilise parents into a campaign, no need to do the hard-sell.

But by neglecting to get the message on workload to ordinary parents, Judith Gillespie fears they are fostering the growth of a "sympathy gap" between teachers and parents. The possibility of a pay strike later this year could wrench that gap wider apart.

All the teaching unions have rejected the two per cent pay rise offered by the local authorities earlier this year and unless a better deal is put on the table by August or September the EIS has said it will consider balloting its members on a strike.

"A strike is something they will not get the backing from parents for. These people are professionals and in other professions, other jobs, people work long hours and are just as committed," argues Hill.

The news is not all bad. Parents leaders, teaching unions and a range of other groups have worked well together in highlighting the threat to Scottish education posed by local government reform. And at a grass-roots level there continue to be generally good links between parents and teachers.

"There may be gripes about one or two members of staff, but most parents are sympathetic, understanding and appreciative," says Gillespie.

Jim Martin, general secretary of the EIS, insists it is at that level that his union maintains and develops contacts most fruitfully with parents. "Whatever we do about testing, we will be making sure we are taking our message to actual parents in actual schools to tell them our worries about testing," he said. The implication seems to be that the EIS can speak to the parents without necessarily going through the SSBA or SPTC.

And if EIS members vote in favour of the conference call for a boycott of national testing – even if there is a pay strike – it is not clear how the mass of parents will react.

As Gillespie explains: "Children obviously progress through schools quite quickly and a new generation of parents has come through since the last boycott. I know what parents were saying two years ago about national testing but no-one can really say what parents' reaction will be this time.

Shooting at the moon

FRANK FRAZER

9 July 1994

It was the most expensive phone call in history. Richard Nixon joked that he made it collect after being put through from the Oval Room of the White House to the surface of the moon within an hour of Neil Armstrong making the giant leap. Not even the President's gags, however, could detract from the sense of awe felt by an estimated 1.5 billion people who had watched live telecasts of the pinnacle of achievement in the space race. "For one priceless moment, in the whole history of man, all the people of this earth are truly one," Nixon told Armstrong and his companion Buzz Aldrin as they stood at attention beside the fuzzy shape of a lunar landing craft.

The world may have briefly shared in the moment of triumph, but it was an American flag the astronauts planted on the moon on 20 July, 1969, and the American taxpayer who footed the $20 billion bill to get them there. Twenty-five years later, the achievement seems as incidental to the lives of many Americans as the struggle by the pioneers to tame the Wild West a century before.

Perhaps middle-class parents derive some inspirational value from the greatest technological feat within living memory as they encourage their children to pursue their own version of the American dream. But getting to the moon has not banished the social consequences of inequality and deprivation most apparent in America's urban ghettos – the message which a group of civil rights protesters tried to put over at the gates of the launch pad as Apollo 11 was being readied for its epic flight.

Even NASA, the US space agency, can no longer survive on the glory of achieving the goal set by President John Kennedy in 1961 – to land men on the moon and return them safely to earth before the end of that decade. He told Congress that no single project would be more important for the long-term exploration of space and "none will be so difficult or so expensive to accomplish."

Kennedy was right about the effort that would be needed for the mission he would not live to see accomplished. At the peak of the Apollo programme in 1966, more that 20,000 companies were involved in related work which supported an estimated 350,000 jobs throughout the US.

Economists might argue that commitment to some new, equally ambitious space adventure, such as sending astronauts to Mars, would not only give a much-needed industrial boost but also provide a sense of direction to hi-tech enterprise which has lost the spin-off expected from Star Wars as defence-related programmes are run down in the post-Cold War era. But there are no plans for NASA to send astronauts to Mars or anywhere else in the solar system, any more than there are plans to return to the moon, which by the early 1970s had served its purpose in demonstrating US space supremacy. For the foreseeable future, the agency's remit is to remain within earth orbit, with regular shuttle flights for short-duration scientific experiments and observations, preceding the proposed setting up of a permanent international space station next century.

But even the future of the space station project was in doubt until a few weeks ago, as NASA's budget was subjected to a fresh round of scrutiny by Congress. It was not only bottom line considerations which prompted political questioning of commitments to long-term research. There was also concern about the proposals to spread the estimated $30 billion cost of the space station project through co-operation with others, including the Russians, whose expertise in long-duration space missions is acknowledged by the NASA professionals.

The plans envisage European countries, Canada and Japan also participating in the venture. But even with the Cold War consigned to the history books, fears about sharing technology with a former potential enemy still periodically haunt the corridors of the Capitol, as the recent debate over the space station showed. For several months this uncertainty cast a cloud over employment prospects at the Johnston Space Centre, near Houston, Texas – home of mission control and headquarters for other activities associated with the manned space flight programme.

The controversy was finally resolved by a sufficiently wide-margin of 278 votes to 155 in the US House of Representatives for Vice-President Al Gore to claim that doubt about US commitment to space exploration had been ended. This removed the risk of cutbacks that would have put a damper on the 25th anniversary of the moon landing later this month.

In fact, no special ceremonies are planned at the Johnston Centre for 20 July, partly due to the wishes of the Apollo 11 crew – moonwalkers Armstrong and Aldrin, and Michael Collins who circled above in the command module – to keep the occasion low-key after a series of public events on previous anniversaries.

Also, there are nowadays few employees who were at the Houston centre or working elsewhere for NASA during the Apollo programme. Some of the last of the moonshot veterans were among those who took a recent offer of early retirement, making way for a new generation of specialists to manage the shuttle and make plans for the space station. "With that, it's really a new world we've got," a NASA official explained.

In all, there are about 3,000 employees classed as civil servants working directly for NASA at the Houston facility. Another 10,000 contractors' personnel are also employed in the buildings or at nearby sites on associated programmes, including design of the new space station.

Though the present operation may not have the glamour to attract the kind of public attention that focused on the first moonshot, there is enough to keep the organisation busy – coupled with the extra traffic generated by the theme centre a mile or so from the main buildings, where visitors can see lunar rock samples, clamber into a mock-up of the space shuttle cockpit or even try landing, using a computerised simulator.

Mission control – the real thing, which visitors can view through a glass panel – is active for several days about eight times a year when there is a shuttle flight – eight being about the number which NASA staff say they can safely handle in a year. Even so, the pace can be quite hectic at times, despite the fact that shuttle missions are planned to a schedule in much the same way as a commercial airline operates – without the competitive pressures of the space race which set the pace of the Apollo programme.

"Today, it's totally different," explains James Hartsfield, a NASA public affairs specialist. "With the break-up of the Soviet Union, we are now co-operating with the Russians. We have had the first cosmonaut on the shuttle and we have two astronauts in Russia."

The relationship between NASA and the Russians will be consolidated next year, when a specially modified shuttle makes the first in a proposed series of dockings with the Soyuz space station. Like all NASA milestones, this will be a high-profile event which fulfils the requirement in the agency's charter to disseminate information to the public on all its activities. In theory that means the US public, which pays for the bulk of the space programme, but NASA officials have found that in practice the agency is regarded as the property of the planet as a whole, as the wider world keeps its activities under close scrutiny.

104
•

Hartsfield admits that there are drawbacks in having missions broadcast live on global television networks: "If we have a problem, the whole world knows. We live in a fish bowl but we've got used to that. NASA makes a good story, whether we are doing something right or something wrong."

Being a government organisation, mainly dependent on federal hand-outs to maintain its research momentum, NASA relied on favourable public perception, if only to influence political masters who are never short of other causes to which resources can be reallocated.

Apart from helping the United States maintain a leading role in aerospace, many scientists are convinced the proposed space station will play a major role in adding to knowledge through long-term studies of the earth's atmosphere and the benefits of weightlessness in creating manufacturing processes which could not be researched on earth. It will also yield valuable information on the long-term effects of zero gravity on humans who might some day have to endure such conditions for a year or so *en route* to Mars.

But in the absence of the space race incentive which supported the moon programme in the 1960s, the agency faces a harder selling job to keep public and politicians alert to the benefits which could stem from the billions of dollars poured into its activities each year.

Perhaps even a low-key anniversary of the moon landing will make a small contribution to heightening awareness by reminding people of the technological spin-off from the Apollo programme which is nowadays taken for granted. Coating for non-stick pans is possibly the best-known example of a product which popular belief attributed to space travel. Others include materials for bullet-proof vests, composites for improved golf club shafts and quartz-crystal clocks.

But Hartsfield is keen to stress that NASA did not invent many of the products with which the space programme is credited. "They were out there already developed. NASA saw them and said it was going to use a lot of them. Thing took off from there."

Studies by economists suggest that the Apollo programme as a whole returned between \$5 and \$7 to the US economy in the form of new industries, processes, products and jobs for every \$1 invested. Other studies have shown that each additional \$1 invested annually in future space research could return \$23 over a ten-year period.

Perhaps the most pervasive of space programme spin-offs was the microchip, which received a boost from NASA's need for lightweight computers without the vacuum tubes which were previously at the heart of electronic cicuitry. It was a small step from developing integrated circuits for the rigorous specifications of the space programme to producing low-cost versions that led to the desktop units which heralded the era of personal computing.

Even NASA is now reaping the benefits of the technology advances it helped to foster. As part of its preparation for future challenges, the original mission control consoles, which have handled every manned space flight before and since Apollo 11, are being retired from service, along with the purpose-built mainframe computers to which they are linked.

They will be replaced by PCs that NASA is buying off the shelf, so that future mission controllers will only need to click on a desktop device to switch from monitoring a shuttle flight to handling a space station with the ease of computer gamesters enjoying the fantasy of navigating among imaginary planets with technology that was beyond reach 25 years ago.

Now there's a name to conjure with

GILLIAN GLOVER

Columbus. Let the name wash over you. Allow those images of ships in full sail, velvet breeches and weevil-ridden biscuits to crowd your psyche. Admire the shimmering blur of the Americas against the horizon. And savour each syllable, because this is a name with a sweep as wide as the ocean and a cachet more distinct than that distant shoreline. It is not, believe me, a name for a newborn 1990s baby boy.

You see, what Lady Helen Taylor and her husband Timothy have overlooked is that we all grow into our names. It's an irresistible fact of life, demonstrated from nursery school onwards. Think back. That pale little boy called Adrian, who is always late for games, is now a hairdresser. Everyone called Adrian *must* become a hairdresser, unless they are especially good at the piano. Then they can serve drinks in dubious nightclubs and wear turquoise socks. Very occasionally they may be permitted to become deputy draughtsmen in the town planning office, but that is rare. Silvie's salon is their spiritual and actual home.

Of course, it need not have been this way. Had Adrian's beaming parents gazed down into his crib and thought: "What a little

Tamburlaine we have here," his life would have been entirely different. Admittedly, no-one would have spoken to him for the first couple of years of his formal education – it's impossible to snigger and talk at the same time, as you no doubt recall – but that very fact would have forced him to adopt all the tyrannical traits of his namesake as early as possible. By the time the boy was six, he would have been pillaging plantpots and torturing iced buns with malevolent bravado. By 11, he would have been a Tory councillor.

Both, and indeed all, such extremes could have been avoided had the new parents opted to call the baby Nigel. Have you ever encountered a football hooligan called Nigel? Of course not. As soon as the child woke up to the impact of having been Nigelled, he would have grabbed his specs and dashed out to renew his library card. So you see how crucial these decisions are.

It is only fair to point out, however, that context is important too. It is infinitely easier to wear elaborately flounced appellations like Araminta or Cressida when attending Kensington tea parties in hand-smocked dresses in the company of one's nanny. In such gatherings one is always fairly certain that there will be someone else with an even more devastating forename. In this much, little Columbus Taylor is fortunate. He will not be tearing through a Brixton playground when he first hears his name taken in vain.

No, the children who really deserve our sympathy are those whose names do not reflect their parents' class and background but their *aspirations*. This makes it virtually certain that they will always be wearing the wrong name at the wrong time. I spent quite a lot of energy recently trying to dissuade a colleague from prefixing the solid and unremarkable surname of Brown with the horror of Claudius, on behalf of his infant son. He thought Claudius Brown had quite a ring to it, and I'm sure as he envisaged himself reclining in his library, leafing through the memoirs of an influential political career, asking young Claudius to join him in a Cognac would have seemed quite the thing. So it's a shame he and his wife currently share a flat in Hyndland, and his political career has not got beyond a glass of wine at the Lib Dem's Christmas bash. Perhaps his own father should have called him Winston.

Even worse than aspirational names are whimsical ones. The kind preferred by briefly glittering celebrities and ageing hippies. Fifi Trixibelle must be a joy for Bob Geldof's daughter, although she may be grateful that she avoided the excesses of Sunshine, River, and Peaches. My personal favourite was perpetrated by

107

two teachers of English at Glasgow's best-known grammar school. Their surname was Butter and they christened their first-born Roland.

But these are only the major explosions of the nomenclature minefields. There is a host of whimpering little anxieties to be taken into account as well. For example, names do date one terribly. When did you last meet someone under 50 called Ivy or Ruby? And how do all those Darrens feel about being named after a character in a forgotten sit-com called *Bewitched*?

More embarrassing than an index to one's age are those names which offer an index to character. Cher called her daughter Chastity, which will be a terrific name for her once she marries, and I'm sure the girl delights in it daily. My own mother was keen to call me Verity. But then a terrible doubt crept into her mind regarding my unfailing honesty. So she chose something a lot safer. Wise woman. I'm sure young Columbus would have appreciated similar restraint.

Sound and Fury

DOUGLAS FRASER

3 September 1994

The midges were ferocious at the Silver Chanter last month. A breathless night at Dunvegan Castle had them dancing greedily. Gentle variations on a theme of sunset red played on wispy Skye clouds. Far across the loch carried the sound of high-pitched battle – the majesty and melancholy of the world's finest pipers competing before the MacLeod chieftain and his guests in the Great Hall.

Few events can tap so deeply into clan history, delighting the worldwide diaspora of MacLeods reconstituted at Dunvegan for their four-yearly "parliament". As they learned on their coach trips, John MacLeod of MacLeod's predecessor, almost 400 years ago, picked a local lad called MacCrimmon to run the local bagpiping franchise. The boy had been brought belatedly into an interclan piping challenge without much time for practice, and in a bid to please the boss, he took a local fairy's offer of a silver chanter and a quick lesson in magical grace-note technique.

For more than 250 years in their piping college at nearby Boreraig, the MacCrimmon dynasty is supposed to have taken a crude musical form, given it substance, method and tradition, and then left Scotland for North Carolina as punishment of carelessly losing the fairy chanter and one of their number in a local cave: only the piper's dog ever emerged, terrified and completely bald. But what was also left was a bequest to the nation of what Hugh MacDiarmid called Scotland's greatest single contribution to European culture: the pibroch, or *piobaireachd*.

This is *ceol mor*, the "great music". By comparison, reels and marches are mere *ceol beag* – light music, akin to late night Radio 2 easy listening. Pibroch is the classical tradition, and strong, serious stuff. You're supposed to need seven generations of piping in your family, and seven years of practice, before you can master it.

But if not so generously endowed by forebears, you can sit there for hours and still not find the words to describe what it's about. Perhaps they exist in Gaelic, but to the uninitiated non-Gael, the pibroch is a musical form of supreme impenetrability. It is like Schoenberg with drones. One observer described sitting on the edge of his seat waiting for the melody which never appears. The pibroch is a sound sensation which sears right to the depths of the soul, and into those furthest recesses of the head which aspirin can barely reach.

All this is a long way from the red-haired, red-faced laddie gie'n it laldie at the Kyle of Lochalsh ferry, or that gruesome cocktail of three out-of-tune busking pipers simultaneously audible from a spot near the postcard salesman at Edinburgh's Scott Monument. To many, such bagpiping occupies a special place in the demonology of Caledonian kitsch. Worldwide, they are identified with the nation, having travelled much of the planet in the vanguard of Britain's imperial regiments.

But the pibroch, the truest form for Scotland's national instrument, is barely known even at home. It is one part of Highland culture which Lowlanders have not colonised. It occupies a musical ghetto. Few know, for instance, that the most prestigious of all competitions takes place at Inverness's Northern Meeting on Wednesday and Thursday of this week. And few Scots are aware of the deep divisions which have opened up in the last two years over the bagpipes' past and their future – a row which has involved bitterness, boycotts, a bid for a closed shop of judges, and a gathering mutiny against the art's military masters.

But first, a Lowlander's mission to understand had led – the night before the prestigious Silver Chanter event – to the Skye Gathering Hall in Portree. The Jock MacDonald Clasp is in progress, its competitors giving their all for a top prize of £100. A few cognescenti listen, heavy in Harris tweed, eyes closed, meditative, feet twitching to the plodding rhythm though one is bootlegging a tape on his ghetto-blaster. Two judges make occasional notes, while a third leans back looks up, his arms crossed as his fingers play his biceps like a chanter.

A small gathering of tourists have joined, preferring the £2 ticket to the £2.80 price of a bottle of Bug-Off for the outdoor ordeal. They expect a hearty blast of *Amazing Grace*, *The Skye Boat Song* and assorted reels to tap their feet to. Few last beyond two pibrochs. A German couple have already experienced this incarnation of Scottish culture, and read novels to pass the time.

A succession of men take to the dimly-lit stage, accompanied only by a large, oriental pot plant, their pipes warmed up in the practice rooms, only allowing themselves some minor tuning adjustments before the off. At such jousts, it is common not to know which of about six short-listed pibroch compositions of 12 to 15 minutes one is going to be asked to play until minutes before one is on stage. It is like expecting a concert pianist to greet the audience, only then to be told which concerto is on the programme.

The point at which tuning ends and the pibroch theme begins takes some discernment, but is most easily told when the competitor begins to pace. This is one of the most intriguing parts of the performance, especially if the music leaves you bewildered. The pace has to be ponderous, over a 15-foot course, averaging 11 steps per minute, out of time with the music and taking at least 30 seconds to turn 180 degrees. It may be worth trying this with the main section of your *Scotsman* squeezed under one arm, just to see what exceptional skill is required simply to move that slowly.

So what is this pibroch all about? Numerous attempts to find an explanation only increase the bafflement. Perhaps they prefer their pipes to speak for themselves, but few players can explain what they're up to. Murray Henderson, a 41-year old New Zealander who makes reeds in Kirriemuir and ranks at the rarified top level of competition, does better than most.

"Each tune is commemorative, whether it is a lament or a battle tune," he explains. "They all start with a melody, the ground or urlar, and variations are based on these melodies – except the embellishments change, finishing with a very complicated variation bringing the theme to a climax. The challenge is to bring out the theme and to bring out the subtle changes of tempo and phrasing to punctuate it. The last variation is more of a technical test."

He continues: "You've got to look to light and shade, the sharpness and softness of getting from one note to the next. In a lament, you want a gentler treatment than a battle tune."

From Fraser Walker, a 16-year-old competitor from Dunblane, comes a reminder that the format was not always thus: "In olden days, you'd play the ground and keep going back to it between each variation. That way, you can have a pibroch going on for a couple of hours and the competition would go on for days."

Eric Rigler, second in the Jock MacDonald Clasp, agrees to explain further. He is 30, Californian, and his kilt belt buckle proclaims him to be pipe major of the Los Angeles Police Department. A former maker of surf boards, he is piper to the stars – recording with Paul McCartney, Rod Stewart and Mike Oldfield – but also spends several months a year on Scotland's competition circuit in pursuit of ludicrously small prize money.

"Judges are looking for your portrayal of the pieces as an artist, but along the way, you must have all the technique as impeccable as possible." says Rigler. "There's also the tone of the instrument and how well in tune it is. There's a lot of hours at home sorting your pipes to get them just right just before you go on – so that if they're going to go wrong, you know how it's going to happen and what you can do about it."

Pipes, it seems, are temperamental beasts. And there's the memory feat as well. Rigler reckons that competitions, including pibroch, march, strathspey and reel, require up to 28 pieces of music ready to play at the drop of a Glengarry.

"The pibroch is a maturity kind of thing," he continues. "You've got to have years under your belt. That gives wisdom and composure. There's a lot more of that, and musical ability, than in the march, strathspey and reels."

Angus MacLellan, late of Strathclyde Police Band, is one of the judges, the one who plays his biceps. He agrees maturity is needed, and is disappointed by its absence at the Portree meeting. It seems too many of the young are spending too much time getting up to technical wizardry in ceilidh bands and folk groups. "A lot of young people are playing on the fast side, although it gives them a dexterity of fingers that we never had," says MacLellan.

What he is seeing creep into the fiercely conservative world of competitive piping is the infleunce of Wolfestone, the Battlefield Band and their ilk, in turn following the Irish folk piping of the Bothy Band and the Chieftains. Over 25 years and with improved amplification of fiddle and flute, piping has changed pitch and broken into mainstream folk music. And it is more than just up-tempo playing that has resulted. Competitive piping has been sent reeling.

Allan MacDonald, one of three Glenuig brothers who rank among Scotland's finest pipers, is a leading rebel who hopes to make big sound waves with the thesis on pibroch he is finishing at Edinburgh University this autumn.

Pibroch, he claims, has been mutated ever since it was written down and put into the hands of upwardly-mobile, urbanised Highlanders early last century. Previously it was only learned by oral tradition, and his research appears to have found a clear link with Gaelic song before Culloden. Pibroch was intended to be lyrical, claims MacDonald, but instead it is sterile and ossified in social structure.

"A lot of pipers find it very boring," he says. "It is an acquired taste, slow and artificial through being standardised, and it's lost the language from which it developed."

It has also suffered from being in military hands. Until recent years, army training and its accompanying discipline dominated the piping tradition, and pipe majors were slightly less than receptive to radical new ideas from their subordinates.

But mutiny has broken out in the lower orders, as younger pipers in civvie street innovate in style. Last month, for instance, Gordon Duncan, a 30-year-old from Pitlochry who has worked with the Tannahill Weavers, Wolfstone and Dougie MacLean, set the piping heather on fire with a sizzling new album which blasts at tradition and has earned him the accolade of "one of Scotland's living national treasures" from respected piping innovator Hamish Moore. Titled *Just for Seumas*, the recording is a response to arch-conservative Seumas MacNeill, whose considered judgment on Duncan's virtuoso playing at one competition last year was to call it garbage.

And it is there the key debate now lies, over such competitions in piping and how they are judged. No other art form, past school age at least, is so dominated by competitions. It has been thus for more than 200 years, and the number of competitive events continues to grow. John MacLeod of MacLeod, who is a London-based opera singer, has challenged this by struggling to turn the Silver Chanter from a competition into a recital, as would be the case in singing. He met a firm rebuke last month from noted piper and journalist Robert Wallace. "The audience and the pipers are there to taste blood," wrote Wallace in the *West Highland Free Press*. "The talk at the interval is not of 'what an enjoyable social occasion,' but 'who is going to win?' Chieftain John Macleod of Macleod has to understand that pipers are brought up in a competition culture. It is, for better or worse, the life blood or our art."

More like a black pudding of our art, retorts Allan MacDonald. He says the only way to make his point and be taken seriously is to win the top awards at the Northern Meeting, which he has duly done. "No-one would be more happy than me to see the whole competition system collapse," he says.

Such collapse has come very close. The piping fraternity has been bitterly split since last year over an apparently obscure issue, but one which could define the future of piping: who has the right to judge in piping competitions. This results from generations of top pipers going into competition only to find their efforts wasted on judges who didn't know much about piping, but they knew what they liked: local lairds, society gents and assorted brigadiers.

Some bizarre results led to a breakaway group, comprising more than half the retired top pipers setting up shop last year under the title of the Association of Piping Adjudicators. They operate a closed shop, refusing to take part in any judging panel that is not entirely made up of APA members. But their closed shop has been closed out. The conservative, establishment figures, linked mainly to the Piobaireachd Society, now dominate the panels.

Many members of the Competing Pipers Association have only agreed to appear in front of APA judges, leaving last year's Northern Meeting almost bereft of numbers or talent.

"There's a lot of bitterness," is the repeated, dark warning. "Quite a lot of people are not on speaking terms. And I doubt you'll get anyone to tell you the whole truth."

Off the record, the language is uncompromising. "There's people whose egos get a kick out of judging us, just because they didn't win the top prizes themselves," says one senior performer. "It was a peasant revolt. Some of the event promoters are pipers, but not up to much, and if you're a brigadier, you're not used to being told the peasants don't like the way you're doing things."

Alasdair Milne, former director general of the BBC and an organiser of the Dunvegan Silver Chanter, says the dispute has opened up a huge gulf, even if pipers are returning to the competitions this year. If it were cricket, he says, the selectors would be imposing some severe fines.

Competitive piping is a small world, a tad parochial and intensely passionate. Young men felt strongly that they should not have to play the only way that judges would accept, says Milne. "It's become fractious in recent years. There are a number of extremely good amateurs who are not subject to military orders or Section 49 of the Army Act, the way most pipers used to be, and who don't want to be pushed around."

114 · Event promoters have, similarly, been unwilling to yield to the APA's trade union-style closed shop ultimatum, pointing out that the association was also engaged in pursuit of sharply increased fees and expenses for its members. "The whole thing's been very bad for the piping world," says Vice Admiral Sir Roddy Macdonald, Chieftain of the Skye Games. But numbers are up this year: "We're not missing anyone in the piping scene that matters."

The stand-off continues. The bitterness runs deep. And the forces of conservatism are not going to give in to a closed shop demand by judges. Flora MacNeill, convener of piping at the Skye Games and a rare woman in this male bastion, is one of those who has by-passed the APA. Mutiny and boycott there may be, but the promoters are still in charge. As she points out: "He who pays the piper calls the tune."

Well, somebody had to say it eventually.

Pillars of wisdom?

SAY "SLEAZE...."

ALBERT MORRIS

1 January 1994

On impulse, I looked at the wardrobe mirror the other day to see how the old year was wearing. It looked bad. The fabric of the months had worn thin, there was a nasty sag in its seat of gravity, the minute stitching was coming apart and the hours had shrunk badly. My fault of course. Buy cheap, you get cheap, and with 1993 I had bought seconds.

Some people like to wear a fancied year all the time. One friend claims that annual quality went out in 1953, that the fabric of succeeding years has deteriorated and that he is content to remain spiritually in that year when the plangent chords of the *Blue Tango* were in everyone's ears, Victor Sylvester's dancing spoors were in all strict-tempo tuition books, Britain's Randolph Turpin won back the world middleweight championship and stiletto heels first tottered into fashion.

I was like that. Long after it had vanished from the calendar, I wore 1963, flaunted its moral and political attitudes with a careless swagger, invited people to gauge the quality of its spiritual and temporal tones and the durability of its domestic and international political fabric, and claimed that the year which saw De Gaulle banning Britain from the EEC, the Profumo scandal erupting and Harold Wilson promising a "white hot" scientific revolution for a socialist Britain was never likely to be surpassed in quality time.

I changed eventually to 1972 when all diaries showed 1979 and although I stuck to 1984 for longer than I should – I was waiting for George Orwell's bleak prophecies to be fulfilled – I managed to catch up with trendy 1993 round about this time last year.

Threadbare stuff it turned out to be, revealing a lack of shining hours for improvement, with the threads of my remarks being snapped as people interrupted me when I tried to interrupt them in conversation and when I found I was given too little time for witty, off-the-cuff remarks, others being too busy making them to me.

That was it. I decided to try on a new year. I was confident that the old Anno Domini Tailors, (sole proprietor F Time) would see me, a gentleman of good-time taste and labelled by outfitters as "small, portly", into fitting and fashionable gear.

I doubted if I had ever seen the old boy's place so busy. There were large queues at the counters for mint-green polyester leisure weeks, the craft-based, individual hours' department was crowded and, in other rooms, people were minutely examining the weave with which they could wear the quintessential attitudes and emotional styles for 1994.

I buttonholed the old greybeard, who was deftly shaping lengths of decade fabric into precise 12-month rolls. "You've got a big cutter there," I observed. "That's about the scythe of it," he remarked, ever one with the gift of the garb.

I told him frankly that I was not pleased with the past year. "It felt as if it had been made for someone else and I was just standing in," I added, as he slung a time tape-measure around me, noted my conservative 60-second minutes and gauged the inside length of my hours.

Someone walked past me wearing a beautiful year, the months swirling around her like twists of silk with Armani-type sexy split-seconds, Calvin Klein-like braces of shakes and matched with magic moments. I liked it and asked for a male equivalent.

The old boy's heavy sigh dislodged time fluff and minute fragments of discarded aeons from his work-scarred time table. "Laddie," he said, "you want something sensible and hard-wearing, in an environmentally sound fabric, which I could knock up for you in a trice, half a tick or, as you would say, two shakes of a lamb's tail."

I nodded resignedly, I never get the years I want but perhaps nobody really does and I suppose I have to fit into whatever is available. As the old-timer cut my cloth with a new-fangled laser blade, I pointed out that weeks nowadays didn't appear to last as long as they did when I was a child. "Six weeks' school summer holidays seemed to last a year then," I observed reproachfully.

The old snipper agreed. "You can't get the quality nowadays," he said. "We were on to International Dateline Techtronics complaining about missing micro-seconds in sidereal days and they said they neither had the staff nor the time to work to our exacting standards. Typical." he added, a tear forming like a stalactite in an ancient eye.

Never mind, my year was shaping up nicely. I wanted it smartly

The Funeral of John Smith MP

Robert Black *picture: Allan Milligan*

Nelson Mandela in George Square, Glasgow   picture: Allan Milligan

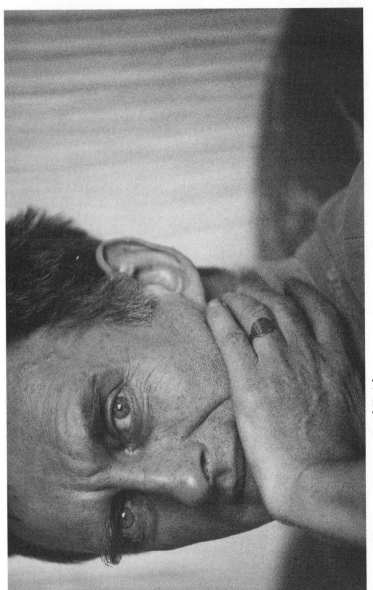

James Kelman   *picture: Paul Reid*

Tiree Wave Classic   *picture: Ian Rutherford*

Cowal Highland Gathering pipe band avoiding a large puddle   picture: Allan Milligan

A grey seal being released onto the beach at St Andrews   *picture: Guilio Saggin*

Peace in Belfast   *picture: Ian Rutherford*

Kelso Ram Sales   *picture: Ian Rutherford*

Longhope Lifeboat Memorial, Orkney   *picture: Donald MacLeod*

Scottish Horse Trials: Bruce Davidson on Happy Talk   *picture: Ian Rutherford*

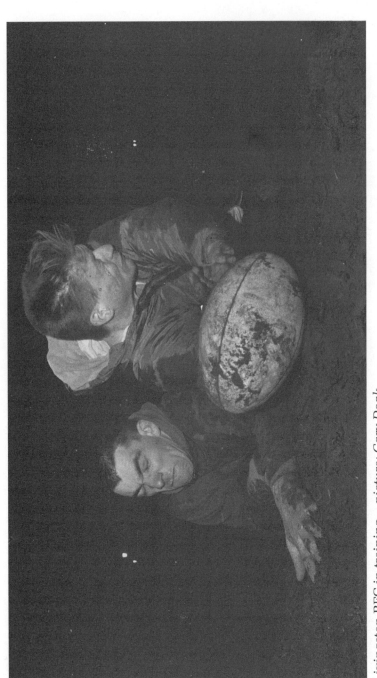

Livingston RFC in training *picture: Gary Doak*

cut on the politically-centrist bias but with matching chips on my shoulders, financial turn-ups for my books and a trendy bit of time-warp to allow for mind changes and memory lapses and with no fraying at my themes.

I also wanted a juncture. Old Time bristled. "Junctures went out years ago. Let me do you a nice half jiffy, a couple of ticks or even a well-cut, English classical arf a mo."

I insisted and at that point it was stitched in, although the old boy grumbled like mad and said it would mean making a large gusset in the silver lining which I had agreed to have fitted at extra expense. Then I tried on the year. It seemed a bit big, but while I felt that hours might sometimes hang heavily, I expected that it would all fit in the fullness of time. All the best emotions had been stitched into its fabric, tolerance shot through with faint impatience, a bit of understandable annoyance, an almost imperceptible hint of irritation, more than a glint of humour, the merest suggestion of gravitas and a lot of hope that this year will be tailored as an improvement on the last.

Like everyone, I have been minutely stitched-up for 1994. Let's button up to face it. Seconds out. Happy new year.

Keeping the torch of Keynesianism alight

KEITH AITKEN

10 February 1994

There is a venerable theory, which I have just invented, that the reason weeny-boppers weep at pop concerts is the disappointment of seeing their idols made human flesh. The air-brushed Adonis is revealed, not as an unattainable god, but as a distressingly ordinary bloke who gets plooks, sweats when he dances and needs a microphone to be heard.

Now, the present writer bears no resemblance to the middle-aged figure whose jowled image heads this column, but he is, alas, many years removed from being an excitable teenager. Still, we all have our heroes, and none of us likes to see their frailty revealed.

Something of the sort happened the other night. There, on *Newsnight*, was a man long admired beyond extravagance, John Kenneth Galbraith. He was in Britain to deliver a lecture at Cardiff and had turned up to be cross-examined by Jeremy Paxman.

Paxman gave the old guru a notably courteous hearing. And yet, Galbraith seemed oddly discomfited, sifting vaguely through an ill-sorted jumble of Keynesian phrases. The Keynesianism, of course, was neither a surprise nor a disappointment: the vagueness, though, was both.

Very well, Galbraith will be 86 this year and has every constitutional right to sound it. Anyway, he was always a better writer than talker, the layman's expert, perhaps the most fluent pen in economics (and much else besides: his autobiography, *A Life in our Times*, counts as a great history of the century, while *Made to Last*, his charming account of boyhood in a bleak community of Clearance Scots on Lake Erie, is one of the best books ever written about the Scottish diaspora).

The thing to do was to turn to the lecture. But that too, sad to relate, was a decidedly mixed blessing. The elegant scepticism was still there ("politicians are often compelled to virtue by the thought of votes") as was the simple decency ("nor should it be socially degrading that one is forced to live on the dole – to think that is a uniquely cruel tendency of our time"). The analysis was less compelling.

Galbraith had been invited to discuss the objectives capitalism should address to create the better society. It is an important debate, which has swollen since the collapse of communism. No-one now seriously disputes the power of the market as an engine: that was the Eighties issue. The Nineties longing is for agreement on how best to connect it up to wheels and to steer to towards a chosen social destination.

This is a debate which Galbraith anticipated in the discussions he published in 1989 with Stanislav Menshikov of the Soviet Communist Central Committee. Then, he identified the problems. Was it too much now to look to him for solutions?

Yes, as it turned out. His description of the "good" society was persuasive, and his account of how far short of it we fall the best thing in the lecture. The route from A to B, however, remained rather sketchily delineated.

Let's start with the good stuff. Galbraith concludes (and it is not too American an observation) that the old class divisions between capital and labour have subsided, only to give way to a new distinction between the contented and the deprived. The latter are excluded not just from wealth but from influence in the democratic process: even though they have most need of that process.

The tendency of Eighties capitalism, he observes, was to heighten the distinction between these classes. The rich got richer, the poor poorer. The comfortable demanded reductions in state provision – on which the deprived most rely.

All this in the name of liberty: "Nothing, let us [not] forget, sets a stronger limit on the liberty of the citizen than a total absence of money," Galbraith writes. "Those who attack the services of the state are usually those who can afford to provide similar services for themselves."

To that he adds one more penetrating remark: that "the hope and reality of economic improvement is one of the pacifying influences of our time". Glancing around a fractious globe, he notes that many conflicts are waged in the name of religion. Its appeal, he reasons, is to suggest that the next life offers better prospects than the miseries of this one: which is why it chimes most with the disadvantaged, and why real hope of enrichment can soothe.

Good stuff indeed. But how to get there? It is here that the discourse becomes both familiar and oddly cursory. What the market does not provide, he says, the state should: specifically, opportunity through education, and decent housing, health care, environmental protection. There must be governmental intervention, through harmonised fiscal policies, to make wealth distribution more equitable and to combat cyclical deficits. Aid must rise, arms trading be curbed.

There is no pleasure in reporting that, to one affectionate reader, this rather echoes the later Bertrand Russell, who used to instruct mankind solemnly that all it need do was embrace kindliness, abolish poverty, declare peace and all would be well. True enough, but a somewhat ambitious manifesto.

Galbraith acknowledges the problem: "This is not a popular political design; there are many in the culture of contentment whose income is secure and who do not find recession or poor economic performance particularly uncomfortable. The good economic society can make no concession to this."

Yes, but can the bad economic society get around it? Can the content be coerced? Paxman gently tackled Galbraith and was rewarded with a mildly tetchy response that just because Keynesianism was old didn't mean it was wrong, and if it was right why bother to reformulate it?

There can be some sympathy with that, but a greater regret. As a distinguished torch-bearer for Keynesianism, and quite its best communicator, Galbraith has spent decades out of fashion, though rarely out of sight.

If, as may be, a changed world is once more asking the sort of questions Keynes sought to answer, the answers may still be right, but the contrary case has changed. The same answers, put the same way, may not inspire. Perhaps Galbraith's real achievement has been to keep the torch alight through harsh times, and it is now for others to bear it forward.

Staying loose while going downhill fast

IAN WOOD

21 February 1994

It seems strange that when it comes to skiting down icy inclines on small sledges, it is regarded as standard procedure for people to lie flat on their backs with their teeth bared and their toes clenched.

Last week, watching the return of the rubber men in the luge event in the Winter Olympics, the thought occurred that what seems to be a high-risk sport can hardly be rendered any less dangerous by having to assume what appears to the inexpert eye to be just about the most uncomfortable, vulnerable and impractical position imaginable.

No doubt, there are reasons for doing it this way, but until it is explained to me lucidly and possibly with diagrams, I will continue to suspect that it might be better to lie headfirst on the stomach, if you follow, so that the luger would point the way he was going and be able to see with relative ease.

Not that what he sees is likely to be all that reassuring, but at least he would be able to see whatever it is without having to peer over his chest and getting a crick in his neck. He would also be better placed to do what lugers do if and when things begin to go wrong – such as get off, hang on, pray or scream.

However, for whatever reason, they luge on their backs, which, apart from looking decidedly dodgy, would seem to make it virtually impossible for lugers to do what the commentator, David Coleman, deems essential to good lugeing. "It is absolutely vital," said David, as a petrified German shot past, laid out like a highly-polished corpse, "to stay relaxed."

This is quite probably true, but to seriously expect a person hurtling at immense speed down a twisty, gleaming run, supine on a souped-up tray, to do so in a relaxed manner, seems, at best, unrealistic. The effort involved in just staying on the luge – to say nothing of staying on the track – suggests a degree of stress and general tautness which would leave most mortals severely sprained in body and mind.

It is one more example of the unnatural demands sport makes upon its adherents. Whenever things become tense, you're supposed to relax. Of course, you don't. You might manage to loosen up to the point where you can actually function, perform the action which is required, but that's about it. Relaxing – really relaxing – is out of the question and it's probably not even advisable that you should.

Where golf's concerned, I find that as I get older, any ability I ever had to relax or at least take things a little easier on important shots is fast disappearing. By important shots, I mean important to me, though not necessarily of any consequence to anyone else. The shot over the water to the last green at the Emirates course in Dubai vaults lightly to mind.

I had the pleasure of playing that splendid course last month. As it turned out, it wasn't a pleasure at all, simply a rerun of the misery which is my golfing lot these days, whether it's Dubai or

Craigentinny. The experience at the last hole at the Emirates was all the more galling because for a while it had seemed as if I might be working up to some sort of highlight.

I'd had the advantage of seeing Ernie Els playing the 547-yard hole the day before and was fairly conversant with the routine. He was at the back of the green with a drive and a 5-iron. I tend to rely rather more on subtlety and shrewd linksmanship than Ernie and so, throttling back, as it were, I played a drive and a 3-wood to a point sensibly short of the water and was left with an easy 6-iron to the green.

I felt the malaise stealing over me on the practice swings. The more I swung, the more wooden it felt. By the time I moved into the address position my legs and arms had gone stiff. It was as if my blood had set. The water, originally a small lake, now stretched for miles. At that moment I knew it would make no difference whether I hit the ball with the 6-iron or with the bag.

As the splash went up, I realised I'd have been as well kicking the thing in and saving a lot of pain and effort.

A ranked outsider on the inside track

RUTH WISHART

14 April 1994

You couldn't really call it a Lazarus job. After all Colonel Oliver L North was never actually politically dead. He ought to have been. By his own now infamous television admissions, while employed as a national security officer with the Reagan administration, he routinely lied, horse traded with the very terrorists "with whom this government will never negotiate", and financed the unsavoury Nicaraguan Contras in express contradiction of a Congress edict. Then, when the Iran/Contra investigation began to lay a trail leading to his office, the heroic marine routinely stole and shredded official documentation which might further incriminate him. In short Oliver North is a crook, a cheat and a proven liar. And now he wants to become a US Senator.

He's not short of the wherewithal. For notoriety read bankability. The book, the lecture tours, the legal fighting fund, have all made him wealthy beyond even the dreams of American avarice. But please sir, Oliver is asking for more. He's telling rallies in support of his winning the Republican nomination in Virginia that he needs their dollars as well as their devotion if he's to have a real chance of fighting the good fight in Washington. In particular he's targeting a very particular constituency of contemporary US politics which embraces a number of "Christian" pressure groups.

The quotation marks are mine, and do not appear in conjunction with an apology. For these organisations in many respects are an occidental variation on the growing trend towards Islamic fundamentalism elsewhere in the world. Both deal in instant cures, both are visited by terminal self-righteousness, and both are assuredly dangerous for precisely those reasons. The American variety, a coalition of sharp-suited TV evangelists, hard-line anti-abortionists and instinctive supporters of all manner of right-wing causes, checks the political purity count of supplicants before agreeing to bankroll them. It is a very effective method of buying votes in Congress should their favoured candidates be returned. North is wooing them assiduously.

And do these "Christian" lobbyists set their face against a man whom only legal wheeling-dealing saved from justice? Not at all. They are apparently mesmerised by North's sickly blend of patriotic piety and square-jawed simplicity. It beggars belief that a man with such a publicly and carefully documented criminal track record should be viewed by huge segments of the electorate as the embodiment of family values. His huskily delivered rhetoric is that peculiarly American mix of hype and homily which comes over like Patience Strong over-dosing on *Reader's Digest*. But somehow it has the faithful passing the collection plate rather than the sick bag.

North is the heir to two strands of American politics, neither of which much flatters western democracy. In the first instance he succeeds men like Haldeman, Erlichman and Dean who served in the Nixon administration and provided new benchmarks for autocratic assumption of control by unelected officials. Their proximity to the president gave them the crucial power of personal access to the throne, coupled with the ability to refuse that same privilege to those with more legitimately acquired rights. North followed that dishonourable tradition of power without accountability. He worked, if you like, for one of the most powerful White House quangos.

The second, more recent tradition, owes much to the universal disenchantment with professional politicians. Ross Perot was the man who most effectively and famously tapped into that infectious support of ordinary voters for the little man slaying the greedy giant of central government bureaucracy. Even if the little man in question happened to be the multi-millionaire, self-evidently feudal boss of a Texan corporation.

Perot recognised the natural desire of the electorate not just for simple solutions to complex problems, but for someone who could seemingly prove that a common sensical calculation on the back of an envelope might have just as much fiscal validity as the weighty deliberations of an army of economists led by a dodgy budget director. (And given the track record of some British Chancellors you can see how the sentiment might translate transatlantically.) He was feisty, different, and personified the public's lack of deference for the established political order. Most significantly of all, he was new.

And in the land where novelty is king, people who have been around the political circuit learning their trade, serving their time, doing the boring public service bits as well as the glamorous sound bites, have a rather depressed share value. Instead of venerating political experience, Americans have developed an instinctive mistrust of it. In a British context that's why so many worthwhile people have eschewed party politics for what they perceive to be the cleaner, greener pastures of community activism. It's why the SDP attracted so many party political "virgins".

Also, in a world of confused morality where yesterday's truism is constantly challenged by today's technology, the popularity of churches and sects which offer to wrap you in a comforting cloak of certainty rather than encourage you to dip an intellectual toe into the more challenging waters of joined up thinking, have an obvious appeal. Offered "solutions" who will vote for doubt?

So, in a depressing fashion, you can begin to see how Col North might (frighteningly) have got something of a double up; he represents the new tone of Bible-belt bullshit and has the incomparable advantage of no known political experience in any kind of elected office. Hell, the man should be running for president. And probably will.

———

No longer such great slaves to racism

ALLAN MASSIE

18 April 1994

Churchill is the only British politician or statesman of the century to survive as a controversial figure. That says something for him. Among American presidents, I suppose, only Roosevelt, Nixon and, for rather different reasons, Kennedy aroused the same sort of feeling.

The historian Andrew Roberts has recently grabbed himself a few column inches by publishing an article in the *Spectator* in which he argues that Churchill was a racist. Considering that the old boy was born in 1874, and served in the British Army in India while Queen Victoria was on the throne, this can hardly be regarded as surprising. It would indeed have been remarkable if he had not, by modern standards, been a racist.

No doubt it is very wrong, wicked and unfortunate, but the truth is that at least until quite recently we were all racists. When, in *The Three Hostages* Buchan has Richard Hannay describe an American Jew, Mr. Julius Victor, as "the whitest man of his race since the apostle Paul", any modern, well brought up liberal must shudder. Yet that was the way most people thought and spoke in those days.

We now have an American liberal as president. Clinton is absolutely the sort of chap who must win the approval of Paddy Ashdown. Yet as a former governor of Arkansas, it is doubtful whether Clinton's attitude towards the American negro is absolutely that which would commend itself to *Guardian* readers. Naturally of course Clinton is aware of the importance of the negro vote; naturally also Clinton is not immune from the fears, suspicions and prejudices of his fellow southerners.

Racism is quite rightly now regarded as an unforgivable sin. It is the one thing of which we are all now quick to acquit ourselves. Yet the truth is that it represents also a very natural and attractive temptation. The belief that our own particular racial group has qualities denied to others is so widely and deeply felt as to be almost instinctive.

At the moment we are seeing what is, I suppose, the most daring renunciation of racism that the world has ever experienced. The Nationalist Party of South Africa which institutionalised racism in its policy of apartheid, has amazingly suffered a change of heart, and now presents itself as a non-racist party. Opinion polls suggest that in the Cape at least this National Party ploy may be successful, but fear of the ANC now begins to disturb the coloureds. Certainly it looks likely that the ANC will win the election, and may not be as respectful of the constitution as the Nationalists have been.

The question is really whether our modern attitude to racism represents a genuine moral advance. I think that, though there is a lot of hypocrisy involved, it may be said truly to be so. The first evidence that we really have made moral progress in the last few hundred years is provided by our abolition of slavery.

There is still, as the evidence of Tower Hamlets shows, a considerable resistance to the idea of the United Kingdom as a multiracial society. Quite clearly the British National Party enjoys some support, but the remarkable thing is how little impact it has made over the years. Back in 1959, the old fascist leader Sir Oswald Moseley made his last serious bid for power, or intervention in politics, when he stood for election in North Kensington, after the race riots in Notting Hill. He got, as I remember, about 3,000 votes, and lost his deposit, not for the first time.

The two things which seem to me evidence of a genuine moral advance are first, as I've said, the abolition of slavery, and second, the condemnation of racism. They have this in common, that they represent a rebellion against the idea of treating human beings as things. Slavery was normal throughout history, and now this has been prohibited, I think we too easily forget its horrid reality. Slavery is, or was, the precondition of racism. Its justification first required a dehumanisation of the object.

Racism is connected with slavery, inasmuch as it also reduces the individual to the status of an object. Individuals stop being regarded as people. They become things – abstractions. And this is what is, so wicked about it: that it denies people their own and proper reality.

One doesn't, I think, have to defend Churchill against the charge of racism. It is better simply to accept that he was a man of his time, and that it was improbable that he should not have been what we would now consider racist. We have made a considerable advance since he was a young man. That is something worth saying clearly. There is a great deal of self-doubt about nowadays. There is lack of self-confidence and a feeling that somehow or other, in ways that we don't understand, we have lost our way. As crime rates rise, and public life seems one way or another to be corrupted, as crimes of violence proliferate, it is easy to despair or find one's only satisfaction in deploring present conditions. Yet the role of Jeremiah is, however tempting, false. There are many ways in which the country and the world are better places than they used to be. One of them undoubtedly is the general condemnation of racism and the realisation that people's qualities cannot be judged according to the colour of skin.

Memories of a chip off the old concrete grain drier

FORDYCE MAXWELL

13 June 1994

I'm not your man for obituaries. In fact I'm so much against the formula that I wrote a spoof one some years ago, describing an imaginary farmer as he really was rather than the way obituary writers would have us believe he had been.

The result was 17 letters from people who all claimed to recognise the ring of truth about late, unlamented, neighbours which more or less proved my point.

But I don't have that problem with Adam Maxwell of Cauldshiel, a figure who loomed large in my childhood and at comforting intervals ever since.

In the labyrinth of Maxwell/Barr/Pate relationships in Scottish and English farming, his was a straightforward one. He was my father's cousin and I have my father's version of what young Adam was like in the 1930s:

"We used to reckon he could tackle Jack Dempsey. When he was 13 he was 13 stones and he put on a stone a year until he was 17."

Most of that was muscle, as it was when I have my first clear recollection of him in the middle 1950s. He was stuck in a ventilator shaft in a grain drier.

Nothing odd about it. Cauldshiel were installing their first grain drier with air blasted along underground concrete tunnels. Deciding he would have only one chance to explore the tunnels while they were clean Adam went from one end to the other.

He got in, but that massively solid frame couldn't back out. What he did do was get halfway through an air vent and stick. He then waited until they chipped him out with a hammer and chisel and much light badinage. It's sitting half in, half out of the tunnel that I remember him first, that and the grin.

A large family with limited resources doesn't go on holiday together. We split up and hit different targets, preferably kindly relatives. My brother Angus and I got lucky. For five summers, while I went from ten to 15, we went to Cauldshiel.

It was a riot. John, the senior brother, Adam, and their sisters Isobelle and Vena, were all unmarried at the time. But Cauldshiel was always full house – squads of children on holiday by the week or by the day, friends, relatives, neighbours, workers, travellers.

Name it, they were there. A bagatelle table in the workshop for dinner breaks, coarse croquet on the lawn, ten-a-side football, cricket, kick-the-can, rope swings, guddling trout, rowdy card games round the huge table at night.

And a bit of work which, in the schoolboy nature of things, always seemed much more interesting than doing exactly the same job at home.

And it was Adam who explained the facts of life to me about machinery. It was harvest time and the sun was beating down. Barley straw was crackling in the heat. The air was full of the sounds of combines clattering up and down fields and tractors carting full loads of grain. Except at Cauldshiel.

The combine stood silent in the yard. Occasionally another piece of metal, a few links of chain or a bolt or two flew into the air from the vicinity of the engine and mill.

The smallest member of the farm staff was tiptoeing round collecting these bits and pieces and putting them in a neat heap which was growing impressively.

Various snorts and snarls with an occasional muffled bellow could be heard from the combine's innards and clouds of dust and chaff puffed out. The heat grew more intense and the nearest field of heavy-ripe barley was shimmering in the haze.

Angus and I watched in fascination. After a few minutes Adam began to appear like a stage escapologist. First his backside, then somehow his trousers and boots and finally he levered himself out by his massive, brawny forearms and looked askance at the world.

He was never, as he agreed, an oil painting but this was something else. His thick bushy hair stood up like an Old Testament prophet's. His weatherbeaten face, arms, open neck and shirt were a mass of dust and grease. One eye was jammed shut with muck and the other savagely bloodshot. He looked again at the sky, at the heap of bits and pieces, at the dead-ripe barley. Then he began to talk to himself in a low voice.

A young, piping voice broke the silence. I realised with horror that it was mine: "Is there something wrong with it?"

It took him a little time to set his mind in order as he fondled a hammer, lovingly. Then he spoke:

"How old are you now?"

"T . . . t . . . ten."

He considered briefly. That seemed to be old enough: "In that case this combine is . . . "

Some of the words were still new to me, but as he warmed to his theme I got the general idea. I too, turned and tiptoed away.

Oddly, that was the image that came back to me when he died at the end of May, the last of that family of four who gave us such memorable holidays, almost the last link with the grown-ups of my childhood.

Odd because outbursts of temper were so unusual with him. Equable, affable, traditional, a securely based owner-occupier in East Lothian, he was one of the few constants in a changing, often for the worse, world then and until he died.

I'll miss him.

Editorial: corruption

TOM NAIRN

26 July 1994

'Remarkably free from corruption' was Allan Massie's verdict on British public life last week in this space. I disagree. British public life – meaning essentially parliamentary life – has long been the most corrupt in the world and is rapidly becoming more so.

Certainly, British back-handing is petty by comparison with world champions like France, Italy and Arkansas: this was the gist of Massie's defence. But that is to define 'corruption' solely in terms of the back-pocket and other material favours. During the late Lothar Spät's cornocupian Christian-Democrat reign in

Baden-Württemberg (e.g.) the currency was private jets and Greek island villas. In Britain it is twopenny consultancies and weekends at 'luxury hotels' (the sort no Spät client would have risked being mugged in).

Honest if threadbare, in other words (or a nation of cheapies, as they thought in Stuttgart). 'It is easy to exaggerate the extent of corruption', concluded Massie, 'If it was not so we should not profess ourselves so shocked by the grubby little episode of Messrs Riddick and Tredinnick'. Just how little has indeed been shown in subsequent revelations about blighters who might have been got to pop a Parliamentary question for as *little* as £200.

In British Parliamentary life non-material corruption remains far more important. Bribery may be secondary, but galloping State egomania is as strong as ever: that is, the febrile conviction of belonging to a sacral elite whose Word is Law. This state of affairs is of course metaphorical rather than literal (as in Kim Il Sung's North Korea). However, the metaphor remains one through which the United Kingdom goes on living politically. In the country of the Unwritten Constitution the daftest backbench windbag can be King (for a day, or at least for a few seconds at Question Time).

Democracy came to Britain early, as a form of elite rule widened out in stages vaguely to include the people. Apologists for this system have always stressed the continuity and stability which it brought. But the obverse of continuity has been, inevitably, the down-loading of anachronism. Rituals natural to aristocratic sovereignty have persisted as ways of coopting popular invasion or subversion. The greater the threat, the more they have been cultivated. From 1928 onwards universal suffrage was captured and ably digested by this curious combination of antique theatre and law court.

One feature of re-programmed democracy is the astonishing self-importance which it bestows upon Members of Her Majesty's Parliament. No doubt Deputies and Senators of all legislatures are susceptible to vanity. But they do not belong to the Mother of Parliaments. That is, they have not been irradiated by original-patent Sovereignty and awarded pastoral sway over "all their constituents". Nor do they act out a confrontational charade modelled on a mediaeval law-court, where debates are 'won' by the forensic mutilation of opponents and survival consists in knowing how to evade one question by posing another.

Many analysts and historians have described the phenomenon.

In his brilliant book *The Eclipse of Parliament* (1992) Professor Bruce Lenman pointed out how today 'The professional politicians, increasingly members of a specialist guild with little grasp of outside realities, remain basically unreformed and intransigent . . . ' There is a corruption here far more serious than small earners on the side. It concerns not money but power . . . not pay-offs but the moral substance of the state, the way in which politicians are still 'bought' out by status and ancestral self-regard. If they are so poorly paid that was only because (rightly enough by the ancestral criteria) cash was considered less important than touching the hem of Sovereignty's wondrous garment (and being elevated into the Best Club in the land).

The past tense is appropriate. For what the £1000-question affair has shown is this system of traditional or tribal status-corruption being rapidly overtaken by banal cash corruption as well. The most rotten of all pseudo-democratic systems could be in preparation. Once we were governed by party-drilled egomanes; now the egomanes are also up there 'for what they can get out of it'. The old rules were those of elite custodianship, self-regarding but also self-restraining: a worthy system, if desperately in need of reform. Now the daylight of the post-Thatcher era is destroying its magic as thoroughly as that of the Monarchy itself.

In Scotland this débâcle has extra significance, since a crucial problem here has always been the spiritual entrapment of MPs. The tories go down pre-processed, and with rare exceptions Clubland sorts the Labourites out in a few days. The roaring radical turns into a responsible chap working hard on behalf of all his constituents. One injection of Real Politics and all his original Scottish passions start to appear claustrophobic: ego-constraining rather than expanding. Soon even a Scottish parliament will look the same way . . . paltry, unworthy of his new self, a retreat rather than a new adventure.

That style of corruption worries me much more than pay-offs, but no House of Commons inquiry will be considering it. 'Without political change of a fundamental kind, necessarily allowing the natives more continuous say in their own governance, no change in the long-established drift is remotely likely', concluded Professor Lenman. It will take more than Blairomania to prove him wrong.

Cheesecloth hippies were too selfish to see through the purple haze

JOAN McALPINE

2 August 1994

She had eyes like the slush on the pavement. Colourless, vacant and watery. Damp, afro curls stuck to her forehead. 'Soggy cheesecloth slopped around bare ankles. The voice, like the hair, was screwed-up. "I'm Sunshine!" she announced to the grim Glaswegian shoppers. "Let me into your hearts!"

It was November, sometime in the late Seventies. I was a school kid with barely enough cultural references to fill a Chelsea Girl carrier bag. But I knew Sunshine was the spirit of the Sixties. And she was way off beam. I pushed on, grateful for cynicism, the Sex Pistols and being born too late.

Sunshine hailed from a cult called the Children of God. They hit the headlines when it was alleged young, female apostles opened more than their hearts for the sake of a quick convert. Who knows why a face in the crowd stays with you. Perhaps as a warning. Sunshine's slushy smile occasionally floats from my memory bank like a bad LSD trip. Her most recent appearances are triggered by repeated references to the W word and Joan Baez. But the Woodstock nostalgia machine is not solely responsible for her salutary return.

The national anguish expressed when two English women were deported to the United States where they face serious charges relating to cultish pranks turns your thoughts to mushy mystical matters.

Susan Hagan, 46, and Sally Croft, 44, are accused of plotting to murder a former state attorney more than ten years ago. They were then fanatical followers of the Bhagwan Shree Rajneesh, who established an enormous commune near the town of Antelope, Oregon. Thousands of the bearded Ghagwan's saffron robed devotees apparently descended on this backwater community, whose only crime was to be a bit dull.

They won control of school boards and even had the police force in the Bhag. Local landmarks were renamed after favourite Buddhas. They tried to seize political control of the county by infecting the local restaurants with salmonella bacteria before polling day. Oregon's state attorney, Charles Turner, was investigating this bizarre vote rigging attempt when it is claimed he was targeted himself.

Luminaries in the media and law – including Lord Scarman – unsuccessfully lined up against the deportation of these women to America. It all happened so long ago, they argue, when Sally and Sue were under the Bhagwan's sinister karmic control.

Besides, Sally now has a top accountancy job in the City and is no longer a threat. Who among us can put hand on heart and say they did not attempt to murder a senior law officer during the wilder excesses of youth?

Except Hagan and Croft were in their thirties when they flung on unfetching orange curtains and prostrated themselves before an old fraud with a most unspiritual addiction to Rolls-Royces.

At least the pair will get a trial. More than can be said of the hundreds of asylum seekers Britain returns to countries where law is just a licence to pull out fingernails. Darker skinned deportees fail to generate the same excitement as respectable white matrons with tangerine togas in their closets.

Alter the characters in this tragi-comedy for a moment. Imagine Britain tried to extradite two Irishwomen on charges of conspiring to murder a Belfast judge ten years ago.

Would the outcry be similar? Would they say: "The IRA is now part of their past. Siobhan has a successful career with Chase Manhattan and wants to put everything behind her."

I don't know whether these dippy women planned to blow Mr Turner away or just meditated on it. But let's make an example of them anyway, for wasting a good education on the wackeries of Eastern religion when they could have done something useful with their lives. Let's show the rest of the Sunshine generation how off beam they all were.

For although Sally and Sue strayed into mumbo jumbo land in the early Eighties, they were Sixties products – aged 19 and 20 in

1969, when all those people sat down in a field with poor toilet facilities.

In the past few weeks, the post hubble-bubble generation have tolerated gloating fortysomethings describe this mundane, if unhygenic, gathering as an act of radicalism on a par with the storming of the Winter Palace or the demolition of the Berlin Wall. Forests of newsprint have been wasted on journalists intent on sharing their mid-life crisis with their children. They compare the "nihilism" of today's teenagers with their own love-in ideals and even slag off "repetitive electronic dance music" as evidence of decline into soullessness. As if Donovan was someone to be proud of.

The Sixties generation cannot blame kids born in 1974 for the current mess. The children of the revolution grew up but failed to build their New Age. Bill Clinton and Tony Blair were their men. At least in spirit.

Now they're here and the world is more environmentally frazzled and socially polarised than any of their gurus could predict. Who's to blame?

In truth, Woodstock and its aftermath were more about destroying brain cells than destroying the system. When the writer Joan Didion explored the counter culture of San Francisco in 1968, she was alarmed at the apathy, emptiness and lack of ability to communicate concepts more sophisticated than "Who's got the weed?"

Political activism was frowned upon – it required a certain amount of lucidity and rational thought. As another chronicler, Tom Wolfe, wrote of the hippy: "He has a very tolerant and therefore withering attitude toward all those who are still struggling in the old activist political ways ... while he, with the help of psychedelic chemicals, is exploring the infinite regions of human consciousness."

The Sixties brought changes, but it was through the hard work of boring, straight campaigners who could think beyond where the next spliff was coming from.

It is little wonder that the real legacy of Woodstock was the proliferation of seedy sects and confused cults. Fuzzy thinking naturally led to an interest in tantric moaning, crystal gazing, Bhagwan chanting, numerology, macrobiotics and all manner of naval and neuro-gazing activities. A veritable directory of self-indulgence. Letting the sunshine into your heart was not a responsible, collective thing to do. It was ego massage. A celebration of individualism. We should not be surprised that these love children went on to become accountants.

They will want to walk, but I hope they never run

TOM MORTON

10 August 1994

A baby sleeping: could anything be so peaceful? The New Female Offspring lies in her favoured position, on her back with arms beside her head, breathing steadily ... wait a minute. Is she breathing? She's awfully still. Maybe I'd better ... and as I've done with the previous four children on countless occasions, I gently shoogle the tiny form to see if there's any reaction, any life. There is. From lungs which seem to have been built on entirely the wrong scale, a sound erupts which makes the ears wrinkle and the eyes water. This is not a cry, it is a great rumbling howl, like an elephant crossed with a wolf, I have woken her. She is alive. I pick her up, feeling as ever afraid that my large-as-hams hands will crush something accidentally. She continues to imitate large angry animals until hoisted over my shoulder and walked briskly about, or transferred apologetically to Significant Other for refuelling.

I have no idea how babies survive their first few weeks. They seem so utterly defenceless and weak, so small and vulnerable. You wrap them in wool, cotton and artificial fibres, they yowl and suck and sleep and sit or lie, and everybody says they're smiling but they're not, they're just gazing out in utter consternation at this completely incomprehensible world of giant breasts, grinning, tweetering heads, and big fingers which wake them from some deep dream of a black, warm, previous womb-life.

This is why I tend to panic when they sleep for too long. I simply cannot believe that they are all right, that they have the capacity to survive without constant monitoring or interference. And yet they do. Soon NFO will lose that wrinkled, appalled look which tiny babies all have and fatten out into blobbiness; soon she will be swallowing hideous jars of food, glutinous, strange combinations such as pear and potato, cauliflower and blackcurrant. Bottles will be applied to her lips and at last, I will be able to see liquid actually disappearing, and know that some goodness other than that utterly mysterious stuff which she gets from her mother is helping the cells to multiply. The whole breast milk thing, with these odd transferences from mother to baby of immunity to disease, dislike of beef bhuna and cabbage, horror of beetroot, excludes and isolates the male, who can only observe in awe, apart. And resist coarse female suggestions that sure, men can, technically, breast feed, or at least soothe, as well. I mean, absolutely NOT! I'm not whipping my shirt off in Burger King for anyone.

Who said I was a new man anyway? Slightly used, fairly reliable, second-hand . . . these are more accurate descriptions. And male breast-feeding is certainly not my cup of tea.

Speaking of which, I remember during the infancy of JM that SO's production of milk had reached almost commercial proportions.

Unbeknown to me, she had stored some of said mystery juice in the fridge in a bottle, to be applied to the greedy maw of JM in her absence. And so it came to pass that some acquaintances arrived for morning coffee, and lo, there was no milk except for this unmarked bottle in the fridge . . . you can guess the rest.

Anyway, as the babies' blobbiness quotient increases, I begin to believe, to hope that they might some day have the capacity to exist on their own, stand on their feet, walk, talk, sing, dance, read, write, watch Power Rangers videos . . . and eventually they'll want to go out on their own.

I know what I did when I was a child. I can remember the dizzying climbs up disused water towers aged seven, the long blind crawls through the sewage system for a new housing scheme, not even thinking about becoming trapped. Tightroping, Blondin-like along the rafters of half-built houses. Dives off the biggest sand dunes in the world, swimming under water with bursting lungs in the warm soup of Troon's unheated, unfiltered swimming pool, emptied only once a week and bearably warm only when murky. Teetering crazily around the outside edge of the lighthouse at the very end of the harbour bar, hugging the old red sandstone while sandshoes slithered on a 4in ledge.

And JM wants to go out on his own, down to the beach or off with his friends to the pier . . . how can I let him go? I know what's out there. I know how narrow my escapes were.

In the end, you have to let them go. The days of gently shaking to see if they're alive have to pass, and out they venture to start taking this gigantic risk of life. The sewage pipes are there for squirming through, the old buildings for scrambling up.

I've never skied. Never gone rock or ice climbing. Later on I know that one of the sons or the daughter will try something detestably dangerous like that, and I'm going to have to let them do it. Or worse, one of them will want a motorcycle.

Well, you can't have one. Yes, I know, I know I've got one, but your dad was 38 years-old before he passed his test, and if that was good enough for me . . . listen, my mother wept every time I went for a ride on my Honda 50 – do you want to put me through that? You do? Oh.

When I was 11, I was told quite clearly by my parents that unless I reached an A or B stream at secondary school (this was just pre-comprehensiveness), I would be sent to boarding school. I promised myself, coldly and definitely, that if I was sent there, I would run away. In the end I made it to 1B2 at Marr College and all the plans filched from my sister's *Mallory Towers* books were set aside. I couldn't bear to follow last week's anguish-inducing story about a 12 year-old boy who ran away from home after being told to clear up his pet-filled room. Thank God, he was found, safe and well, and is now happily feeding his guinea pigs. The horrors, the horrors out there facing a 12-year-old runaway, things only now, as adults, we know exist. I hope none of mine ever run. But they will want to walk ever-increasing distances away from that gentle shoogle of reassurance, from mother's milk and apron strings, to try all the things their parents never did, never could. And I cannot, dare not, stop them.

Ignoring the hard facts of an active sex life

JAN MOIR

19 August 1994

How nice it would be if more couples could behave like Tony and Wendy Duffield, the charming, self-styled sexperts featured this week on Desmond Morris's *The Human Animal* television series. "We are not porn stars, we are researchers," they moaned in unison, after the nation had been subjected to a graphic portrayal of their most private sexual moments – all in the pursuit of science, you understand.

What was most interesting was that Wendy and Tony needed some extraneous stimulation to get them going for the BBC cameras. The couple have already made a sex video called *The Lovers Guide*, they edit a sex problem page, run a sex helpline and have built an entire career around their supposedly bottomless passion for each other. At Chez Duffields – we are led to believe – poor Wendy can hardly get around to filling the kettle or pegging out the washing without fabulous sex taking place every five minutes or so. Where does she find the time to put on all that make-up?

But sadly, the curtain was the only thing to go up when the couple began filming for the programme. Perhaps this is understandable, for most sensitive people would find it difficult to indulge in even the mildest form of monkey business with the sinister figure of Desmond Morris looming large. However Mr and Mrs Duffield – troupers to the last – brought the concept of foreplay to hitherto unknown frontiers. Before the cameras started rolling, he pedalled like billy-o on a bike to work up a good sweat while she pepped herself up with some strategically placed ice cubes.

Interestingly enough, ice cubes have always done the trick for me, too – but only if they're swimming around in half a bottle of gin. And, pray tell me, who wouldn't need a very stiff drink to allay the horror of being approached by a man strapping on a camera rather than a condom and sitting two O levels, rampant promiscuity (his own) and two failed marriages as the reasonable CV for a respectable sexpert? Any woman with any sense would tell him to get back on his bike and not stop pedalling until he reached the open sea.

But the point is that however suspicious you might be of Tony Duffield and his gross exhibitionism masquerading under the banner of sex education at least, when put in a sexual situation, he managed to show some form of discretion. How nice it would be if some members of our older generation could follow his example.

Why, only nine months ago, Jack Nicholson, 57, walked into a Hollywood bar, ordered a Jack Daniels and got the waitress pregnant before last orders.

He sent some flowers to the hospital where she gave birth this week which proved what a lovely, old-fashioned gentleman he is, in spite of what anyone says about him being an old goat with the sexual urges of a maladjusted primate.

Closer to home, our very own George Best, 48, went to a party last Sunday and dumped his girlfriend of the last seven years when he met a 22-year-old blonde air-hostess called Alexandra. Once the football legend spotted her across the room, there was no stopping him. He dribbled across the carpet and scored with a classic opening line. "I love you," said George. "I have never met anyone so charming and considerate," said Alex which, apart from anything else, doesn't say very much for air travellers.

Like all the greatest sportsmen, Bestie has fantastic reflexes which propel him into action at the slightest provocation. Me George, You Blonde seems to be his rather basic maxim – and why not? He once went out with a gorgeous female called Princess for three weeks before he sobered up and realised he was dating an Afghan hound. All he needs is one glimpse of a shaggy main of fair hair and he's off, halfway down the aisle before some spoilsport ref blows the whistle and points out that he's already married, or somesuch trifling detail.

Perhaps Desmond Morris should forget Tony and Wendy and make his next documentary about Jack and George and their fascinating motor responses instead. At least he wouldn't have to hang around waiting to call for action. At least he wouldn't have to hang around *at all*.

What sexperts and anthropologists always ignore is that the real problem with sex is not the act itself, but the consequences. Who cares if it's good, bad or indifferent sex when the aftermath is what really matters. Forget about babies, what about the terrifying spectre of the discarded lover hell-bent on seeking revenge, the skeleton in the closet that rattles on for years, long after you've forgotten what you saw in them in the first place?

Whatever your feelings about Bill Clinton, it is hard not to sympathise with his current predicament. Gennifer Flowers, who claims she once had a 12-year affair with him, is now determined to embarrass him at every opportunity. In a rather cringe-making attempt to emulate Marilyn Monroe's paen to John Kennedy she has poured herself into a clinging silver dress and sang a breathy rendition of *Happy Birthday Mr President* which will be broadcast across America to "celebrate" Clinton's 48th birthday.

No matter that the silly woman is making a bigger fool of herself than she ever could of him, the whole embarrassing spectacle is enough to make you padlock your knickers and stay celibate for the next few decades or so. But even that might not keep you out of trouble. Actor Jon Voight is currently being sued in the American courts because he refused to have sex with his female business partner. Now that really is scary.

143

Westminster Commentary

IAIN MACWHIRTER

2 November 1994

Political storms, such as the one currently raging in parliament over sleaze, generally blow themselves out in one of three ways: as tragedy; as boredom, or as farce. Despite the discomfiture of Mr Peter Preston later today as Tory MPs vent their spleen over his alleged forgery, it is difficult to see the Aitken affair now going anywhere other than up its own orifice.

Previous *affairs de sleaze* have not ended so comically. The last round began, you may recall, with Major's back to basics initiative at the 1993 Tory party conference. It ended – after a succession of bedroom antics involving various members of government, in tragedy, when Lord Caithness's wife shot herself, allegedly after discovering his marital infidelity. Then the Tory PPS Stephen Milligan died while apparently indulging in a bizarre autoerotic practice. Suddenly, it wasn't funny anymore.

The Pergau and Arms-to-Iraq inquiries ended in tedium. The public's (not to say journalists') capacity for complex stories is limited. Consumer resistance builds up rapidly as more and more documents are leaked. After the foreign affairs select committee (sitting, note, in public) had established that arms and aid had become entangled in the Pergau Dam affair, the story got lost in a morass of fact and fiction; interpretation and obfuscation. Something similar happened to the Arms-to-Iraq affair. Once Lord Justice Scott and Presiley Baxendale QC began their exhaustive examination of government documentation on machine tool exports to the Middle East, we all soon lost the place.

Mind you, when the Scott Inquiry reports in January, or thereabouts, it could still turn into a tragedy for some of the ministers who signed the public interest immunity certificates that sought to keep the affair out of the public domain.

But our present sleaze storm is rapidly degenerating into low farce. Now that Peter Preston, the editor of the *Guardian*, has been found in bed with Mohammed Al-Fayed with only a cod fax to maintain his journalistic decency, it is becoming increasingly difficult to remain indignant about Aitken's bill at the Paris Ritz. Labour are backing off rapidly.

Some opposition MPs may add their voices to Tory denunciation of Preston in today's emergency debate. This debate will focus on what John Major yesterday called systematic deception, fraud and collusion. That may seem rather strong condemnation for faking a letter, but a lot of MPs – and not just Tory ones – get very worked up about this kind of thing. Many MPs live in fear that their notepaper might be forged or stolen and that documents might be prepared linking them with causes, or persons, of dubious character. Like, one is tempted to say, Mr Al-Fayed.

In the lobbies last night, Tory MPs were imagining all manner of grizzly punishments for the *Guardian* editor, who has now resigned from the Press Complaints Commission. These ranged from expulsion of his newspaper from the house to Preston being prosecuted for forgery. These remedies are mostly fantasy. But Preston could well find himself up before the house privileges committee, along with Al-Fayed, assorted cash-for-questions members, uncle Tom Cobbleigh MP and all.

With or without Labour MPs in attendance, this inquisition could lead to Preston being brought to the bar of the house. No, this is not one of the many alcoholic bars for which the palace of Westminster is famous, but a literal bar which marks the boundary of the debating chamber of the commons. Miscreants are traditionally hauled here by the serjeant at arms to face the high court of parliament. It sounds like something out of Gilbert and Sullivan, and probably would be much funnier if it happened. According to the House of Commons Library, the last journalist to suffer this punishment was John, now Sir John Junor, the right-wing columnist, back in January 1957. The charge then was that he had written an article in the *Sunday Express* which cast doubt upon the honour and integrity of MPs. Which shows how far we've come. One can hardly imagine the committee trying to press this charge today: the entire press gallery would be queuing up at the bar. In 1957, Junor got off by making a grovelling apology to MPs.

If Preston refuses to do likewise he could, in theory, be locked in the famous gaol that still exists in the clock tower that houses Big Ben – if it's still standing. But the last person to be locked up there was Charles Bradlaugh in 1880, so it's reasonable to suppose that Al-Fayed's favourite journalist will escape being clapped in irons. Some Tory MPs were hoping Preston would be referred, like the Harrods' boss, to Barbara Mills, the Director of Public Prosecutions. That would call for more than an apology. But one suspects that even Major would hold back from such a declaration of war on the press over what looks such a relatively trivial matter. Cod faxing is not, he might say, a hanging offence.

Perhaps the best thing would be for Tory MPs to turn up on the day of Preston's appearance at the bar with bags of rotten fruit to hurl at him. That was pretty much the mood in the tearooms last night. But righteous indignation aside, Tory MPs were, in reality, much relieved at this latest comic turn of events, and not just because it is so agreeable to see the tables being turned on the reptiles. Tory MPs believe that the questions surrounding Aitken's sojourn at the Ritz have been obscured by this own goal by his tormentors.

Whatever their ultimate significance, real inconsistencies have emerged in the various accounts given by Aitken about his hotel bill. What was a minister of the Crown doing in the company of so many Middle Eastern businessmen with connections to the arms trade. Batting for Britain? We'll now probably never know the truth of the story. As for the mysterious brunette apparently going around Paris with bundles of used notes paying ministerial hotel bills, that is pure Inspector Clousseau. The Paris Ritz, however, may assume the status of an informal part of the constitution, like the Speakers' Court, the press lobby and Number Ten.

Elsewhere on the sleaze front, bathos ruled. Minister Is Part Time Dentist announced the splash in the *Guardian* yesterday. The housing minister Sir Paul Beresford is – shock – revealed to be moonlighting as a tooth-puller. Perhaps he is the man to the root of the matter.

Person to Person

IT'S ANOTHER IDEA BORROWED
FROM CLINTON...

Norman's major difficulty

IAN WOOD

Ian Wood on the script that has left the man called 'Hollywood' looking time and again for a happy ending

If ever a man was qualified to be the subject of the classic gift-catalogue poser about what to give the man who has everything, it is Greg Norman, yet in his case the answer is easy. A few more major championships would do.

Since he first began to appear on the international circuits in the late Seventies, the rangy Australian, now 39, has looked a champion. That may have been part of the trouble. Blessed with looks, power, talent and presence, it seemed that all he had to do was turn up and trophies would be thrust upon him.

Immediately dubbed "Hollywood" by his colleagues when he played the European Tour, the tall blond Queenslander has always known how to play the leading role. Success had come early, and with considerable ease. A natural athlete, he turned to golf at the age of 17, and was playing off scratch within two years. When he turned professional in 1976 he gave a hint of thrilling things to come by winning the fourth event in which he entered – the West Lakes Classic in Australia – going into the final round with a 10-shot lead. Two years later he topped the Australian Order of Merit.

The money came readily enough, the Ferraris proliferated, and the image grew ever more vivid in the public mind. With everything apparently in place the impression was that someone had only to shout "lights, music, action", and he would be off and running. Not that he hadn't been getting along at a fair lick up to then, but Norman now had his eye on the major titles, the ones which write golfers into the history books.

In this context, he has had a fairly frustrating time. After losing out in a three-way play-off for the 1989 Open at Royal Troon, he was asked by a fellow Aussie: "Greg, do you feel the game owes you one?" He replied: "One? It owes me about bloody five."

He had just shot a record 64 in the final round – opening with six straight birdies to tie his compatriot Wayne Grady and the eventual winner, American Mark Calcavecchia. After all that, his hopes vanished when an enormous drive lodged against the face of a bunker he thought he couldn't reach on the fairway of the eighteenth in the first four-hole play-off in championship history. He'd begun the play-off with two birdies before dropping a shot at the third, the short seventeenth.

Norman had, of course, made his breakthrough at Turnberry three years earlier, and now, as he returns to defend the title he secured for the second time at Royal St George's last year, he must regard the Ayrshire links with some affection, not only as the scene of his first major victory, but as a place which afforded a sort of sanctuary from the slings and arrows hurled at him by outrageous fortune in other parts of the golfing world.

In the spring of 1986, he'd bogeyed the last hole at Augusta to lose his chance to tie with Jack Nicklaus, who won his sixth US Masters title at the age of 46. The following year, even as he mentally donned the Green Jacket, Norman was obliged to peel it off again as Larry Mize pitched in from miles away to win on the second play-off hole.

Indeed, the Australian has lost play-offs in all four majors – to Mize, Calcavecchia, Fuzzy Zoeller (over 18 holes) in the 1984 US Open at Winged Foot, and to Paul Azinger in last year's US PGA, a championship which was also dashed from his hands in 1986 when America's Bob Tway pipped him by holing out from a bunker at the last hole.

The resilience and extraordinary ability of the Open champion can be gauged from the fact that in that year, 1986, he won, besides the Open, the European Open, the World Match Play Championship and four consecutive events in Australia.

That resilience was never more in evidence than when he fought his way through a form slump which stayed with him through 1991, a season which saw him drop from the top of the US money list in 1990 with $1.6 million to 53rd with $320,000. By the autumn of 1992, by dint of much hard work and a few swing changes, he had revived sufficiently to win the Canadian Open.

It was this new Norman who, at Royal St George's, clinched his second major title, his second Open, with a last round of 64, the best final round ever uncorked to win an Open. He had got under way with rounds of 66, 68 and 69, and that was the first time a champion had broken 70 in all four rounds.

Everything about his performance was of the highest class. It had to be, for nothing less would have prevailed against the quality of the challenge he had to withstand. This time even Nick Faldo, three times champion and the man who had put Norman to flight in winning the 1990 Open at St Andrews, could do nothing about it, though he could hardly have defended with more distinction: rounds of 69, 63, 70 and 67.

In the business of collecting national titles, a little luck is generally required along the way, and Norman hasn't had much. However, Royal St George's confirmed his stature as a major figure in golf, and now, as champion and world No 1 he returns to Turnberry, the course where he first joined the game's elite.

If it was the last round that set the welkin ringing in Kent, it was the second round in Ayrshire eight years ago which did the trick. On a cold, blustery, unpleasant day, with Turnberry's Ailsa course bleak and forbidding, Norman scored 63 – rated by five-time champion Tom Watson as among the best he had seen.

Gary Player said of the 4-wood shot he hit to two feet at Carnoustie's fourteenth on his way to winning the 1968 Open that it was so straight he had to bend sideways to see the flag. Norman must have had a crick in his neck after that masterful round, for everything seemed to cover the flag.

Ridiculously, the 63 should have been a 62, and could even have been a 61 because on the eighteenth he three-putted, having set himself up with yet another reasonable birdie chance. That wobble came out of the blue, and it was to have its echo in last year's Open when he missed a tiddler on the seventeenth just when it seemed he could do no wrong.

This tendency to have these sudden little lapses may go some way towards explaining why he's such a compelling figure. It suggests a vulnerability amid all the power and dash, and ensures that this most spectacular of champions, who can spread wonder and consternation with equal facility, is never ever boring.

Andy Goldsworthy

RUTH WISHART

16 April 1994

It may be as permanent as the extraordinary drystane dyke snaking through a Cumbrian forest, or as ephemeral as the icework already losing form as the sculptor steps back from his creation. But common to each piece of artistry from the hands of Andy Goldsworthy is its unsullied rapport with the materials and landscape from which he draws inspiration.

No unnatural substance is permitted to intervene in the creative process, no artificial aid in its construction. "It would be pointless to use anything else," he says, apparently startled at the suggestion he might intrude some "foreign" material brought to the site of his outdoor work. "If I make a red pool, it may be startling at first, but beyond the shock it tells a truth about the river and the rocks. It has a resonance about the way things are made. I chose the pool and ground the stones in the water, but there are echoes of the way the pool is formed by stones in the water, a resonance with the natural order."

He works with everything from leaves and snow to sand and stone, with branches, thorns, slate. And his tools are his hands. Unless they are involved, the chemistry he seeks between his imagination and the natural world eludes him.

His hands, he says, are what gave him a voice, what made an inarticulate young man find the words: "I was never academic. I went to a modern secondary school, I had difficulty getting into a foundation course in art and failed three times before I got into a degree course. But last year I was given an honorary degree at Bradford where I first studied art and I realised they must think me reasonably articulate now. And that's because of my hands. They've been the key for me to both speaking and writing; they've been the vehicle to understanding so much." That process of enlightenment began when he was 18, and had finally found acceptance at Preston Polytechnic in Lancaster.

Four miles from there were the spreading sands of Morecambe, a summer magnet for optimists in pursuit of the great British summer, but a perfect winter habitat for a man for whom space and relative solitude were to become so important. He made his first outdoor work there from the wet sands, surprised to see it swiftly washed into oblivion by the incoming tide, amused at how little knowledge he had of the natural rhythms of the area in his impulsive beginnings.

Twenty years later, knowledge of the area where he lives and works in rural Dumfriesshire is absolutely central to his creativity. His firm conviction is that familiarity breeds comprehension; that visiting and revisiting the same spot affords ever greater clarity of vision and ever more knowledge of the cyclical forces of nature, which are what drives him to push forward to more and more unexpected frontiers.

"I need to return to the same places again and again, because only by doing that will nature show me how much I don't know. Only by doing that will I be able to have some understanding of it. I think that what is important to most artists is concentration and energy and for me it is a mistake to try to apply that energy to too many places, rather than go deeply into the one."

So when he accepts invitations to Australia, he returns to the same red-earthed hill where he has worked so often before. Doing so, he says, gives him a real affinity which a solitary expedition wouldn't afford. Going back for Andy Goldsworthy means going back precisely, to the familiar embrace of a particular landscape, a hill, a river or a forest with which he hopes to establish a lasting relationship.

In fact the trips themselves, usually to prestigious exhibitions such as the ones in Paris and San Francisco which will follow his current ones in London, are regarded as something of an unwelcome invasion of his preferred game plan. "People assume that these trips must be important to my art, that's not really the case. It's pleasant to go there of course, and the journey may alter me, because we are all changed by travel. But when I travel I merely see things differently, it's at home that I experience real change. When I leave home for the London exhibitions the leaves will be coming out in Dumfriesshire and I won't be there. I won't see that part of the season. I resent that."

All further evidence of that acute sense of place which so informs his work at all times and in all media.

Yet within these unflinching foundations lurk many paradoxes. Works, especially intricate works with leaves anchored by thorns or tree trunks stained a dramatic crimson with ground stone, which you suppose to be the result of meticulous pre-planning, turn out to have been merely the product of instinct allied to serendipity.

Sometimes, because he has been waiting for a snowfall, or for the river to have dropped, he will have a reasonably clear idea of what the day and his hands will fashion. More often, the work will change in concept during the process, taking on a direction only partially dictated by Goldsworthy. And if nature slips into the driving seat, he is content: "I couldn't possibly try to improve on nature, I'm only trying to understand it by an involvement in some of its processes."

Neither is he driven in the manner familiar to some other artists, powered by the need to free ideas jostling for attention in overcrowded imaginations. What propels Goldsworthy to work every day, even – and sometime especially – when the elements are at their most unfriendly, is a huge curiosity, an insatiable appetite for knowledge about life forces, cycles and the under-exposed possibilities of the outdoor world. Sometimes circumstances dictate that he will work on indoor installations in his studio, or preparing exhibitions. But working inside is apparently a process that continually drains energy. Outdoor projects, in contrast, provide constant renewal and creative nourishment: "One is breathing out, one is breathing in."

His latest installation combines both, a sandstone installation whose component parts were numbered for reassembly in a London gallery.

"I chose stone as the subject of my new book just because it seems so unflinching, but in fact it's not so much about stone as what flows through stone."

Visual proof lies in the Baird and Stevenson quarry at Locharbriggs, where he assembled the pieces for his London show. There, among the stone which characterises buildings like the Kelvingrove Art Gallery or the Burrell Collection lie his "herd of arches". These are free-standing semi-circles assembled from stones split along their grain and roughly carved into flat blocks. Which somehow acquire the precise degree of tension necessary to defy gravity.

Just as he will return and return to places, so is he content to explore at length the different properties of the materials he enjoys: which leaves at which part of the tree afford most flexibility, which types of wood can be made to do what, how basic shapes can be transformed by different colours. The effects are as dramatic as they are unexpected – soft, red stone rubbed into the sides of seaweed-covered rock, a trail of dandelion heads laid out on low water, a long stone encased by dyking, or enclosed by brightly covered leaves.

Sometimes the most satisfying images are simply the result of trial being superseded by error; Goldsworthy is a man who proves the contention that every problem is an opportunity temporarily disguised. And sometimes major works just grow from minor experiments. Those who visited and marvelled at his 1990 retrospective in Edinburgh's Royal Botanic Garden may recall a room divided by a curtain of horse chestnut stalks anchored with thorns, featuring a round hole. That emerged, he tells you, from idle curiosity about whether he could bridge a two-foot gap between two trees using such materials. Now the Edinburgh wall qualifies as only a small scale example of the technique when compared with its successors.

Yet while he rejoices in the lessons to be gained from repetition, he guards against merely repeating pleasures when there are new techniques to be explored. "Although sometimes I'll have deliberately backed myself into a corner in order to provoke a reaction. It's like a catapult, the more you draw it back, the more you shoot out of it."

155

Curiously, it is the ephemeral works – the icicles shooting horizontally from rocks, the snowballs impregnated with colour, the wet sand thrown from beneath the water to be caught by the camera in flight – which are, he says, the very core of his work rather than more permanent monuments like the slate stack and circular dyke assembled by the Scaur water near his home. "It's that ephemeral work, the kind that is often done in a day which is the source for me, it's where I learn. I never believe that kind of work to have intrinsically less value than something permanent. In fact I think my work is moving more and more in that direction. It's like those wet sand throws – there is such intensity involved, such perception. Even talking about it now brings that intense sensation vividly back for me."

For such works, immediate photography is obviously essential. But everything he does is photographed, the "mistakes" as well as the triumphs. In his studio are hundreds of carefully filed, numbered and dated slides dating from his earliest work in the Seventies. This is not merely a visual record but an important chronicle of his personal odyssey. Photography, as he explains in his new publication, fulfils an important social and intellectual need in addition to providing the visual evidence. If for some reason the film doesn't come out, he says he feels dislocated and that in some fashion the work is only half finished.

In illustration, he tells you about going out one recent Sunday, despite the fact that the weather was dire, and despite expecting a visit from gallery representatives from London. The compulsion to make the work was such that the entire group wound up helping him bend the branches and secure the necessary stones.

"And when I was finished, I was covered in mud and absolutely exhausted. But I had to find the discipline to photograph it as well, even though it was going to be a difficult shot done in three parts in bad light. But it had to be done as part of the visual diary which helps me understand the thread running through the work. And any artist needs time to think about a work they've made. And sometimes in your mind, you convince yourself that it is a good work. The photograph will tell you if your mind is being truthful with you."

He is at a stage now where he feels he can explore natural phenomena more successfully by doing less to them. "I could never just be a spectator, I'd always want to be involved. But the more I understand, the more I realise you cannot change the force. But I can be a witness to it."

No Saint Nicholas

PETER JONES

27 April 1994

When Sir Nicholas Fairbairn, MP, stands down at the next general election, the country will lose one of its most colourful political figures. Peter Jones charts the decline in public life of the brilliant lawyer who two decades ago seemed bound only for glory.

Twenty years ago, Nicholas Fairbairn was first elected MP for Kinross and West Perthshire, with a brilliant legal career behind him, a vast and engaging hinterland of artistic achievement all around him, and the glittering prizes of politics in front of him.

Twenty years on, aged 60, he is to quit the House of Commons, having gained little in terms of advancement save the knighthood routinely dished out to MPs with a failed ministerial career, noted now only for occasionally rising to his feet to make eccentric contributions in the House, and outrageous contributions outside.

To those MPs of all parties who knew, admired and feared the diamond-sharp Fairbairn wit and intellect of yesteryear, the shambling, truculent character visible to any television viewer of Scottish Questions in the Commons today is a matter of huge sadness and regret for a dissipated talent.

To newer arrivals to the Opposition benches, the odd glimpse of what can still be a penetratingly forensic mind is not enough to outweigh their general, amused view of someone who is more often an embarrassment to his party and the Government.

The decline of Fairbairn dates from his fall in 1982 after three years as Solicitor-General for Scotland. His offence was to have spoken to the press before speaking to Parliament of the reasons why the Crown Office had decided not to proceed against youths accused of raping a Glasgow woman.

He might have survived with the apology to Parliament he had to deliver had it not been, according to contemporary accounts, a floundering performance at the Dispatch Box. There was also the matter of his private life hitting the headlines the previous month when his Commons secretary, Pamela Milne, attempted to commit suicide in his London flat. Though both she and Fairbairn were single at the time and there was nothing wrong with their affair, the potential for lurid coverage of his unconventional private life reducing his standing as a Government minister must have been a factor in Margaret Thatcher's decision to dismiss him.

But in an interview with *The Scotsman* last year, he offered a different, bitter explanation, contending his resignation had been enforced by underhand manoeuvrings by two senior ministers and grandees – Francis Pym and William Whitelaw.

He said last year: "I was hurt, diminished, defamed, maligned, but determined those greasepole climbers weren't going to win." Just how bilious he felt towards Whitelaw was revealed when he described him during the 1992 general election as representing "what I despise most – sanctimony, guile, false ingenuousness, slime and intrigue under a cloak of decency for self-advancement".

That was after Whitelaw had cancelled an election visit to Perth following a speech by Fairbairn asserting that the Scottish National Party's view of Scotland was one where the "Greek, Tasmanian, or the bastard child of an American serviceman" would have more say in an independent Scotland than native-born Scots who had emigrated.

Whitelaw said they were "very extreme views". Many felt them to be racist, though Fairbairn denied it. The remarks were designed to cause a stir, having been faxed to newspaper offices earlier in the day, and certainly succeeded in putting Fairbairn on the front pages.

The burning resentment he felt over his dismissal from office coloured much of his back-bench activities. Some of his most scintillating performances came during the committee stages of the Scottish Law reform Bill, put before the Commons while Malcolm Rifkind was Scottish Secretary.

Day after day, night after night, Fairbairn used all his legal knowledge and experience to assault clause after clause, cleverly and wittily. The bill's provisions were analysed and dissected, shown to be often superfluous or destructive, to the confusion of ministers and the delight of the Opposition.

It was largely through his efforts, that large chunks of the bill, those dealing with liberalisation of divorce, extension of police powers of entry, and the ending of the solicitors' monopoly of conveyancing, had to be dropped.

And yet there seemed to be another edge to Fairbairn's critique, an edge aimed at the ministers behind the bill – Rifkind and the then Lord-Advocate, Lord Fraser of Carmyllie – both lawyers. If Fairbairn's intention was to demonstrate how his superior legal mind had been deposed from the law officer's post and replaced by inferior legal minds (Fraser followed Fairbairn as Solicitor-General), then he succeeded by his emasculation of the bill.

That Fairbairn had no love for Fraser was shown during the internal Scottish Tory battles when right-winger Michael Forsyth was made chairman in 1990. When the Left mobilised to oust Forsyth by beefing up the Scottish Tory Reform Group, Fairbairn vigorously criticised Fraser for taking the group's presidency. His accusation that Fraser was demeaning the Lord Advocacy by presiding over "a motley collection of revolutionaries in drag", was meant to support Forsyth but helped to bring him down as it was faxed out from party headquarters, clearly putting central office into battle against a wing of their own party.

The deposing of Thatcher more or less completed Fairbairn's disaffection from the establishment. As he voted in the contest which led to her replacement by John Major, he declared: "We cannot change diamonds for paste or gold for fools." Perhaps the only surprise was that it took him until this year to denounce Major as a "ventriloquist's dummy" and "not up to the task".

For many in his party that was an outrage too much, one more item in a history of outrageousness for which, sadly, he will be remembered rather than his achievements.

Sir Nicholas: In His Own Words

I appreciate that in my dealings with the press, I may have made errors of judgment. – resignation letter, January 1982.

I said to her, do not forget that you yourself were an egg once. Some of us regret its fertilisation. – remarks to Edwina Currie, who resigned office after comments she made about eggs.

Sabres of paradise – his description of the male sexual organ.

I'm not crazy about the concept of monogamy. Life is about chance. A wonderful game of chance . . . shall we go to bed? – to female journalist, 1991.

They are glorious, different and competent, and thank goodness for it. So let us not talk about women's issues – the only thing that women issue are babies. – discussing women at Scottish Grand Committee, 1993.

Are women so feeble that they have to be protected? Not at all. They are tauntresses. – rejecting anonymity of rape victims, same 1993 debate.

I can trace my family in Scotland back 1,200 years, and it is rather irritating that a second generation Irish potato labourer's grandchild should tell me what is good for my country. – comment on SNP candidate contesting his constituency.

Sexually attractive no, but certainly bonny. – on Margaret Thatcher.

They all look as though they are from the 5th Kiev Stalinist machine-gun parade. – on women MPs.

The greatest peacetime leader this country has ever seen. – on Margaret Thatcher.

More like a ventriloquist's dummy than a Prime Minister. – on John Major

Bach to Basics

MARY MILLER

16 May 1994

Miller's tale: as a doctor, theatre, opera, film and television director, Jonathan Miller is a polymath grown bitter when it comes to music; his work in this country is now mostly offbeat – at small, privately run venues. Bach's St Matthew Passion, *semi-staged in Glasgow and true to the original, is an opportunity he has grasped with moving results.*

He doesn't believe in God but Jonathan Miller has prepared the Last Supper as a musical repast, to be served in Glasgow.

Jonathan Miller's street smells. On a warm May evening, heady lilac competes with a comforting whiff of cat pee. Walking towards his house past a row of cars which look to have been immobile for some years, a cross-eyed Siamese yowls on the wall, currant bushes trail over on to pavements crunchy with withered blossom, and there is the sense that Miller has somehow designed the perfect pretty-city set for his large family to live in. It is a neighbourhood where swank and brains co-exist peacefully, in tall genial houses with interesting happenings in their basements. One walks peering in at au pairs in leotards practising aerobics, at replicas of *Provençale* kitchens where terrifyingly smart women stir mixtures in distressed terracotta bowls, at a middle-aged lady practising the cello. Miller's house, it turns out, is the least designed of the lot.

Nervous about meeting him, I had been assured I wouldn't get a word in edgeways – hardly comforting for a committed interrupter – and that he would enthuse, rave, intimidate, fly. He answers the door from a dark hall, looking as though recently sheared – startled, trimmed yet baggy. Silence. He looks down and stretches out a hand. For a moment, I think he is going to bless me. We sit down in just the sort of room you would expect; all kelims, pictures, books, faint gloom, full of fat sofas. He is very quiet, very gentle.

We are to talk about Bach, about his staging of the *St Matthew Passion* which comes to the Tramway in Glasgow this weekend. He begins to talk very calmly and sensibly about how the initiative – from the London agent Ron Gonsalves – took root. My nerves increase. When is he going to begin to, well, be Jonathan Miller, the verbal mugger, the Great Man?

Patiently, he explains how his wife, 30 years ago, encouraged him to listen to *oratorio* and how he loathed the very English performances, with huge choral societies "like the Conservative Party at prayer". Bam! We're off. He continues: "Then I heard Paul Steinitz's version, all much smaller – but still with the atmosphere of Hampstead yielding up its dead, with their scores in their hands. Then John Eliot Gardiner and Norrington and people came along with early instruments, and it all got *much* better – none of that peculiarly awful camp sensibility, just a lovely Protestant austerity."

Miller has, in fact, interfered very little with the Bach. The musicians and singers sit in a circle, and he is startled at the "almost erotic relationships which emerge, when the soliloquising arias and the obbligato instruments perform to each other." He has insisted on rapt attention from those who are not performing, a sort of smiling co-operation, which he compares to jazz playing. It sounds hell – all meaningful gestures and soppy eye contact. But no – the effect, from a young group of remarkable singers and players, is extremely moving.

We watch a videotape of the performance and Miller, nearly in tears, leaps in with comments: "You see, I wanted the sense of everyone sitting round a camp fire, people telling a story and getting up to do ramshackle charades, to show what happened." We watch. The performance is beautifully lit. "Look at that girl, she's practically *fellating* that flute, look, the singer's getting closer . . ." So, as his players share the musical material, Miller shows us the Last Supper as a musical repast.

The Tramway, with its shed-like, stained walls, excites him enormously. "A secular space, you see, the sacred side doesn't touch me at all. I don't believe in God – for me, this is just a story like the French Resistance, or from Warsaw, as people were rounded up for Auschwitz. It's just pain, torture, sacrifice. Someone knowing that they will be betrayed, let down; that their death is inevitable. It could happen, now, in Argentina, or somewhere."

"The idea of the Son of God is something I don't understand. I really don't believe in anything at all." Isn't that brave, to have faith in nothing? "Brave? No, it's no more interesting than not liking spinach, or being colour blind."

In fact, he loathes the idea of loading performance with "other luggage". Beethoven's *Fidelio*, in focus at the forthcoming Edinburgh Festival, provokes a stream of Miller-mauling. "It's such a bloody awful piece – a load of silly kitsch. It's not about totalitarianism or glorious women – it's a romance about one man getting another's guts. People get hold of all kinds of stupid political ideas. They fail to hear the tone of the music – it's the world of Goya, of Napoleonic conquest, of disappointment in a liberty gone wrong.

"But what do we get stuck with? Prisoners emerging from gulags – a hijacking of deeply horrible things, things which belong to *this* century, and should be dealt with with long tongs. They don't belong to the theatre, and very long sequences of excuses and permissions need to be granted before we pillage such events for the purpose of art or entertainment.

"I hate these ambitious young men who repackage art with a cargo of 20th-century horrors – it's sanctimonious and frivolous, like thumbing a lift on a hearse. Worse, if you've emerged from a race, a few of whom managed to avoid gassing; it's hitching a ride on the Belsen-bound cattle truck."

The room is nearly dark. He has fallen silent and looks miserable, his face collapsed into a fleshy mope. Dare one ask a question? Then he looks up. His face reassembles so I dare: how are we, then, to represent past horrors to our young?

"With decent, sober, clear documentary accounts of what happened, that show that ordinary architects and engineers, fully aware of their actions, built crematoria to burn and gas people. You say 'this is what happened, there and there.' *Schindler's List* was an abomination. Maybe when it's all as long distant as the sack of Rome, someone, perhaps, might write something after deep and meditative self-examination: an elegy, maybe."

The previous artistic administration at English National Opera – he refers to them as "the Ceaucescu Regime" – who put Miller out and forced him to base most of his work abroad he targets particularly as those who directed opera for their own self-congratulation. The Jonas, Pountney, Elder triumvirate have now moved on – but their parting manifesto, a curious, glossy idealogue called *Powerhouse*, Miller describes as disgusting. He is bitter about his present – his work in this country is now mostly offbeat – at small, privately run venues like Broomhill and Harewood. The recent ENO *Rosenkavalier* only materialised as the tail-end of an unfulfilled contract, and though he will return to the Royal Opera House "they've only condescended to let me revive *Cosi fan Tutti* because it's cheap".

He is emphatic that theatre directors – so long as they have a sense of the genre and a musical instinct – can benefit opera: "Someone must illuminate that awful, pawky, facetious, silly, worn-out opera *schtick*, all the old junk which the old school of directors offloaded. At least directors from the stage know how to make things look real. But some of the abominations at the opera have been perpetrated by people who have never been allowed near a play. Then these stupid malignant twits who write about music for the London papers coo and simper, and they all ponce about being pretentious together."

163

So what would he like to do – what is best? "Oh, it's all too late now. (He is 60 in July.) I'd like to paint, write, look at the history of science." He doesn't *look* playful. He looks like a retriever, sloped home from some bog having lost a pheasant. "I know, I'm rather gloomy now." Does the state of the arts in this country compound this? I'm not remotely interested in the arts. I'm not certain that they have a state and if they do, it's not in the least an important clinical condition, any more than athlete's foot." He sniggers – "aesthete's foot, rather.

"All I want is to do some good, intelligent, pottering around. I think people who think their work is important, that they'll leave a mark, are appalling.

"Really, I don't like Britain much." I sense adjectives, lining up and jostling. "It's become rancorous, dirty, envious, third-rate and unkempt. I'd like to live in small-town America, where all the silly prejudices of the US are softened and people acknowledge that they live in an occupied country. I enjoy working in Europe; I like the Donizetti I did in Monaco but the audiences were a group full of hateful, beknighted, over-privileged spoilt children. And, abroad, I feel orthopaedically disadvantaged by language – I talk with a bad limp."

By now the room has filled, Rachel, Miller's wife, is indicating politely that Miller should remember to eat. Someone needs a contract, lost in a roomful of paper and Miller, looking, finds a book he must lend me which in fact his wife has been hiding from visitors. He pats her cheeks.

He shows me the door and watches me leave with his sad dog look; the look of a dog who thinks it may just have had its day. Bach and baroque music, though, has offered him a bone. Just watch – we'll see him jump for it.

The Scoop Master

JOY COPLEY

18 July 1994

One of Britain's leading political journalists retires at the end of the month. He isn't a household name but Chris Moncrieff of the Press Association has been an influential reporter without parallel.

Chris Moncrieff stopped dead in his tracks. He could hardly believe his eyes. Blue luminous elephants were lumbering along Blackpool beach at dawn. Political editors are used to heavy nights on the town at party political conferences, but this was ridiculous.

Moncrieff is a man of great stories. The ones he writes as the most prolific political editor in history and the personal ones he tells, which have the tears rolling down your cheeks.

The blue elephants turned out to be real, not an hallucination. They had been painted as a gimmick by the Tower Circus owners and were exercised each morning at 5am.

When Chris Moncrieff retires this month after 32 years at Westminster, the Palace will lose an institution.

As the political editor of the Press Association news agency, approaching 63, he works from 6.15am to 11.15pm seven days a week writing history making political stories and scoops.

He is a "Boys Own" style reporter, a type of Billy Whizz who never stops. He only ever takes two weeks' holiday a year – and even files stories he stumbles over at the seaside.

He always forgets to eat and his colleagues buy him pork pies and sandwiches, which he scoffs over his computer, which is riddled with crumbs and bits of crisps. They have learned by experience never to bring him anything hot because he never stops long enough to eat it.

Such is his output, that when he retires two mere mortals will replace this colossus. Moncrieff talks in stentorian tones resembling Andrew Sachs of *The Good Old Days* and sounds as if he is permanently filing copy, sometimes stopping mid-sentence to spell out words.

But he does not look like a jutting-jawed action man reporter. He is affectionately known as Rumpled of Westminster because of his crinkly suits and friendly craggy face.

As an agency man his work is mostly invisible to the public, despite the fact he is often first with the news and his lightning reports form the basis of many of the stories in the regional and national press, radio and television.

The scrapes he has been in and the lengths he will go to file a story when following prime ministers around the globe are the stuff of cartoon strips. He once managed the herculean task of filing copy on a fuel stop in Siberia.

There was the time he was almost clubbed to death by an enormous Russian wearing pink pyjamas in a Moscow hotel. It was 4am and Chris was screeching at the top of his voice to make himself heard above a crackling telephone line, the story of Margaret Thatcher's visit to Moscow. The angry Russian burst into his room and told him to stop or he would floor him. Chris calmed him. Shoved him out of the door and risked life and limb by continuing to phone the story with one hand firmly on the door handle.

Once he was even mistaken for the prime minister of Poland. Standing between Thatcher and the Solidarity leader Lech Walesa in Gdansk, he was described as "the grim-looking Polish prime minister" in one newspaper.

He has to stick like glue to the prime minister of the day which means he misses out while on trips abroad. Political correspondents can sometimes take the odd hour out to savour the sights. But not PA.

"I went to the Falklands and never saw a penguin; went to Egypt and never saw a pyramid and to India and never saw the Taj Mahal," he says, "I was always too scared of missing something".

On sensitive trips he can often be the only reporter accompanying the Prime Minister. He was sitting in a pub in Fleet Street one minute and off to the Falklands with Margaret Thatcher the next.

Hours later, when he arrived exhausted he could not find a telephone for his story. So he hijacked a lift on an army motor boat to a requisitioned ferry anchored in the turbulent sea off Port

Stanley. After hauling himself up the side of the boat, he then managed to persuade an officer to let him use the phone. Finally he pulled out a crumpled £10 note to pay for the call and was told it cost a staggering £275.70. With a trembling hand he wrote out a cheque and still shaking lost his balance clambering off the boat and splattered straight into the icy sea, where he was eventually plucked to safety by the army.

Of all the prime ministers he has worked under including Harold MacMillan, Alec Douglas-Home, Harold Wilson, Edward Heath, James Callaghan, Margaret Thatcher and John Major, he found Thatcher the best.

"She was without a doubt the best from a journalist's point of view. Wherever you went there was always a story with Margaret Thatcher," he said.

Political reporting has changed since he first came into the House and found it "horrendous". "I applied for a transfer out of the place as soon as possible, but then the place sort of grew on me".

In those days there were virtually no press releases or explanatory handouts, which nowadays are like confetti. "Even on Budget Day, there was nothing. You ran straight out of the chamber, into a telephone box and began dictating from your notebook . . . praying at the same time."

The now almost daily press conference by the political parties were a rarity up to 15 and 20 years ago.

167

"It took the parties a long time to catch on that they had a captive audience. They must have been a bit thick-witted," he chuckled.

To say he has travelled the world, rubbed shoulders with the great and the good and has broken many stories, including the leaked Department of Trade and Industry letter which attempted to discredit Michael Heseltine in the Westland helicopter affair, he is modest, completely unpretentious and without side.

When ministers and MPs want the world to know something they ring Moncrieff. Denzil Davies, the former Labour defence spokesman, rang him, somewhat tired and emotional in the middle of the night to launch into a tirade against Neil Kinnock and announce he was resigning.

MPs who wanted to complain and tut-tut about Michael Foot's duffle coat at the famous memorial service rang Moncrieff to whisper their unhappiness.

It is hard to decipher what makes this driven machine tick. His emotional self remains something of an enigma. Ask him why he works such gruelling hours and does not take even half of his holiday entitlement he looks slightly puzzled and taken aback as if the question had never crossed his mind. "I really don't know", he says. His wife Maggie, who he met when she was playing principal boy in *Robin Hood* at Newcastle Theatre and married in April 1961, has the patience of a saint.

"We have never had any bother or upset about the hours. She has been in the acting business, which is the same hare'em, scare'em rough and tumble life," he said.

It is amazing that after these years he still retains a puppy dog enthusiasm for his job.

"When most small boys wanted to be train drivers I always wanted to be a reporter. I never ever feel that I am on a treadmill, I love writing stories."

When he retires he will still write obituaries for PA and do some lectures and be a regular pundit on Radio Talk UK. He is very generous to others and in the words he constantly uses about others . . . Chris Moncrieff is "a very fine man".

Dancing with the Wolf

BRIAN PENDREIGH

15 August 1994

Sometimes people are not what they seem. I had read a dozen articles on this guy, and they could have been about a dozen different men. They were like pieces of a jigsaw that didn't quite fit. I needed a lead. I was sitting in the office alone at midnight with a notebook on my desk and some cheap red wine on my brain when it came to me. It was a thought that led me to Chinatown in the small hours of the morning. It was there I found my angle on Jack Nicholson.

The tabloids had portrayed him as a party animal, wining and dining and dancing the night away with women young enough to be his daughters. Those were the older ones. Most were young enough to be his granddaughters. But sometimes people are not what they seem. Nicholson was 37 when he found out he was illegitimate and the woman he thought was his mother was really his grandmother. His real mother was the woman he knew as his big sister. Both were dead. It was too late to talk about it.

He said it was not important anyway.

Several London papers carried detailed diaries of everything he did there last month, a sort of Nicholson gazette page as if he were royalty, which he is, passing among his subjects buying a meal here and a copy of *The Big Issue* there. These accounts came complete with timings – 11pm Thursday, on the dance floor at Tramp with a "a succession of pneumatic but unknown young females"; 3am Tuesday, drinks in his £550-a-night suite with Naomi Campbell and Kate Moss.

He was photographed with a grin you could park a stretch limo in. Master of the chat-up line. "Have you ever danced with the devil in the pale moonlight?" It was the image the tabloids wanted and they made sure they got it. And Joker Jack helped, of course.

But it was not the Nicholson I met. It was not the Nicholson in the notebook on my desk, talking about taking time off and needing to clarify aspects of his life. These women with whom he was seen in London were not the women he had loved and left; or loved and lost. Seventeen years he spent with Anjelica Huston before leaving her for Rebecca Broussard, a waitress and small-time actress who gave him two children.

But he insisted on keeping his own space. They lived in separate houses a few minutes apart. And then the year before last she ended the relationship and got involved with a younger man. Nicholson recently completed another film with old flame Huston, but she is married to someone else now. Nicholson is photographed with a bimbo on each arm and one to spare, and a grin that says: "I don't care, I'm Jack, look what I can do." But that is not what he was quoted as saying in *Vanity Fair* when asked if he still loved Broussard. "Of course," he says. And there is more: "You're left. You're abandoned. And you're not going to be over it for another year – whatever the f*** you do . . . they do . . . she do. If it takes that long, I'm willing. I don't think I got the time, but I'm willing to do the time. I'm going to give my need the time."

169
•

He does not "do much press", as they say, but he meets a few of us in London's Dorchester Hotel, primarily to talk about his new film *Wolf*, one of this summer's few big-budget adult movies. Nicholson's character Will Randall looks like a man, but he is really a wolf. Nicholson arrives, wearing slacks, polo shirt, dark glasses and two-tone shoes. Charm oozes from every pore and he sweeps me up in that devilish grin as if he knows me of old, from the days in Chinatown. "The classic werewolf myth is that it's a sexual myth primarily," says Nicholson, "a male sexual myth; and that he kills – through the cycle of the moon – eventually kills the one that he loves." But *Wolf* also draws on Native American mythology, Nicholson explains, which is more literal in terms of transformation, not man into werewolf but man into wolf. Nicholson studied wolves. "I know the alpha-wolf concept," he says, "the fact that, because of the way a pack is formed, one male and one female basically do all the f***ing." And is there a wolf in Nicholson? "There's something of the wolf within us all, I think." He says he has its baleful gaze, but does not go further.

He does not restrict his comments to the film. He talks about the press and the state of the world and of masculinity. "Everybody is for the minority, everyone is attacking the white male and the white male is the only minority on the planet, simple as that." He seems philosophical about uninvited press attention. "False implications in the press have cost me important relationships," he says. He believes there is an industry of informers selling tittle-tattle. "They pay tremendous amounts of money to people for stories, whether they are real or not . . . I don't think I would be able to resist that amount of money if I was starving, if all it required to survive is to say 'I heard this or somebody sucked that'." Nicholson is hunted, the wolf is hunted. Does he feel endangered? "Well, I've always felt a little bit endangered." I think he likes this. "But then I'm very complicated in terms of self-protection." He talks about sex and the gaps in his life, but he talks cryptically. He gives you pieces of a jigsaw.

We dance in the moonlight of riddles and I am left to work them out at midnight a few weeks later in the office, like Jake Gittes, just me and the ghosts of past cases.

This is one guy you cannot just phone up with a few supplementary questions. He is one of the biggest stars in the world, and one of the richest.

He made £40 million from playing the Joker in *Batman*. He got a percentage of profits. It was such an astute deal that he got a further £20 million from the sequel and he was not even in it.

Instead he did *Man Trouble* for $35,000 for his old friend Bob Rafelson, who directed him in *Five Easy Pieces, The King of Marvin Gardens* and *The Postman Always Rings Twice*. Before Nicholson was famous, they had co-written and co-produced the film *Head* for the Monkees.

Nicholson would have got more if *Man Trouble* had been a hit, but it flopped.

Nicholson is a very loyal person. *Wolf* is his fourth film with director Mike Nichols, an association that began with *Carnal Knowledge* in 1971.

Wolf was written by Jim Harrison, a novelist who has been a friend of Nicholson's for 20 years and who claims he wrote it after waking up one night in his cabin in remote Michigan and thinking he was turning into a wolf.

Wolf is a medium-size hit in America, though Nicholson is not infallible.

He has had a fair number of flops, including *The Two Jakes*, the sequel to *Chinatown* that he directed himself. But he has also given a string of unforgettable performances in unforgettable movies – *One Flew Over the Cuckoo's Nest, The Shining, Terms of Endearment, Hoffa*. There is a genius in some of those performances that borders on madness. He has won two Oscars and been nominated for ten. Katherine Hepburn is the only actor or actress nominated more often.

But Nicholson was in his thirties before he became a star in 1969 as the lawyer who jacks it in, dons an American football helmet and goes on the road with Peter Fonda and Dennis Hopper in *Easy Rider*, the film that tapped into the Sixties' freewheeling, dope-smoking counter-culture so successfully that it became one of the most profitable films of all time.

He had been acting in films for more than ten years by then, including Roger Corman's *The Raven*, alongside Vincent Price and Peter Lorre, and *The Terror*, with Boris Karloff. Now Nicholson is back in the horror genre. "There are lots of cycles," he says. "I played many disturbed teenagers for Roger. I don't think I ever got to play a monster in one of his movies." By the late Sixties, Nicholson was also beginning to make a minor name for himself as a writer. His scripts included *The Trip*, a film about LSD, starring Fonda, Hopper and Bruce Dern, who were going to team up again in *Easy Rider*. Nicholson's initial involvement was as one of the producers, until Dern dropped out. Shooting had started before Nicholson took over Dern's role. In the five years between *Easy Rider* and *Chinatown* his fee rose from $2,000 a film to $1 million.

It was apparently just after *Chinatown* was completed that Nicholson heard of a man in New Jersey claiming to be his father. There is still some doubt over who his father was, but it was at that point that a surviving aunt confirmed his sister was indeed his mother.

And so to *Chinatown* a film of lonely sax play and lonely sex play, all about people not being what they seem. Nicholson's character, private detective Jake Gittes, is in love with Evelyn (Faye Dunaway), whose husband has been killed. Evelyn appears to have imprisoned her former spouse's lover Katherine and there is a violent confrontation, with Nicholson laying into Dunaway as she alternately claims the girl is her sister and then her daughter; and then her sister *and* her daughter.

It transpires that Evelyn had a child by her own father, played by Anjelica Huston's father, John Huston. And in the end Evelyn is killed and Jake is left alone, devastated, and someone says to him: "Forget it Jake. It's Chinatown." Patrick McGilligan says in his recent book *Jack's Life* that Nicholson only found out about his sister/mother after *Chinatown*, but it is as if Nicholson is trying to exorcise his pain on screen. And in 1986, Nicholson told *American Film* magazine: "My films are all one long book to me . . . It's all autobiography." He has made 23 films since *Chinatown* and rates some of his most recent among his best. "I'm in top form at the moment," he smirks. However he maintains he is still open to suggestions about his acting. "It's just that not that many people have that many ideas that are better than my own." Then he adds: "I'm only kidding." There are hints of uncertainty in his arrogance. Asked why he has not directed more films, he says: "There's a little thing lurking in the back just saying to me I could direct this worse." He has worked continually for "seven or nine years". In that time his relationship with Anjelica Huston ended, and the one with Broussard began and ended. He complains about the long hours and the pressure. Is it worth it? He responds that of course it is, because the upside is that he can now take a year off work. "Not many actors are that successful," he says.

"It's not like I'm retiring. What I would be looking at is life. And that's really the material of the movies that you make. I mean,

I'm not specifically gathering information around the topic. But I'm kind of taking time off, so that maybe my life fills up or some things clarify and become easier to express." What was it he said to *Vanity Fair*? "You're abandoned. And you're not going to be over it for another year . . . If it takes that long, I'm willing. I don't think I got the time, but I'm willing to do the time. I'm going to give my need the time." I take a taxi home from the office and fast-forward through videos of *Chinatown* and *The Two Jakes*. A 17-year-long relationship had ended.

At the end of the sequel one of the principal characters turns out to be Katherine, the daughter of Jake's dead lover from the first film. Katherine's husband is dead too and she asks Jake if she will ever get over the pain.

"Does it ever go away . . . the past?" And Jake says, a little flippantly: "Well, I think you have to work real hard on that one." Katherine leaves his office, but as she begins down the stairs, his door bursts open and he stands there, the handsome face now fleshy with good living, hairline receding, bags under eyes. But what a look. Katherine's question is written in his eyes. The mouth is open. There is something more he wants to say: "It never goes away," he tells her. And he looks like he knows. You play that scene again and again. The pain never goes away.

He does know. In the end you want to cry, and you call it a night.

Sometimes people are not what they seem. That is the angle. It always was the angle, in *Chinatown*.

173

Subverting the saints

PETER CLARKE

23 August 1994

The man who envisaged 'rivers of blood' in Britain has now produced a text of far more Apocalyptic scope. Peter Clarke considers Enoch Powell's new book and predicts that it will change Christianity for ever.

"God chose the Jews because of their verb structure," Enoch Powell told me. I can't pretend to understand the argument, but I liked his jest. Like so much of Mr Powell's conversation, it consists of imaginative leaps that are part joke, part truth.

Now he offers us a new translation of St Matthew with a detailed commentary. It shimmers with intelligence. I used to think Enoch Powell would be remembered most for his (as yet unpublished) love poetry. Now I know it will be for his exegesis on the New Testament.

Without Greek, you are lost. A little bit of Hebrew helps. The main skill is to burn the mental furniture. The New Testament is not reportage or a narrative of events. It is the theological means by which Judaism broke out of its confines to convert the gentile world.

In Rome around AD100, certainly after the destruction of Jerusalem in AD 70, the first Christian gospel was written. It is now lost. The gospel according to Peter was the text from which Matthew was drawn. All other gospels are sub-edits of the lost scrolls.

Literary and textual criticism is the application of pure intelligence. Reading the Bible in English is merely a pollutant or confusion. Latin is no help either. The key texts were written in Greek by people whose knowledge of Hebrew allowed a few schoolboy howlers. Their purposes were doctrinal.

Enoch Powell's study of the evolution of the gospels draws nothing from the manuscript divergences of the last 1,800 years. The crucial texts are Roman, but in Greek. The recent archaeology of desert papyri has no relevance other than to confirm the torment of Judaism after the sacking of Jerusalem. If you have fluent Greek and a good knowledge of Hebrew you are one of a very small number of people. The most striking quality of John Tyndale's translation of the Bible, from which the King James version was derived by his committee, was the loneliness of the man. So it is with Mr Powell.

His Greek and Hebrew have been proofed by Professor Edward Ullendorff and Doctors Henry Chadwick and William Horbury, so we can be confident he is sure footed in his translation. Yet this astonishing volume is without a bibliography as his brain-journey has been so alone.

I remember Mr Powell in his study in South Eaton Place with his Greek New Testament and his lexicons. This is archaeology at its best. No dirty hands, just the play of intelligence over texts so covered in barnacles of assumption and prejudice that his conclusions seem utterly subversive.

He started reflecting on the curiosities of the Greek gospel texts as a precocious pupil at school in Birmingham but it was, I think, the conversion of the Tory Party to socialism by Edward Heath that turned Enoch Powell's imagination back to Matthew. If the Conservative Party was renouncing its purpose in favour of powers that would dissolve Parliament it was more rewarding to wrestle with the challenge of the New Testament instead.

The alternative was the Shakespeare myth. He says it is plain no one person could have written the corpus attributed to an Elizabethan impresario who died bookless. The writer of *Hamlet* is demonstrably not a Warwickshire lad and the author of *Coriolanus* had to have lived a political life at court. I still hope we will see an Enoch Powell textual assessment of the members of the committee who composed Shakespeare.

It seems the authors of Matthew were writing as a team. Their task was to reconcile different stories that had grown up and to satisfy the followers of the Baptist. The Jesus figure had to be true to Jewish prediction and to the embrace of the non-Jew. We see there are inconsistencies and oddities but we feel his Bronze Age followers did a creditable job of conveying the divine messages. For those brought up Jews it is baffling that Christendom has fallen for a lot of fairy tales but mildly pleasing. Davidic King myths have beguiled most of the rest of the world. Mr Powell's cool reasonability opens up appreciations I had not imagined.

I had not realised so much was pure allegory and known to be allegory by its authors.

The healing of the centurion's son and the parable of the labourers in the vineyard illustrate it well. Jesus does not have to cross the sea from Palestine in order to convert. His healing is done by conversion, by the word, by missionaries. The writers were missionaries in Rome. The equal payment of labourers hired at the eleventh hour ceases to be merely irritating once you appreciate it represents the gentiles reached by the gospel at a late stage in the salvation-experience.

All those daft anti-capitalist sequences about the "poor" being favoured over the "rich" and camels passing through the eyes of needles stand up as luminously sensible when they are seen to be metaphors for Jews reluctant to convert non-Jews. Jesus never enjoined poverty on his followers – nor did the 1st-century Greek writers. Mr Powell's translation and commentary has the surprising effect of making the Jesus stories the more impressive.

Forget the supernatural and the miracles as preposterous magic. The miracle is textual. The miracle is the break out of the peculiar ideas of the Divine that were Judaism (the rich) into the gentile, Mediterranean world (the poor).

Enoch Powell often found pieces of his textual jigsaw fell into place when he was doing other things. Polishing his boots was often fruitful. A Hebrew allusion could suddenly make sense when he was sploshing in the bath. I like to think of him applying his singular mind sitting on the Opposition benches in Parliament reflecting on verses in St Matthew while Government ministers explained their latest surrender to the European Commission.

This book would be a formidable achievement for a full-time scholar but it is the fruit of a mind engaged in the daily hurly burly of politics. After constituency duties were performed there was time to read and study. The library at the Commons is great fun for parliamentary excavation but of no theological utility.

The cunning secret of Mr Powell's fertile regimen was to avoid the temptation of an office in the Commons. His life is conducted with the greatest efficiency and modesty in his home.

I remember saying to Mrs Powell that I could not understand how a person of his intelligence could believe in the transparent nonsense of the Bible and the sanctimonious twaddle of church-manship. I surmised it was merely prudent for a Conservative politician to defer to the Established Religion.

I learned how serious a student of Christianity he was and that he had travelled from the atheism of his young adulthood.

When I have talked to him about his work he exhibits the quality of authentic scholarship. He speaks without jargon and in simple lean sentences. For him the realisation the Jesus figure was stoned to death but that the Romanised crucifixion was theologically necessary has its own astonishment. The banal-minded like me grump that we have been misled by clerics and teachers. Yet the greater mystery revealed is the purposeful nature of the early church struggling to escape Jewish ritual observance and to encompass the Roman world.

The Evolution of the Gospel omits the work of Paul and we have no glimpse of how or why Constantine employed the power of the state to nationalise the youthful church and make it obligatory. Mr Powell's focus is only on the primary nature of St Matthew's gospel and to show it must have been derived from a post Petrine text.

It is no arrogance on Mr Powell's part that he seeks no confirmation from other philologists or theologians. He seems almost without vanity. He has a dignity and self-assurance untouched by fashion. So he went digging by himself to see what he could find without the companionship of preconceptions.

I am so partisan I can be discounted but I believe this is a book that will change the world. For those dazzled by the lapidary beauty of the bible and carrying the debris of childhood teaching it may seem a brutal book. The superstructure of the church and its doctrines are built on clever copywriting by Hellenised Jews writing in Rome.

It seems too coarse and vulgar to ask if the Jesus figure existed. The answer is no, the stories are all allegory, but the evolution of the text is as near a miracle as mankind will ever experience. When Enoch Powell the politician is a footnote in the following centuries his textual critiques will have transformed Christianity.

The contemporary mind sees religion as mostly error but we are richer only because the Jews exorcised the other petty Gods. Mr Powell shows how they made the journey. Do as you would be done by. The rest is all commentary.

177

Iain Banks

GILLIAN GLOVER

19 October 1994

In search of the real Iain Banks, best-selling author of Complicity, *Gillian Glover finds the personality who devised the connoisseur's guide to horrible death disarmingly boyish.*

By the time you read this, two more people could be dead. Or a Greenock librarian may have sought a culture sex-change and opened a chip shop in Gdansk. Last week, Iain Banks could not be sure. Today he will know, because his new novel is 24 hours into its gestation.

"I've allowed myself a week to come up with a plot," he explained. "But I haven't a clue what it will be. All I know is I'll start writing on Monday the 17th of October. That's the day I've set myself." So the Banks computer, both literal and metaphorical, is already lit up, because Banks meets targets the way other writers meet for coffee. It is 11 books and ten years since *The Wasp Factory* was published, and Banks has turned 40: an age when the *enfant* should finally part company with the *terrible*. Not in his case, however. Banks is 40 like Dennis the Menace is 40 – a chronological footnote to a continuing display of exuberant, youthful pyrotechnics.

I had wanted to visit him at his home in South Queensferry. That, I was sure, would let me catch sight of the real man: the personality who devised the connoisseur's guide to horrible death which constitutes much of the narrative in his last novel, *Complicity*. There was sure to be a vast black leather sofa, a collection of 19th-century surgical instruments, a whole shelf of books about the plague, maybe even some specimen bottles ... At the very least, he would harbour a suspiciously voluptuous pot-plant.

So it came as quite a disappointment when he insisted that we meet in an Edinburgh restaurant. The fact that the protagonist of

Complicity also ate in Viva Mexico was scant compensation for missing all that psychologically loquacious furniture.

Nor did this misplaced zeal easily convert to a commentary on Mr Banks' personal appearance. He looks like a genial university lecturer. The sort whose enthusiasm for Real Ale keeps pace with his academic endeavours, and who spends his Sundays working on the prototype of a car that runs on processed urine. This is the left-wing conscience in full plumage: beard, glasses, chunky sweater, checked shirt, and jeans. It was a relief to see that he was wearing a long, rather arty raincoat, especially since it wasn't raining. You can always ask harsh questions of men in raincoats.

Harsh, obvious questions about childhood and the sort of games wee boys must play if they are to grow up to write so lovingly about torture and mayhem. Banks smiles at the familiar territory. He is an only child – a circumstance which he believes did help make him a writer. "It makes sense. You are forced to live in your own world. But it's not a nightmare world. I liked school, liked the teachers. Liked my pals and my parents. It doesn't make good copy, but I was happy." He lowers his voice confidingly, "though, of course I did torture wasps occasionally."

He recalls a launch party for the publication of *Canal Dreams*, when an American approached him and said: "I can see you must have had a really disturbed childhood." Banks disagreed, but was pleased to add: "My Mum and Dad are both here. Why don't you ask them? A few moments later his mother's voice rose indignantly over the babble, "Och, no. Not at all. Iain was a very happy wee boy."

So happy, in fact, that when he should have been dropping out, tuning in and styling his rebellion to the throb of 1970s rock music, he was nipping home from Stirling University every second weekend so his mum could do his washing.

But he did enjoy one obsession: an absolute determination to make his living as a writer. The subjects he chose at Stirling – English, philosophy and psychology – were assembled as those most useful to a future novelist. And after graduating, he pressed the "hold" button on any other career by taking a series of bizarre casual jobs. Hospital porter, rope-and-gangplank sorter for Clyde steamers, lawyer's clerk, barman – the whole job-centre waste-paper bin. "I missed out on grave-digger, though," he sighs,"I always wanted grave-digger for the CV."

He had written four novels before *The Wasp Factory*, none of

179

them published; so disappointment must have bleached some of the rosy shading from the picaresque vista of his twenties. But he resists the idea. "The only major disappointments in my life have been the last four election results."

One flick of the conversational catapult, and he's free! Forget classroom *angst*, let's concentrate on bar-room politics. Not that Banks reserves his views for drinking sessions; but the glee, the volume and the absolute conviction with which he communicates them does smack of 19 pints and a pie supper. He uses the word Tory as if peeling it off the sole of his shoe. It is perhaps the sheer force of his laser-powered socialism that has so far doomed its translation into fiction (not to mention fact).

He is candid about the flaws of *Canal Dreams*: "It just didn't work as a political novel, though it's quite effective as a thriller." Similarly, the passages of political comment in *Complicity* creak and wheeze. But Banks is sure to persevere. Those who wear an honorary woggle round their hearts always do.

To be fair, this irrepressible boyishness is a huge part of his charm. When he talks about his passion for gadgets, he is the wide-eyed seven-year-old explaining all the gears on his Christmas bike.

"At the moment I'm thinking of getting one of those Night Sight things from the Innovations catalogue. You know, so you can see in the dark. I've just got to have one. But it's 500 quid, which is quite a lot to spend on a gadget, when I don't know what I'd use it for. Maybe I could start a career as a peeping Tom . . ."

And, while on the subject of aberrant sex, there were some meticulously crafted examples in *Complicity*. Banks laughs. "I've just got a vivid imagination. Honest, I don't experiment at home." Of course not. But one has to make sure it is all physically possible: for example, how did he check on the effects of injecting a large amount of semen into the bloodstream? He shakes his head. "I didn't. I'd be too embarrassed. I just thought it through. If anything replaces your blood so that it can't carry oxygen to your brain, then you have a stroke.

"Ideally, if some nutter actually does that, it won't work. I don't want someone to stand up in court and say 'my client was a normal person until he read a book by this person Iain Banks'. But it was an ancient idea – it goes back 15 years or more, only when I thought of it, it was so horrible, I couldn't find a home for it. But in *Complicity* it happens to a pornographer with an interest in snuff porn, so your moral sense says: OK. Green. Go for it. Otherwise it's gratuitous. But not here. I wanted this to shock."

Did it shock his wife? "She hasn't read it. She thinks *A Room with A View* is too violent." So she doesn't know what goes on inside the Banks cranium? Surely, after only three years of marriage, discovering the terrible truth could be grounds for divorce? "We've known each other for 14 years," he counters. "Though I can't say too much about her. She likes to stay fairly private." Intriguing. A Mrs Rochester in a turret room, perhaps?

Well, no. Nice plot twist, but the characterisation won't work. Banks likes his women strong and determined: "I've always had this weakness for strong women. Women who aren't subdued, who have a bit of aggression. It's the only thing I look for in women that I don't in men. I don't like aggressive men at all. You get such an advantage as a man anyway, the aren't-I-wonderful thing all comes with the hormones. But with women it's different, a basic self-belief makes a woman interesting." He stops himself in horror. "God, this sounds as if I admire Maggie Thatcher . . ." and it takes several minutes of multiple expletives just to exorcise the notion.

It does not concern him that his wife has not ingested the entire Banks *oeuvre*. Perhaps he's relieved. "My Mum has read them all," he says with pride. He rates time for reading as a luxury, though a necessary one for a novelist. After all, it was a newspaper report about an American widow whose body exploded at her cremation because the doctor had forgotten to remove her pacemaker, which gave him the idea for the opening of *The Crow Road*.

Even so, reading is not the principle luxury Iain Banks would input into the data discs of Utopia. For that we need the string sections of several symphony orchestras and a CD-Rom sunset. "My real luxury would be an equitable economic system on the planet so I could spend my money on gadgets with a clear conscience, knowing that it wasn't needed to feed little children or supply clean drinking-water. Yes. That would do nicely, thank you very much."

He seems totally sincere. But while awaiting Armageddon and the New Order, he just nipped off to buy "a really amazing watch". After all, when the end is nigh, one likes to know one's timing is absolutely right.

181

Regally yours

A LITTLE CANNABIS WOULD SOOTHE YOUR NERVES, MA'AM .....

When Paul met Sheila

FORDYCE MAXWELL

"G'Day cobber, noice to see yer this arvo. Fancy a tinnie?"

"Er . . . well, if you put it like that, why not? Nicely chilled, is it?"

"Colder than a polar bear's bum, mate. Here. Get that down yer. Cheers."

"Mud in your eye, as we say. Now about . . ."

"Ah, ferget the old diplomatic rhubarb for a few minutes. Now we're together again, and I haven't forgotten the last time, let's get to know each other a little. Watched Neighbours recently?"

"Well, actually . . .

"Bonzer stuff, mate, bonzer. And Sylvania Waters?"

"Really, I . . ."

"That Noelene! Larff! that's your genuine Ozzie bint, mate. You don't get many of her to the pound, I'll tell yer. And that geek of a husband! He makes old Phil look like a pussycat. And what about the cricket?"

"Look, can we . . ."

"That's some team, I'll tell yer. Shane Warne? See that ball that bowled Gatting? Pitched a yard outside leg stump, turned square, turned two corners, went round the wicket keeper and bowled him. Thought I'd split me strides. Took two Fosters and a XXXX to calm down. And young Slater? What a batsman."

"Please . . ."

"Aw, don't come the raw prawn, mate. Don't go into yer Crocodile Dundee act. Have another tinnie . . .

I'd love to, your Majesty, but could we possibly spend just a few minutes discussing the constitutional position of Australia?"

Institution already dead by its own past standards

TOM NAIRN

12 July 1994

"I could see his point of view"; "Seemed a decent fellow, *I* wouldn't mind him being King"; "Best of luck to him, he does a lot of good". Many readers must have heard such comments since Prince Charles starred in Jonathan Dimbleby's TV film ten days ago, and quite a number may agree.

I urge them to think again. It seems to me that the programme was a nauseating failure precisely *because* so many viewers had these reactions, predominantly in good faith. Because (in other words) the film partly achieved its purpose of rehabilitating Prince Charles and (more important) his "candidature" for the UK Crown when his mother dies. Had it failed in that aim – for instance by showing the prince as a buffoon and Dimbleby as a mere lackey – then the monarchy's future, already in doubt, would presumably have vanished altogether.

As it is, many are now saying: "Things aren't so bad, it may last a bit longer." This is, of course, why the film was made. And its true awfulness lies in the fact that the reasons it advances for such a recovery of faith *in the institution* are absurd. On one level it appealed to the public's good faith with a portrait of an individual "not as black as he's been painted"; at another, it utterly abused that faith by implying that Charles's individual traits may somewhat resurrect the British Crown. With a decent well-meaning fellow up there the show can be reprieved: throne, constitution, some kind of alter (or maybe altars) – the gist of "all we hold dear".

"Baloney" is one answer. For well over a century, apologists for royalty have been repeating that one of the best things about monarchy is its inevitability: Britons are spared all the fuss and bother of presidency since the King or Queen of the moment is delivered (like the rest of us) by nature. What but a natural family can epitomise the nation so humanly – in a way free (above all) from politics? Just what the midwife delivers in the sense of personal idiosyncrasies is unpredictable, but was also thought to be of secondary importance: the institution and the symbol were what really mattered.

No longer! Now an heir-apparent feels impelled to broadcast what was really a presidential-type campaigning appeal to the nation. Idiosyncrasy has become all: put up with me (since you cannot elect me) for I am, contrary to what my estranged wife has been suggesting, quite a decent sort. Now, Prince Charles may indeed be that, have his own angle on all the scandals and (as the film rather laboriously insists) be quite nice to unemployed youth and other deservers. The point is that an institution reduced to making this sort of plea is already dead by its own past standards.

The British viewing public was in effect being asked to vote for Charles as King, with their hearts if not yet with a ballot-slip. There was a touching moment when one saw the prince standing amid the ruins of the Windsor Castle fire: "Tempting" throbbed the Dimblebonian commentary, "to see this as the symbol of a stricken institution." The rest of the film was devoted to resisting the temptation. In fact a symbolic state institution which can be kept going only via Charles's dotty benevolence and patent-medicine quirks is not simply "stricken" but deceased.

If we are to be asked to vote, let it be done properly. This implication was present in the programme, though only as a sub-text. After all, its abusive, sympathy-stealing "campaign" contained the possibility that viewers might not have yielded up their hearts, as well as an invitation to the Murdoch press and the Princess of Wales to resume hostilities. "Trapped by Destiny, one day to be King" boomed the opening titles, prefacing a portrait of relentless duty and disciplined Usefulness in the People's cause. The reply won't be long coming: "OK – *let him off!* Give someone else a chance!

Hence succession (and sovereignty) are no longer inevitable. We have been given a say. Or rather a quasi-say, since it was equally plain from one of the filmed conversations that Charles has no intention whatever of pre-abdicating and giving anyone else a chance. So he remains inevitable: this emotive ballotting will make no actual difference – except that, if the public can

187

be got to like him a bit more, then life may be easier for the poor chap.

National service, old-fashioned building, organic farming and anti-bureaucracy – such were the familiar recipes accompanying the prince's confession of close yet not over-precipitate friendship (gulp) with Mrs Parker-Bowles. For Christ's (or maybe someone else's) sake, I want actually and not empathetically to vote against this possibly quite decent man. He just won't do for king/president. Where are the other candidates? When will they be given a Channel 4 maxi-budget to plead their cases?

For that we would require a constitution, one of those written down jobs defining (if that's what people want) the precise functions of monarch or president. But this is the very last thing the prince wants, in spite of those famous multi-culturalist ramblings. John Habgood, Archbishop of York, got it right last Sunday, when he pointed out Charles hadn't actually meant disestablishment. "As a country without a written constitution we depend more than most on symbolism ... and on subtle linkages between Crown, Parliament and church. None of these are unalterable, but we need to get out of our minds the idea that it is possible to make a few simple changes without the risk of triggering off a whole series of other changes which might be far from what we want ..."

Sorry, Habgood, it's too late to shut Charles up. The damage to the subtle linkages is done. I just can't get the idea out of my mind that a few simple changes (like getting rid of him) might trigger off lots of others. And be exactly what many people want.

Golly Gush

GILLIAN GLOVER

Meet Barbie and Ken, says Gillian Glover, the heroine and hero of the new Royal book whose only merit is its ability to raise a snigger.

Draw down the blinds and drape the nation's monuments in black; this is a dark and shameful day. A once-proud dynasty has reached its nadir and the wanton destruction of that nobility touches each one of us. The House of Windsor? Don't be ridiculous. I'm talking about the house of Pasternak. How can it be? How could it possibly have happened ... that someone by that name should write such appalling prose? Forget unmasking the imposter Anastasia, I demand a DNA test on sometime journalist and all-time queen of clichés, Anna Pasternak. Only then will they be able to rest easy in Vladivostock.

Of course, the literary merits of *Princess in Love* were never likely to be its principal selling point. The first man claiming to have been enticed to bed by the Princess of Wales could always depend on more than a smattering of polite interest at his local golf club. So Major James Hewitt can scarcely be surprised at the volume of response his revelations have aroused. The very building bricks of Britain are shuddering to cries of "cad", "bounder", "treason" and similar everyday expressions of disapproval.

Yet this is not an antique tale of courtly love. The blunt, cudgelling pen of Ms Pasternak has gifted the narrative real immediacy. She transports her reader instantly to a fabulous land for formulaic phrasing, and there amid the luxuriant adjectives and teeming adverbs, she sets down her hero and heroine. Surely you recognise them? They're Barbie and Ken, fresh from the toyshop with all moving parts intact.

Barbie is very pretty, she has yellow hair and long legs and she is a princess. Ken is very nice looking too. And he's big and strong. Here is a bit when they don't know each other terribly well yet:

"She was like a frail bird whose wings had been torn apart, who no longer had any hope of flying or enjoying any freedom again. To stay alive, she knew she had to talk. She could not go on living in the murky shadows of her secrets, secrets that were threatening to consume her. And beside her was this man, this man who seemed so whole and uncomplicated. He was open and strong, every part of him representing the normality that she longed for . . ."

Later on, after all their adjectives have been introduced to each other, they get much more friendly:

". . . she could not get over how he looked at her. That gaze of such kind, deep longing and delight, his eyebrows slightly arched as if he just could not believe how lucky he was to be with her. That thrilled her to the core, her exhilaration tainted only by pangs of sorrow as she reflected that her husband had never once looked at her like that."

No, please don't laugh. Barbie gets to be very fond of Ken. She even invites him to her palace, *and* she has a bath before he arrives. Ms Pasternak knows that sort of thing. She probably interviewed the chambermaid who changes the towels to make sure they were damp. Perhaps it was the chambermaid who told her what the princess was thinking in her bath, because Ms Pasternak certainly seems to know:

"As she lay in the bath, she thought of James – his strong physique, his height and those broad shoulders which he carried well and which gave him the physically nonchalant air of the loose-limbed and athletic, his thick auburn hair which swept up and back from his kind, sensitive face . . ."

Golly! Barbie is so carried away at this point she hasn't even noticed that her illustrious relative Dame Barbara Cartland has dropped in. Which is a pity, because she stays right till the very end of the story, and uses all the Kleenex.

She offers some advice while she's there, though. And Barbie and Ken make use of this advice on page 57. A Very Important Page. The sort of page that has to be organised properly, tactfully – dare one say royally?

And so the regal resolution of the jolly friendship between the pretty princess and the gallant captain is this:

"Diana stood up and without saying a word stretched out her hand and slowly led James to her bedroom."

A two-line gap, roughly equivalent to the slamming of the

190

bedroom door, allows the reader to ingest the importance of this gesture before the narrative gets up for a drink of water and resumes:

"Later she lay in his arms and wept."

Well, wouldn't you? Our reasons for tears may be different from the princess's, of course, but Ms Pasternak guesses this and helpfully pinpoints the trauma:

"She wept bitterly for that part of her that had died with Charles's rejection, that delicate bud of youthful optimism and confidence that has been ripped cruelly from its stem before it had had time to open."

No doubt Ms Pasternak was anxious lest her readers impute any lack of expertise on the gallant major's part that might reduce his inamorata to tears, and so we are delicately informed that orgasm did occur:

"The second the rapid vibrations had coursed through his blood, he had become part of her ..." and *"she had revealed herself so completely, had travelled with him to where she had never been before ...."*

Such restraint! And never, you may be disappointed to learn, do things become more explicit. Yet the picture that emerges as a whole from this sorry exercise in vulgarity is very explicit indeed, and utterly biased.

Throughout the book James Hewitt has cast himself via his obviously infatuated writer, as saviour of a disturbed, neurotic, bulimic, immature and reckless woman. The light of benign approbation never flickers over his heroic demeanor.

The letters which he claims to have from the princess are carefully paraphrased, no doubt to avoid a legal injunction, yet Pasternak can still bring herself to write on the last page:

"The world would judge him harshly in its ignorance, when all he was was a kind, weak man who had done his very best."

And what is this "very best"? A multiple betrayal. A book that is a literary, thematic and moral tragedy. A book whose only merit is its ability to raise a snigger. In fact, an ideal monument to the standards of Major James Hewitt.

Common failings bring royal house down

RUTH WISHART

25 August 1994

Granny is pushing on a bit. Same age as the century; apparently *compos mentis* unless you count cutting around in chiffon frocks in midwinter as signs of terminal eccentricity. Then again at 94 she's not about to help the family get it together really. The daughters are a bit of a mixed bag you have to say. The eldest still has what it takes. No discernible hint of bad behaviour after forty odd years at the helm. Not a lady to set the nation's pulses racing though, and not guilty of much in the passion stakes herself unless you count a lifelong affair with the more blue-blooded equestrian superstars. Little sister has had a somewhat chequered career by comparison. Thwarted in her first choice of husband, divorced from her second, and subject thereafter to rumours of other adventures, some involving gentlemen of a less than noble bearing.

Then there is the son-in-law. A short fused, tact-free zone with a tendency to spend lengthy periods of his marriage travelling alone or with friends to assorted destinations like South America. Just what he does when he gets there, and with whom, is apparently the subject of the latest Kitty Kelley unauthorised biography. Since Ms Kelley's speciality is character assassination (Frank Sinatra and Nancy Reagan lie among previous literary corpses) there is little doubt that the revelations will not be welcomed by Her Indoors.

Even so, with all their foibles recorded and otherwise, that quartet might still have managed to keep the show on the road, still managed to convince the great British public that theirs was not to reason why, merely to remain grateful that their country still enjoyed the privilege of being ruled by one of the last remaining, functioning Royal dynasties. Even when intermittent mutterings about their financial arrangements bubbled up in the public prints, the general consensus seemed to be better by far to hang on to nurse for fear of something worse. (The something worse usually being cited being the awful spectre of a President Thatcher.)

But frankly the next generation has now well and truly lost it. All the nation's soap operas rolled into one bizarre set of relationships. How can serried ranks of citizenry still stand in sycophantic lines in order to be "received" by an assortment of princes, duchesses and princesses royal almost all of whom have behaved in a manner which you wouldn't begin to tolerate in your own offspring? How can we pretend to be a real grown up collection of nations when we continue to genuflect before a first family so fatally flawed that nobody can possibly take them seriously, with the possible exception of the editors of those newspapers who cannot believe their luck in having such a rich source of endlessly titillating copy from the one household?

The latest chapter of Dianagate really is the last tacky straw. I have not the smallest clue whether or not the estranged wife of the heir to the throne is given to making nuisance telephone calls. I have not the smallest degree of interest either. The only significance of the story it is possible to detect is that in using a daily newspaper reporter to refute allegations in a Sunday publication she displays an almost total lack of judgment. Forgiveable in the young bride who got pitchforked into the Royal circus and advised the only training available would be of the in-service variety. But scarcely excusable in the adult mother of two who must be more aware than anyone else in the country of the impact and the implications of speaking directly to the press.

Announcing her retiral from public life eight months or so ago seemed the shrewdest possible move if what she genuinely craved was privacy and growing up space for her sons. But so many of her appearances in newspapers since then seem the result of stage management that you have to wonder if she knows how to breathe any more without the oxygen of regular publicity. Having another set of birthday snaps in *Vogue* for instance is hardly a fast track to anonymity.

And what are we to make of Charlie boy? Marrying the wrong woman for what seemed the right reasons and thus laying down the foundations for the kind of toe curling scandal which emerged with the Camilla tapes. In fact, toe curling scandals have become something of a trademark, given the sorry saga of the duchess being financially advised in a topless condition in her holiday home. Neither has Fergie's husband acquired any kind of reputation for properly joined up thinking, seemingly caught in a time warp of adolescent humour.

Sister Anne seems the only one of the bunch to conduct any rational sort of lifestyle and she too fell at the marital fence before making a second attempt at a clear round. Now it seems that Edward, long thought not in the market for matrimony, is about to give it a whirl with a woman who appears to have been cloned from Diana, at least in the physical sense. Four children, three failed marriages, one still unmarried. It has to say something for their upbringing. Perhaps the previous generation of royals, much like the rest of society, just stayed put in bad relationships.

And that really is the point. They have turned out to be much like the rest of us, and now that the genie of press intrusion into private Royal lives has leapt rampantly from the bottle that becomes only too apparent. They commit adultery and get involved in unsuitable affairs. They plot and scheme against their former partners. Some of them are none too bright and some of them are frankly batty. Given all of which it's plain daft to behave as if they're different or special. If they retired from the Royal fray, just think of the benefits. They'd get a bit of peace at last. And so would we.

Foreign fieldwork

BEFORE

AFTER

High

To the future

FRED BRIDGLAND

4 May 1994

*The victory is won but the struggle not yet over for president-elect
Nelson Mandela and the newly democratic South Africa. Once his
cabinet is in place, there are promises to be delivered.*

Ice-covered surfaces are not dangerous for people who know
how to skate, Friedrich Nietzsche once observed. "The past few
months have shown that South Africans, if they are proficient
at little else, are world-class skaters," notes *Business Day*, South
Africa's own daily version of *Financial Times*.

The country has managed to glide, leap and perform triple axels
around and over all sorts of obstacles – carnage in the townships,
bombs, incipient secession, negotiations, walkouts, rumours of
coups, looting. Finally, it held its first universal suffrage election
and landed squarely on its feet, power passing graciously from
the last representative of the old apartheid era to a black man
who created the guerilla army *Umkhonto we Sizwe* (Sword of the
Nation) and who accepted the burden placed upon him as head
of state with equal chivalry.

At one stage it looked as though the South African skater would
keep falling over and never complete its unique general election
routine. Catastrophe stared the country in the face as calculations
showed, 24 hours into the general election count, that at the pace
it was proceeding it would take eight-and-a-half years before the
result was known. But some judicious bending of the statutory
rules has enabled the pace of the count to be raised from that of a
snail to that of a lumbering tortoise. If the country's luck continues
to hold, the count should be completed in time to enable Nelson
Mandela to be inaugurated as the first black state president of
South Africa at an official ceremony in Pretoria next Tuesday.

Mr Mandela will be hoping the country's run of luck continues once he takes up the burden of office and begins what is already being dubbed "The Second Struggle" – the delivery of extravagant promises made by the African National Congress in terms of providing jobs, building houses and providing electricity, running water, sanitation, free universal education and improved health services.

His first job will be to construct a 27-member cabinet, which under the terms of the new constitution, must include a certain number of opposition members. All parties represented in the new 400-member, all-race National Assembly who won more than 5 per cent of the national vote are entitled to representation in proportion to their share of the national vote: five per cent earns one cabinet seat, ten per cent two seats, and so on.

The National Party of outgoing State President FW de Klerk is guaranteed, as the second largest party in the new parliament, the position of second deputy president, De Klerk will fill that position in the "government of national unity" whose life will run until 1999 under the terms of the new constitution. Beyond that De Klerk wants his party men in security, economic and financial affairs posts. Mandela is likely to acquiesce, except when it comes to the finance ministry. The finance minister will be the linchpin of the ANC-dominated government. He will have to decide where the resources come from and how they are allocated to enable Mandela to carry out the ANC's ambitious Reconstruction and Development Programme (RDP).

International investors and the local business community would like to see the present incumbent Derek Keys retained as finance minister. Mr Keys has nursed South Africa's fragile economy and brought inflation down from near 20 per cent to single figures: during the transitional period he has worked closely and successfully with the ANC. But ANC radicals are opposed to such an important post being given to a member of the "auld enemy". Mr Keys might well be happy anyway to pass up what looks like being a poisoned chalice. The finance minister will have to say no, no and no again as ministers come to him for funds for pet projects and he will have to tell them foreign exchange reserves are distressingly low, that money does not grow on trees and that trade unions will have to be told that the "liberation dividend" does not include big wage increases. South African workers are less productive than Chinese workers but earn five times as much: how, the finance minister will ask the spending ministers, do they

198

propose under such circumstances to attract the foreign investment necessary to kick start the economy and, in turn, underwrite
the RDP?

Increase taxes, the spending ministers will say, especially those
who are steeped in the easy answers of Fabianism and Marxism.
But income taxes are already very high. A married man earning
80,000 Rand (£15,000) pays 24,700 Rand (£4,630) income tax, a
single person 27,390 Rand (£5,130). Marginal rates of income tax
are 43 per cent from 80,000 Rand upwards. The International
Monetary Fund has warned that if whites and foreign-owned
businesses, who already contribute 90 per cent of tax revenues,
are squeezed any further they will lose incentive, begin leaving
the country and gross tax revenues will shrink.

It will therefore take an ANC man with a strong position within
the movement to stand up to his colleagues. Increasingly, it
looks as though Mr Thabo Mbeki, the ANC's director of foreign
relations, will be appointed finance minister. Mbeki, intelligent,
erudite and charming, has an honours degree in economics from
the University of Sussex and is well known and liked internation-
ally. The problem for Mbeki is that it would leave the way open
for ANC secretary-general Cyril Ramaphosa – his rival to succeed
Mandela, now in his 76th year – to be appointed first deputy
president. If president-elect Mandela were to die in office, the first
deputy president would automatically step into his shoes.

The succession is a difficult issue, for both Mbeki and
Ramaphosa are well qualified. In both, an affable manner hides a
tough inner core which was vital for survival in the brutal game
of liberation politics.

However, apart from great issues, the new government will
have to decide on some rather more trivial matters. Place
names, for example. Cape Town's DF Malan Airport is unlikely
to keep its name for long. Daniel Malan was the Afrikaner
nationalist who became prime minister in 1948 and launched
the authoritarian apartheid regime which lasted until De Klerk
started dismantling it from 1989 onwards. The Hendrik Verwoerd
Building, a major part of the parliamentary complex in Cape
Town, will quickly be renamed. Verwoerd, prime minister from
1958, was the main architect and philosopher of apartheid. It
was during his rule that Mandela was sent to Robben Island,
visible from parliament's rooftops, for life. The town councillors
of Verwoerdburg, a pleasant new town near Pretoria, have been

trying to find a new name for their municipality for some months.

John Vorster Square in Johannesburg could only be retained in the same way that Auschwitz has been preserved in Poland – as a monument to mankind's capacity for evil. Mr Vorster succeeded Verwoerd as prime minister when the latter was stabbed to death in Parliament in 1966. The police station at John Vorster Square became notorious as a place where many black opponents of apartheid entered alive and came out dead. During the reign of the infamous interrogator Brigadier Jan Swanepoel, many allegedly leapt out of tenth floor windows to their deaths.

The renaming is unlikely to be wholesale. Streets named after Afrikaner pioneer Paul Kruger and British imperialist Cecil Rhodes will live on. But the Kaffir River and the small settlements of Kaffirs Kraal and Kaffie Drift will surely not be part of Nelson Mandela's new South Africa.

First with no equal

MICHAEL PYE

21 May 1994

Jacqueline Bouvier Kennedy Onassis served her country in an extraordinary way – an American First Lady who demanded a kind of attention her people were not entirely used to giving. She lived a large Cinema Scope life and became a legend, a heroine. But there was a price: she hid herself in the myth and lived and struggled for the sake of fame.

Jacqueline Bouvier Kennedy Onassis had the model life for a

modern novel – celebrity, sensational fortunes, murder, sexual intrigue and quite ruthless shopping. She encouraged very few people to find the remarkable woman caught there in her own story, sometimes struggling visibly.

Men defined her, even after they died. She was bullied by the clatter of flashbulbs when all she could hear was the sound of the shot that killed JFK; she was known to jump at gunshots, even at the theatre.

Her life was suspended that day in Dallas. She became a widow who had to play at sainthood in order not to compromise her income from the parsimonious, and intensely political, Kennedys. She was praised for her meticulous mothering of John, jun and Caroline Kennedy, but not when she sought to provide for them. Her decision to remarry – to Onassis, a shipowner under investigation by most western intelligence – became an international scandal.

The notion that she might later take and hold a job, as a publisher's editor, seemed absurd. And yet she was, I think, a rather good commissioning editor; but I'm influenced by the one project on which we both worked, which we both adored, but which her bosses would not buy.

Above all, she was public property. The name was so easy to value that the makers of Gloria Vanderbilt jeans once asked her to endorse a line of Jacqueline Onassis jeans (they got no reply). The face, in its time, had put paparazzi in the line of Greek gunboats for a saleable shot. In her last years, when her private life was transparent – the companionship of Maurice Tempelsman, a politically astute diamond dealer – a picture of Jackie on a boat, even Jackie on the street was still worth serious money.

She complained, even sued, to stop these intrusions, but she also knew she had made her own trap.

She'd been a rather amateurish photo-reporter once, snapping the famous, quite dazzled by the sight of Lauren Bacall dancing with General Omar Bradley (and by the sight of a sidelined Humphrey Bogart looking crossly on) while covering the Coronation. She understood the political use of publicity, and sometimes the need not to get it.

This kind of celebrity hides substance. In the White House years, we'll never entirely know if it was indeed Jacqueline Kennedy who persuaded JFK to liberalise immigration laws, who successfully pushed the notion that the US should sign a test ban treaty or that Washington should sell wheat to Moscow. There's evidence she did all this, that she acted as "the White House liberal" against the tendency of JFK and his closest advisors, but there's also an archive of evidence that she was uninterested in politics – the political wife, thumbing a copy of *Vogue* in the limo while her husband stomped about trying to get elected.

There's ambiguity even in the moment after the assassination itself – when she always claimed to be cradling her husband against harm, but film shows she was actually crawling desperately out of the car, kicking what was left of his head. The celebrity – the legend – absolutely insists she was a heroine.

This legend was her own work. It was she who, weeks after the assassination, persuaded the writer of *Life Magazine* to write that the Kennedy years were like Camelot (she did so by quoting lyrics from the musical, not Mallory; indeed, the womanising Kennedy makes an odd candidate for the virtuous King Arthur).

A certain diffidence, or arrogance, or perhaps emptiness helped this process along. Jacqueline Bouvier Kennedy Onassis dropped friends easily, suffered fools hardly at all, wore a kind of social blinkers on public occasions so she could better cope with the main event. The publisher John Fairchild says she could open her pupils photogenically just at the moment the flashbulbs went off – hiding any inner self. This blank invited interpretation.

She could seem frivolous, or a guardian of old standards. "Mrs Kennedy," one lofty critic wrote, "remained attached to an older tradition of aristocracy and obligation" – unlike, say, Nancy Reagan, another woman who gave interviews about the new White House china and was famous for wearing clothes. The Kennedy presidency – the son of an Irish crook married to the daughter of a failed stockbroker – was glorified in retrospect.

In the process, Jackie O redefined celebrity in America. She demanded a kind of attention that Americans weren't entirely used to giving. "Jackie invented the idea of American royalty with the help of her court," Fairchild says. She did so, partly, in self-defence. In the mid-Fifties, Truman Capote found her "sweet, eager, intelligent, not quite sure of herself and hurt – hurt because she knew that JFK was banging all these other broads".

After the assassination, she was more than royal. Bob Colacello remembers the crowds around her at a museum: "They treated her more like a saint than a celebrity, and it had a lot to do with the way she carried herself."

When she announced her marriage to Aristotle Onassis, it was as though an icon turned courtesan. She said later that Onassis "rescued me at a moment when my life was engulfed in shadows" – Robert Kennedy had just been murdered, and her income from the Kennedys seemed mean and conditional – but it's also true the pre-nuptial agreement included $3 million in cash, because in the words of the document itself, $20 million "might easily lead to the thought of an acquisition instead of a marriage".

Saints and royals matter mostly because of need. In 1960, Jacqueline Kennedy was frivolity, youth, possibility – the late flowering of a generation held down by depression and war. Her rather shaky taste, her vague knowledge, seemed to be everything European (as opposed to suburban, effortful American) and everything graceful – aristocratic, almost.

That was invention, too. She's a Bouvier, from the Bouviers who claimed quite grand French ancestry by the simple device of confusing their own true ancestor (an 18th-century ironmonger from Grenoble) with a crested landowner of the same name but a much earlier century. The Bouviers' long, social climb was done mostly in bed – through marriage into clans like the banking Drexels. It was remorseless, and it ended badly with Jacqueline's father.

John Vernon Bouvier III, otherwise known as "Black Jack" was a gambler, a prodigious womaniser, a man who kept up a good front without examining how he might pay for it. "Black Jack" was a stockbroker, and Jacqueline was born a few months before the great Wall Street Crash. His womanising strained his marriage – into a practical Irish family that owned apartment blocks – and broke it while Jacqueline was only seven.

If you know only this, you know much about Jacqueline Kennedy Onassis. Almost from her birth, money was an issue in her family; her father lived not so much beyond his means, but without even considering them. She fused extravagance and love. Manners also mattered, but in order to keep up a good appearance – social convention, rather than kindness.

And there was the excitement of a wild father, but also the tedium and strain of coping with the messes he left behind. When JFK was running for president, Jacqueline had to worry the press might discover her father's other children, by a wartime romance with a married Englishwoman. When she married the promiscuous Kennedy, she deliberately turned down more comfortable,

203

more reliable men, but this time she also made sure there was money.

Very early, she learned the carefulness that often marks out people whose parents separated when they were young – who felt a little guilty, and very scared, and learned to show nothing of this at all. She also learned not to hope too much. "I have come to the conclusion," she once said, "that we must not expect too much from life."

She was salvaged by her mother's second marriage – to an Auchincloss, a descendant of the Scottish yarn merchants who became grand in 19th-century New York with the help of railway shares and enormous quantities of manure ("nitrates", the politer books say). Her carefulness now looked like manners, her socialite ambitions like the logical thing for a young, female Auchincloss.

So she was Number One Debutante of her year – a title which, in the iron snobbery of New York, reflected her Auchincloss and not her Bouvier connections. She danced, she went to Miss Porter's school, she spent a year at the Sorbonne, she smiled a lot, she went to Vassar and resented not being able to go away for the weekend like you could from town. She became the social asset that Joe Kennedy reckoned could win the presidency for his son John: the social mountaineer who knew what other social climbers need.

That concern with appearances would sanction a taste for fashion in the Sixties, which the puritan Fifties, busy struggling with the H-bomb and the Red Menace and Patricia Nixon's "good Republican cloth coat", had managed to suppress. A new kind of social column started with Jacqueline Kennedy – one which mentioned what people spent as much as who they dined with.

Middle America was hot to know what she wore, which made frockmakers care about dressing her, which turned frockmakers into a new kind of star – no longer helpful higher servants to the toffs, but the best taste-makers America had. To judge by the discounts Jackie O demanded in every grand store, she saw no harm in profiting a bit by her place in the promotion.

After all, she believed in celebrity, of an older and rather more serious kind – CinemaScope lives, projected on a huge scale. That was how she thought of JFK. "Only bitter old men write history," she said. "Jack's life had more to do with myth, magic, legend, saga and story than with political theory or political science."

By living up to him, she hid herself in myth – lived and struggled for the sake of fame, and died without escaping.

The bodies count

MICHAEL PYE

27 June 1994

Remember that two people died brutal deaths. Remember the blood on the pathway and the screams. Remember these things, because everything else surrounding the O J Simpson murder case is conspiring to diminish the horror.

205

Remember the blood that washed the pathway, the way the knife bit into the two bodies. The cops say the woman was cut so badly around the neck that her head almost fell away. The man had been slashed more than 20 times. On Sunday 12 June, something shocking happened in LA.

Such shocking things happen every day, of course. But this woman was Nicole Simpson – a glorious Californian blonde, living comfortably with cute children. The man was a waiter Ronald Goldman, but he was buffed and young; he'd been an Armani model. The two were beautiful, until they died. And it was the wrong place for screams and such terrible deaths: a grand suburb of Los Angeles, a protected place.

Remember these things, because everything else conspires to make us forget the horror. Nicole Simpson's ex-husband is O J "The Juice" Simpson, a football hero, an actor, a hero. From the start, O J Simpson was the only suspect in the case, and celebrity was on a collision course with reality and justice.

There's a war of publicity going on, but also a hum of true sentiment. Heroes get loved too much to go to the gas chamber, people say. Yet this hero kept his jobs and his reputation even after he'd been convicted of battering his wife. Men who batter their wives sometimes kill their wives – "often", some women's groups say. For the first time, a pedestal figure faces such charges.

The prosecutors worry they can't wash away the grin, the charm, the trophies. The defence worries what's said about O J the wife-batterer. And everything has its audience.

The day Simpson is meant to surrender to the police, he gets in the back of a white ford Bronco with a gun to his head and a friend drives him. The friend talks him out of going to Nicole's grave, tries to take him to the police. And while the Bronco creeps along freeways, followed by a wedge of cop cars, watched by the TV helicopters, the crowds get to the freeway overpasses and they're cheering. They're shouting for The Juice. They just love this guy so much, they could consume him.

They even love him so much, they try to imitate what he's accused of doing. At least twice so far, in Memphis and in Atlanta, men have gone out to kill their ex-wives because, as one said, "Women just do that to men like that and it's a damn shame".

So, long before any trial, there are two TV films in development. The first book comes out this week, called *Fallen Hero*. Asked how you can write a book before there are facts and what happens if O J Simpson isn't found guilty, the publisher says: "We'll deal with that later." There's a second quickie book coming which is, say the promoter, "about how people who live in the glare of the media have to live with the media".

For all this is public, like celebrity garbage, celebrity affairs, indiscreet celebrity moments in night-clubs (don't ever dance together if you're famous; the headlines can make a dance into a passion). We own every bit of pain and horror.

Two dozen lawyers turn up on TV analysing the case ("It's workfare for lawyers", one says.) There's furious jockeying to be the trial lawyer because Simpson's main adviser, Robert Shapiro, is better known for backroom fixing than for courtroom histrionics. Maybe there should be a woman lawyer: that would signal that O J isn't a monster. Maybe that would look too manipulative.

Or maybe Shapiro will go ahead alone; already he's proved good at humanising Simpson. He asks for a pillow for an old football injury. He pats O J's shoulder like a caring uncle. He asks for a doctor to look at what may be a swollen lymph node and even the judge gets caught up: she asks if Simpson's family has a history of cancer.

On the other side, there's a telegenic LA county district attorney, Gil Garcetti, a man with too many careful bones in his face, like the classic local news anchor. If Shapiro can't lose, Garcetti can lose big. He didn't get a conviction in the Menendez brothers case. He didn't do well in the trials that followed the Rodney King beating. He's an elected official and he has to win this case; but he has to win against a hero.

So he tells the cameras his case is "solid. I can't discuss the details, but we have good solid stuff." And behind the scenes, a rival district attorney, for the city of LA, releases tapes of Nicole Simpson, sounding scared and resigned, begging the cops last year to come and take O J away before he hurts her. You hear the dispatcher asking if this has happened before and Nicole saying: "Many times."

The city DA has his reasons for releasing this tape. It hurts the prosecution because it's prejudicial, but then in 1989, when Simpson was convicted of battering his wife, it was the city DA's office that made the mistake of asking that Simpson be spared jail, do community service and get therapy. Simpson ate lunch for his community service and literally telephoned in his therapy. It wouldn't do for this new case to go smoothly; someone might start criticising.

The cops also chat, to their old press buddies, the police blotter squad. We've been told Nicole Simpson and Ronald Goldman were killed with a sword, a 15-inch serrated knife, a military entrenching tool. We heard all about the hunt for the murder weapon, in underbrush opposite the Chicago hotel where O J Simpson spent the night. But now it seems the cops don't have a murder weapon at all.

We heard about a bloody ski-mask – a horrific image, a man killing wife and friend with his face deliberately blanked out. But then the defence demanded that the mask be produced, the prosecutor told them: "There is no ski-mask." We heard how O J's body was a mass of scratches, but it seems he has cuts only on his hands. The blood groups on the ground, in the white Ford Bronco, are apparently too common to make a conclusive match.

If somebody thought all this would help the prosecution, the're wrong. Defence lawyers hate grand juries, who sit to hear preliminary evidence in private, hand down indictments and don't say why. Grand juries are notoriously open to the daily browbeating of prosecutors. But the grand jury on O J Simpson has been sent home by a judge who says they have all kinds of prejudicial information that the prosecutors didn't even mention and in some cases couldn't. The jurors were joshing daily with the assembled press.

There's almost always a period of pretrial publicity that would be thought shockingly prejudicial in Scotland (Monroe Freedman, a law professor, says: "The supreme court has established that inflammable, inadmissible evidence does not prejudice a trial"). So it takes extraordinary circumstances for a grand jury to be disbanded; nobody can remember when it happened last.

Simpson's case will go, not to the grand jury, but to preliminary hearings this week, when the prosecution has to show its hand and the defence can challenge and question. Until then, we're left trying to read that face, the face of a man who's been sick too long, or someone on lithium. It's blank, the eyes closing. The face naturally goes on magazine covers but only *Time* magazine sees a need to alter it, to make it darker. Nothing racial, *Time* insists; just art. Just the way someone tragic and murderous is meant to look.

It seems odd we can't read the face, because Simpson has made a living out of convincing us, showing how much he wants to hire a Hertz car, doing pratfalls in low comedy or, in a TV pilot that's only just finished, playing a heroic Navy Seal. He controls what we think about him for a living; it depends on how he's cast.

Before that, he was a TV sportscaster, the one who explains everything. And before that he was an icon: the football hero with a smiling charm and prodigious speed, the purest form of celebrity. We cast him as a hero, but all we know is 90 minutes running and blocking; we make up the rest. Suddenly that blank and exhausted face starts to look like a mask.

For there are "police sources" up in Buffalo, New York, who say O J was lucky not to get nailed in two 1975 drug raids; in one, the football hero left his friend's flat minutes before the cops crashed in and found cocaine and marijuana. That buddy, Michael Militello, told reporters that O J did indeed snort cocaine in the 1970s. The headlines renamed The Juice: Snow-J.

We start to read the details of O J's marriage to Nicole. Here's the big football hero, around the time his knees begin to give out, out cruising. He meets Nicole Brown, a quite stunning 18-year-old who's come up from the 'burbs to check out Hollywood. He's married still, but she moves in. This isn't sport sex; this is passion, confusing and maddening, and it lasts. Five years later, with a suitable pre-nuptial agreement, they marry each other.

Nicole quit junior college because O J wanted her with him. She's worked two months as a waitress, two weeks as a sales clerk in her whole life. Her family came to be tangled up financially with O J depending on him one way and another. She let O J control what she wore, who she saw, where she went. "When he was around," a friend says, "she would tense up. She watched every move she made and every step she took." "I've always told O J what he wants to hear," Nicole said in her divorce case. Anyone who's ever worked with battered women will tell you these are the first clear signs of trouble.

That trouble came quickly. Nicole Simpson wasn't perfect, of course; she could be foul-mouthed, self-regarding, a bit impatient. On occasions, if she saw Simpson with another woman, her temper could be furious – chasing O J down the street, howling about why he couldn't at least choose someone pretty to cheat with.

But that's character. What O J Simpson did was crime. Here's Nicole Simpson's psychologist, Susan Forward, who comes forward to say that O J stalked Nicole, stared in through her windows, went after her baying: "Whore, whore". He could be infuriated 1,000 ways, none of them predictable. "Maybe one day she forgot the dry cleaning." Forward says. "Or there was a cute gas station attendant. He was having affairs. That was classic projection – blaming the victim for what he had done."

The LA police confirm a 1985 incident when Simpson broke the windscreen of his own car with a baseball bat after a fight with Nicole. "I broke the windshield. It's mine," Simpson said. In 1989, on Hogmanay, Nicole called the police; they found her hiding in the bushes, with a black eye, a cut lip, a bruised cheek and the mark of a handprint on her neck. Friends remember that the bruises weren't uncommon. Nicole, too, belonged to O J.

There are tapes of the night in 1993 when Simpson broke down the back door of his former wife's house and came in ranting, because, it seems, he'd seen a picture of one of her ex-boyfriends. For even when the Simpsons were divorced, they were together, because Nicole, it seems, still loved the man and the man just would not let go. They tried to reconcile and knew it was impossible.

Now Nicole, like O J, worked out at The Gym, an institution in west LA, a town where hard bodies and good looks just get you past the door. She'd jog in the mornings with her women friends but "they had nothing to do but shop and hang out with the kids," Jeff Keller, a model who also used The Gym, now says. Nicole collected a circle of people who were much like she had been when she met O J: liking life, looking good, chilling out.

One of them was Ronald Goldman, one of the actor/waiter/model class of person, working at the Mezzaluna restaurant. The two knew each other and Goldman was good with the Simpson kids and liked sporting about in O J's Mercedes, but it seems that's as far as it went; each liked the company of someone cute.

On Sunday 12 June, Nicole ate at Mezzaluna and left her glasses behind. She called and happened to get Goldman, who volunteered to bring them over. Neighbours say there was quiet after he arrived, then screams, then quiet; and the path to Nicole's comdominium had been washed down in blood.

Did O J do it? We can't possibly know; every "fact" is a manipulation, every "statement" equivocal. If wife-batterers sometimes go on to kill, that doesn't mean you can execute a man for wife-battering, in case. It's alarming to think that a man can stay a hero, even after the cops have been called at least eight times to save his wife from him.

You feel edgy sympathising with this man. He's a hero and a brute. But the courtroom mikes are open and, when the judge goes into chambers, we hear Simpson asking the bailiff not to take him back to the holding pen. "I'd do anything to stay out of that cell," he says, and says it again. "I'll sit here and read." He's used to going anywhere, doing anything, and now his world comes down to a cell that's plain paint and steel.

There's pathos there. But then you remember those two cut bodies on the pathway, the blood and the screams. Caring for O J's troubles, even if he is innocent, no longer seems the most important thing.

Shelter in the storm

SARAH WILSON

16 July 1994

At the huge Benaco refugee camp in Tanzania, Red Cross workers do what they can for sick and injured survivors of the Rwandan massacres. Sarah Wilson joined a Scottish nurse on one of her daily forays into the brutalised East African country to collect emergency medical supplies

Liza Coghill careers around Rwanda's mountain roads at break-neck pace. In a country where violent death is appallingly commonplace, her speed seems reckless. It is not until later, travelling with a more sedate driver, that a possible explanation emerges. At less then 40mph you can see pieces of human flesh by the roadside. You can smell the rotting bodies. Travel faster and the flesh becomes indiscernible, the smell of death vanishes.

There is another incentive to make up time while the road is good. Coghill never quite knows what she will encounter on her daily forays across the Tanzanian border, but it is a safe bet she will meet delays. Each morning, she loads up with an array of emergency medical supplies and a very flexible itinerary.

With the front-line shifting day to day, the atmosphere in Rwanda is still very tense. Coghill is often stopped at check-points and forbidden to go any further. "I was blocked at the border for a month," she says, "which meant people were suffering a lot of malaria unnecessarily."

She usually travels alone but when she takes a journalist the Rwandan Patriotic Front rebels insist on sending a minder along. Though she is fairly blasé about her daily journey, the soldier is reluctant to risk travelling into the interior unarmed. Eventually he agrees to rely on the Red Cross emblem for protection.

The 32-year-old Scottish nurse, from Moray, arrived in Tanzania less than two months ago, after the worst of the massacres across the border in Rwanda. At her refugee camp base, fellow aid workers recall the appalling brutality. There are stories of injured villagers being pulled out of aid vehicles and macheted to pieces.

Since Coghill arrived the carnage has decreased in scale but not ferocity. People whose feet have been torn off by mines are beginning to appear alongside those with machete and arrow wounds. "Cuts across the back of people's necks are common," she says, "and wounds around the ankles."

As a Red Cross worker, Coghill avoids assigning blame. But villagers in Rwanda, from both the Hutu and Tutsi tribes say most of the attacks were carried out by the Interahamwe militias – led by an extremist faction of the mainly Hutu government. They suggest the ankle wounds are caused by attempts to sever the achilles tendon.

It is said that this technique – revived from medieval times – allows the killers to claim more victims. The wounds stop people from running away while the militias deliver the *coup de grâce* to others.

Coghill continuously restocks the supplies of dressings at local clinics. She frequently sees infections, including gangrene. With whole villages constantly on the move in fear of their lives, sanitary conditions are often poor – making people more vulnerable to disease and infection.

There are few hospitals operating in Rwanda, and there is often little the nurse can offer other than first aid. If she finds someone who needs urgent hospital treatment, her jeep is usually the only means of getting them there.

But in most areas the killers have now come and gone and diseases are more common than wounds. Measles, diarrhoea, and cerebral malaria are rife. Sometimes she reaches a village which has been cut off for weeks only to find that the inhabitants have been moved by the RPF rebels. With the militias still roaming the countryside the rebels need to keep people together if they are to mount an effective guard against further tribal massacres.

Each evening Coghill returns to Tanzania and her tent in the Benaco refugee camp, just across the border. It is a secure place to sleep, but accommodation is spartan. There is neither running water nor electricity. The dining area is lit by a generator but for her tent she has only a torch.

It is far from the front line but killings still take place in the camp which surrounds the Red Cross compound. One evening, rumours that a well-known militia leader was being held by Tanzanian authorities prompted an emergency meeting in the mess tent.

Everyone was told to pack and be prepared to leave quickly if trouble flared up. Many of the refugees are thought to be former Interahamwe members and tempers can easily flare. There was a near riot the previous week when the refugees thought the militia leader was about to be expelled from the camp.

But Coghill is used to such knife-edge conditions. For six months she worked in Nagorno-Karabakh – a troubled ethnic Armenian enclave in the former Soviet republic of Azerbaijan. She prefers working in a war zone to a large British hospital with oppressive bureaucracy. A job in the accident and emergency department at St George's Hospital in Tooting, South London, put her off. "I still think there's a role for me in Britain but I would like to work in a town somewhere like Gloucester," she says.

Coghill is not the only Scot drawn to the Rwandan relief effort. The Benaco refugee camp, looking after 350,000 people – the largest number in recent years – is run by Sheila Wilson from Paisley in conjunction with the Tanzanian Red Cross.

Together they helped set up the miles of huts made from grass, sticks and plastic sheeting that are the refugees' only shelter. A veteran of several foreign conflicts in Asia and East Africa, she left Somalia for Tanzania – originally to look after Burundian refugees.

The Rwandan crisis erupted just as the Burundians were beginning to drift back home. Wilson remembers: "There was to be a meeting in the Rwandan capital, Kigali, on 8 April to close the camp. Can you imagine?"

Two days before the planned meeting, the city was transformed. On 6 April the massacres began after a fanatical Hutu faction assassinated Juvenal Habyarimana, the Hutu president, because they feared he would be soft on the Tutsi minority.

Within a few weeks, people were flooding across Rwanda's border to escape the carnage. More than a quarter of a million people crossed the Tanzanian frontier in 24 hours. "Everything was a priority," Sheila Wilson recalls. "We knew we had to get food distributed or security would break down."

A first aid post was quickly established and latrines dug and, so far, the camp has staved off predicted outbreaks of diseases such as cholera. But the atmosphere is far from calm. The few Tutsi refugees who have escaped extermination and reached Tanzania do not feel safe.

Given that Benaco accommodates nearly twice the population of Aberdeen within a few square miles, it is surprising there is not more trouble, Wilson says. "It is like a city without a police force or a judiciary. Of course we have a crime rate, but it is not high."

But it is difficult to imagine how the country will overcome the legacy of half a million people massacred. One of the worst and saddest repercussions of the carnage in Rwanda is the scores of children who have witnessed unspeakable crimes. Not only will they carry psychological scars for the rest of their lives, but the task of looking after them will be formidable with so many adults killed.

There is a small orphanage at the camp which takes in children who arrive without any relatives. Its youngest charge is less than two years old.

"Children are not orphans for six months," said Coghill, "they are orphans for 20 years."

When dress code gets a bit wearing

JAMES MEEK

10 October 1994

We are not like other men. And when I say "we", I don't mean only men from Scotland: this affects England, Wales, Ireland, parts of North America and a few other places. Belgium perhaps.

The place is Grozny, capital of Checknya, after dark. In the dimly-lit lobby of the Caucasus Hotel, there is no sound save the low murmur of four women in leatherette armchairs and a correspondent dialling Moscow, unsuccessfully, over and over again.

There is a commotion at the doorway and another correspondent wanders in, fresh from the airport.

The two men greet each other warily. They have two things in common. They are both from the United Kingdom. They are both scruffs.

Unlike the new arrival, whose dress is best described as moderated grunge, the resident has made an effort. He is wearing a jacket. The jacket is OK, Fulham Road Market, beige, but the shoulder pads are loose, it's getting old, somewhat stained and crumpled.

It's tokenism. He's only pretending to be smart. Under the jacket is a creased denim shirt, a pair of frayed blue jeans, and, on his feet, the real giveaway: scored, mud-spattered hiking boots. But the Frenchman upstairs – ah, the Frenchman.

He shares our discomforts. He travelled on the same aeroplanes, by the same cars, to this grimy brown building with its odour of dusty bedcovers and its trickle of cold water. And he isn't crumpled. He walks the streets of Grozny in an immaculate teal-green blazer, creaseless fawn slacks and a smooth white cotton shirt. The shoes I forget; moccasins, I imagine. With the gleam of polish.

There are two issues here. How do they do it? And secondly: so what?

As far as the second goes, it would be interesting to trace the idea that to be scruffy is to be somehow holy: from anti-materialist Greek philosophers, through Christian and Marxist attitudes towards the ragged poor, through 20th-century glorifications of the proud starving artist-intellectual, until by the time I was a student it was accepted that to be scruffy was to identify, contradictorily, with champions of the masses and aloof Nietschzean outsiders at the same time, when, in fact, most of us were neither. We just had donkey jackets.

In an excellent television documentary some years ago about television images of the poor in Britain, Beatrix Campbell talked about the irritation producers felt when poor people they interviewed dressed well and looked good.

It's easy here in the former Soviet Union to commit parallel insults: such a poor land, such a dirty land – wear hiking boots and a lumberjack shirt at all times. Might there not be mud there? Might there not be war there? Why should they care that I dress like a slob when they have no money?

The idea that getting from Moscow to Grozny with a suit and tie is logarithmically more difficult than achieving the same feat going from Moscow to Edinburgh does not stand up. They do have coat-hangers in Chechnya.

You could justify interviewing President Djokhar Dudayev of Chechnya clad as if for a Sunday afternoon coffee in a student flat on the grounds that you care nothing for his tinpot trappings of power. But you would not expect him to come to your office in a lime-green synthetic fleece, a pair of jeans and scuffed Timberland boots, would you? The trouble is that, having decided not to be a scruffy traveller, the curse of your ethnic origins asserts itself. A scruff in a crumpled suit and tie looks worse than a scruff in denims.

There is always a crease that defeats me. The pale, awkward people from north-west Europe are surrounded, it seems, by a puckering of space-time which warps and crushes cloth and attracts dirt.

What was the Frenchman's secret? A rigid suitcase with hangers, and skilled packing? A travel iron? An arrangement with the leatherette Furies in the lobby? I know I could have all these things, put on the perfectly smooth clothes and within minutes have disruptive vortexes working away to crease and wrinkle. It's something you have to be brought up into. Our culture trapped us between the self-shabbifying elderly, the chaotic non-uniformity of school uniforms and the carousel of cheap fashion.

To put it another way: women stopped ironing our clothes for us and we couldn't be bothered to do it ourselves.

The only way we can avoid being scruffy, it seems, is to dress up – like the captain of the yacht club, like Terry Thomas, like Noel Coward. But a bow tie is too much for Grozny.

I'm afraid the token jacket stays – It's better than a parka.

Sporting chances

AND YES — THAT LOUD WHINING NOISE
FROM THE WILLIAMS RENAULT CAN ONLY
MEAN ONE THING — NIGEL MANSELL IS BACK

One kick away from the victory

GRAHAM LAW

7 February 1994

Graham Law examines the strategy which came so close to winning it for the home side.

The juggernaut of emotion was still careering along the Calcutta Cup fast lane as disbelieving spectators made their way to the Murrayfield exits after Scotland's 15–14 defeat in a contest which, although not overflowing with quality rugby, was the ultimate in theatre.

Sir William Sutherland, chief constable of Lothian and Borders police, turned to his companion in the SRU committee box and, perplexed by the game's cruel denouement, admitted: "Even our officers have discretion."

England had committed grand larceny courtesy of Jonathan Callard's injury-time penalty – controversially awarded by New Zealand referee Lindsay McLachlan for handling in a ruck after a tackle – and Scotland, who had played with the sort of demented fury which gave a nation back its pride, were scunnered.

Hard-headed realism also demands that today we should reflect that had Scotland landed penalty chances the near 50,000 souls would have been spared that painful finale and that the press, yours truly included, would have had much word-eating to do.

Alan Sharp, the Bristol loose-head prop who starred like a seasoned veteran rather than the debutant he was, sat in disbelief in the dressing room. A hard man who has had a few run-ins with Her Majesty's authorities, he was in tears.

He had reason to be. The attachment between nation and Scottish team which had all but severed in the wake of the miserable displays against New Zealand and Wales was restored with a gutsy vengeance. Here, however, let's not jump on the ex-internationalists' bandwagon and credit director of rugby Jim Telfer with everything short of the immaculate conception.

Telfer has frequently stressed that his role has been more of a watching brief. Apart from one session in the early preparation for the game, Scotland coaches Douglas Morgan and Richie Dixon – as Telfer related – have been directing operations.

Let's take two facets of their pre-match routines. Dixon asked his father-in-law in the Berwickshire port of Eyemouth to acquire a fishing net in order to instil in his charges' minds that they had to get lower on the drive.

Dixon had used a net in the past at Stirling County and, pegging it to the ground and setting it at a demanding height, he had his forwards going back and forth under it, hitting tackle bags when they emerged.

The quickly taken free-kick from Kenny Milne on the quarter-hour – when he took Ben Clarke with him as the Scottish pack made a dynamic wedge – was every bit as memorable as the Fin Calder tap penalty in the 1990 Grand Slam game and owed rather a lot to that Dixon drill.

Don't just take my word for it. Lock Shade Munro, who, cast as front-jumper after his excursion to the middle in Cardiff, looked very much the part, declared: "There has been a song and dance about who's done what. But that's just what it has been. Richie Dixon takes the forward sessions and he should get the credit. The reason we did so badly in Cardiff was our fault, not the coaches'."

Scotland's tackling has been brittle of late, but that charge could not be levelled at the weekend. Morgan had piloted live tackling, akin to a game of British Bulldog, during one session which had ended with a host of walking wounded.

Thus on Saturday we could marvel at some classical tackling. Kenny Logan's ninth-minute downing of Tony Underwood set the tone at a key stage in the game where England opened full throttle and matters seemed ominous.

Scott Hastings induced a turnover on Phil de Glanville with his stern engagement. Rob Wainwright, who completely over-shadowed Neil Back, bowled his opposite number over, spawning loose ball, which allowed Paul Burnell to show some soccer skills as he frightened the life out of Rob Andrew.

Gary Armstrong chopped the menacing Tony Underwood after the winger had countered, and Logan (on Carling) and Gavin

Hastings (on Martin Bayfield) indulged in further heroics, when Andrew's interception seemed likely to punish Townsend's one moment of indecision.

England's lineout, 12–4 up at the interval, was a shambles in the second half, Bracken being subjected to some nightmare tap ball, principally from Martin Bayfield. The Scottish lineout rediscovered much of last year's authority, taking the second-half count 13–6.

The scrummage, too, was a considerable improvement on Cardiff, much to the obvious pleasure of Armstrong, who preyed on Bracken like some emaciated wolf. The scrum-half, surprise, surprise, performed as if he had never been away.

His game was not totally error-free. He was briefly afflicted by the same "yahoo" obsession – shades of 1984 – with hoofing the ball downfield as Townsend and Gavin Hastings. Especially during a 20-minute spell in the second half there was a case for variation and movement, a point Morgan acknowledged.

Any criticism must be tempered, however, by the fact that Scotland were continuing to create considerable anxiety in English ranks, neither Callard nor the Underwood brothers personifying security under the barrage.

Armstrong, candid as ever, reckoned referee McLachlan had made the correct decision when he penalised the scrum-half for a second deliberate movement after John Hall had nailed him inches short of the English try line in the wake of an attacking first-half scrummage and television evidence vindicated that assessment.

England may have moved more ball than Scotland, but while the hosts were inclined to over-egg the pudding with high Garryowens, England equally demonstrated a form of tunnel vision with the secondary battering-ram assaults of the likes of Victor Ubogu and Ben Clarke.

There were occasions when it seemed quick spread might have been rather more effective.

Bottoms up for Scots in World Cup

ALAN FORBES

9 May 1994

Scotland will have a football team at the World Cup after all. Our team members are already lining up to have their bottoms polished for the occasion.

In the inch-high world of Subbuteo football a polished bottom is essential for that sliding tackle, the glide into open space and the spin on a sixpence. It beats legs any day.

Scotland's international stadium at Hampden Park was a seething cauldron of pent-up emotion yesterday as the nation's top 32 table football players battled it out to represent Scotland at the Subbuteo World Cup finals in Chicago in June. More than 30 people packed into the Queen's Park social club to witness deft skills of finger flicking.

In games of two halves, each lasting ten minutes, the players were whittled down to the final pair, old friends Kenny Scott, 21, and Derek Sansome, 18. This final was only the latest of several hundred matches that the pair have played against each other.

They live on the same street in Coatbridge and have spent many hours playing table football in Derek's father's garage. Yesterday's match, however, had high rewards – a trip to the United States and a chance to play against other footballing nations . . . which is more than our "real" football team can expect.

Kenny and Derek have won a similar number of victories against each other. Yesterday the game began with aggressive forward sliding by Derek's players, but Kenny's plastic goalie-on-a-stick made two miracle saves from close range.

In the third minute, however, Derek's players finally broke through Kenny's defensive shield and scored a dramatic goal (it was impossible to identify the scorer). The social club immediately resounded to applause.

At least one of Kenny's players hurtled to the floor (over 100ft, in terms of scale) in an effort to equalise. But to no avail as Derek emerged the victor and will fly to the US with his tiny team, in Scotland strip of course.

Also flying to the World Cup is Bob McGiffen, general secretary of the Scottish Subbuteo Association. He is a technical adviser to the international body, advising on new rules for the game.

Mr McGiffen said the game is competitive but good-natured. He admitted that some players had been known to get upset in defeat but there had been no sendings-off or reports to the procurator fiscal. Crowd trouble was unheard of, largely because the spectators are made of plastic and can be stuffed into a box.

Table football has not been immune from cheating, however. Alec Anderson, the company's Scottish salesman, revealed that some years ago players had added lead to their players' bottoms to add spin and weight to their tackles.

Mr Anderson also confessed that Subbuteo has been slow to introduce black players to its teams. That should be rectified within the year.

Another introduction will be players in Scotland's new strip. It seems the tartan design was difficult to copy in miniature.

223

A tactical team talk

BRIAN PENDREIGH

18 June 1994

In a traditional working men's bar in Glasgow, two Rangers fans are discussing who they will support in the World Cup finals. One says the Republic of Ireland. The other, momentarily lost for words, pretends to shoot him. "Holland," he says. He tells me about his divorce. And then he starts to cry.

Not just a watering of the eyes, but big tears rolling down his unshaven cheeks. He wipes them away with a crumpled cotton hankie. But more is to come. It is not unknown for someone to break down in tears during an interview, but it is usually in response to a more penetrating question than "Who will you support in the World Cup?"

For Scots, knowing who to support in the World Cup used to be a simple matter of patriotism. A generation grew up under the impression that Scotland always qualify. In recent tournaments there has been the added dimension of England's presence, with Scots offering passionate, though temporary, support to whoever they were playing. But who can Scots support this time in the absence of both Scotland and the Auld Enemy?

The World Cup finals are not without British interest. The Irish attack will be led in their opening game against Italy's millionaire footballers tonight by the Motherwell striker, Tommy Coyne, less than a year after his wife died and he quit football.

Coyne's is a remarkable story, combining the wish-fulfilment of *Roy of the Rovers* with the life-and-death drama of *Brookside*. Coyne was born in Glasgow and could have played for Scotland if they had wanted him. He won his first cap for Ireland at the relatively late age of 29 after manager Jack Charlton established he was eligible through his granny.

Coyne's life was shattered last summer by the death of his wife shortly after the birth of their third child. He walked out on his club, Tranmere Rovers, and came back to Scotland with his children, before returning to football six months ago after a cut-price transfer to Motherwell. In April, he scored the goal that gave Ireland a historic away win in Holland.

"Tommy Coyne is going to score a hat-trick, with two overhead kicks," says Andy Galloway, an arithmetically-challenged trainee electrical engineer from Motherwell. "Most of the games, I want the underdogs to win. I'm fed up with Germany and Argentina." Anything else? "Respect to the Motherwell posse."

Coyne's presence in the Irish squad has stirred interest in Motherwell even among those who do not normally follow football. "I'm not a football fan," says Stephen Cogan, "but I'll watch some of it for the spectacle. I'll probably give Bobby Charlton's side my support," he adds, as if to illustrate the limit of his interest.

"I'm happy to see Tommy being there," he adds. Cogan might get his Charltons confused, but in Motherwell Tommy Coyne has achieved that status where a single forename suffices, like Elvis and Marilyn.

Coyne is one of two Glaswegians in Ireland's squad – the other is Ray Houghton of Aston Villa – and one of three ex-Celtic players – the others being Tony Cascarino and Pat Bonner, a favourite at Parkhead for years who will probably play for Kilmarnock next season.

Joe Callaghan, a 30-year-old council cleansing worker, is a Celtic fan who will support Ireland. "I'm going over there," he says. To America? "To Dublin, I'm going to Dublin to watch the Italy game." But the game is in America? Callaghan is off to Dublin to watch it on television, along with 13 other members of the Motherwell Celtic supporters club. "It's a better atmosphere."

His grandparents were Irish and he considers himself half-Irish, half-Scots. Hundreds of thousands of Scots have Irish blood. Celtic was founded by Irish immigrants and the Irish tricolour flies over Parkhead. Would fans of other teams be so ready to back Jack's lads – Rangers fans for example?

The Rosevale bar in Partick is a famous "Rangers shop". "Traditional ales and spirits," it says above the entrance. The customers are all men, the bar staff all women. Do they have LA? "No."

The first two customers to whom I spoke said they would support Ireland. "Jack Charlton is doing what the Scottish team should have done. He doesn't give a shit about fancy football. He just goes in there and gets results," says Bill Browne.

"I think they'll get to the quarter-finals," says Charles Brennan. Browne says: "With a bit of luck the semis, because he's got his Weetabix with him." "Shredded Wheat," interjects Wilie Daly. But it turns out Browne and Brennan are Celtic fans. Daly is a Rangers fan.

Will he support Ireland against Italy? "Twenty-two Catholics? I'd have to be neutral." What if Ireland were playing Holland? "I would need to support the Dutch," he says. Why? Someone else volunteers the name William of Orange as if talking about some particularly attractive Dutch play-maker. Daly seems to acquiesce.

Bobby McLean and Samuel Cameron Baillie are standing silently at the bar with their pints. McLean resembles George C Scott, Baillie looks a little like Reg Varney from *On the Buses*. There are red marks on his shirt like blood.

McLean would support Ireland. "They're the nearest team to

us," he says. He also likes Brazil. "Holland," says Baillie. Not Ireland? "No." He is not influenced by the local connections? "You keep reverting back to Ireland," he says. "I think you're Irish . . . I bet you've an Irish name," he says.

He requests proof of identity. "Plenderleith or something. Alright . . . You must support the Protestant team." He smiles. "I was only making a joke there.

"I want to see Holland win, but see this pub team across the other side of the water . . . I'm not going to mention the word, but it begins with I. They didn't get there on merit." Baillie expounds his theory of an international Catholic conspiracy, involving English nuns signalling to Nazi bombers and a Polish referee sending off Mark Hateley to stop Rangers winning the European Cup.

One thing leads to another. "Two pints and a Coke, please." He tells me about his divorce, keen to air his grievance. He cries, he laughs, he puts his arm on my shoulder and wants to make sure I have his name correct. "Samuel Cameron Baillie."

On the outskirts of Edinburgh, the Gyle shopping centre is full of old women with no opinion about the World Cup and couples with children, like William and Lisa Tutty. They are Hearts fans. "I think most people in Scotland will be supporting Northern Ireland," says William Tutty. He corrects himself. "The Republic of Ireland."

"You can almost compare them with Scotland. They are a small country. I think in general people go for the underdogs . . . and I think being close at hand."

Lisa Tutty says: "I would support Ireland because it's a British country and it's not England." William Tutty: "It would be nice to get some new blood . . . It was good to see Cameroon almost beat England last time. In all honesty I would like to see America doing well."

There is a difference between supporting England's opponents and wanting Ireland to lose. If England had not had the misfortune of getting cuffed by Holland and Norway they would be one of the best teams in the World Cup, probably *the* best, and their commentators would be happy to explain why, at great length.

By the sort of fluke that keeps cropping up when you play games on grass instead of paper, Ireland are there instead. Like Cameroon they are underdogs. While Italy draws heavily from European club champions AC Milan, Ireland calls on players from Portsmouth, Bolton and Motherwell.

Deciding who to support in the World Cup is not just a question of football. Geography and religion come into it. But most Scots will, quite simply, back the team expected to lose. After all that is what we have done in the last five World Cups.

Uncertain squad to face Freuchie

SARAH CHALMERS

25 June 1994

Grant Laing thrust his hands into the pockets of his oil-stained overalls and shifted the weight from one foot to another as he pondered the question: What is his greatest concern about tomorrow's cricket match against Freuchie?

Car mechanics at Spittalfield are not used to providing the media with sound-bites and the 31-year-old captain was momentarily stumped. Then it came to him. His eyes opened wide and he let out a belly laugh, exclaiming: "Our biggest worry is if everybody turns up."

At Glendelvine, cricket is a serious business when a match is in play: the rest of the time it is a good excuse to go to the pub. But tomorrow the tiny Perthshire club is pitted against the mighty Freuchie, one of Scotland's most dedicated clubs, in the Scottish final of the British Village championship.

And the captain's concern over numbers is a legitimate one. Not all of the team can play on Saturday and Sunday every weekend. Two weeks ago, by the Saturday night, only eight people had committed themselves to Sunday's game at Huntly.

Undeterred, Mr Laing commandeered a couple of local lads at the pub, too inebriated to realise what they had agreed to, who turned up next morning at 8:30 complete with white sweatshirts and a bottle of Irn Bru, to give it their best shot. The team lost, but the crack at the pub made up for it.

And to be fair, a sense of humour may be one of the few weapons Glendelvine's David has against Freuchie's Goliath. The Fife club became the first Scottish team to win the national championship at Lords in 1985 and made it to the final again last year.

They are regularly in the final of the Scottish section and now boast six teams. They have a professional coach and practise religiously several times a week.

Glendelvine, on the other hand, usually have to wait until the morning of a match to see if they can produce one team (once the local farm-workers know if they are working that day). Their only coach is the four-wheeled one which transports them to their away matches, and their star player is David Brown, 56, a former welder who gave up his job because he was bothered with his back and knees.

Glendelvine itself is not even a village but an estate, owned by Sir Gavin Lyle. In 1921, the then laird, Alexander Lyle, a keen sportsman, gave a portion of land to form a cricket ground.

The ground lies halfway between the tiny villages of Caputh and Spittalfield and is reached via a gap in the hedge which opens up to reveal a partially pebbled track leading to the ground, and a blue and white wooden hut (with matching scorebox) which serves as a clubhouse.

Sandy Baird, 44, a council worker and team player, goes to the ground most evenings to look after the wicket and keep it free of rabbits. His father Eck looks after the outfield and has been the scorer for more than 25 years and his late mother Jessie used to make the teas.

Glendelvine will enjoy themselves tomorrow and if they win, that will be a bonus. But they are not quite the rookie team they claim to be. They made it to the Scottish final in 1972 and again last year. Then they had Freuchie struggling at 64 for four when the unfortunate Russell Brown ("no relation", insists David Brown) dropped a catch.

They are taking the team mascot – their supporter of more than 30 years, Jock Tait – on the bus for moral support. But if all else fails, there's always next year, by which time, as Mr Laing points out: "Freuchie might be too big to qualify as a village of under 3,000 whereas Spittalfield will be lucky to get above 200 residents."

Foundering in the wake of high fashion

IAN WOOD

3 July 1994

A feature of fashion is that those who actually follow it are blind to how daft it can make them look. Daft, that is, to anyone who has lived long enough to see fashions come and go and be in a position to make valid comparisons.

I have seen many comings and goings and while untouched by most of them – red flannel next to the skin is my motto and if it isn't falling apart, wear it – I have taken note and reckon I know a disaster when I see one.

There was a day when Wimbledon was, sartorially speaking, pretty safe. Everyone came out in pristine white, looking like so many glasses of milk and very summery and restful it all was. This changed with the onset of professionalism and gradually the eye became programmed to accept, without shrinking excessively, splashes of colour, lurid logos, baseball hats and risque shirt-changing scenes beneath the umpire's chair. However, in one of my increasingly rare glimpses of the tennis extravaganza the other day, I chanced to see Andre Agassi, the hunky Californian and darling of the shrieking teenies, strutting his stuff against somebody or other. Like a man jolted out of a deep sleep, I awoke, as WS Gilbert would have it, with a shudder despairing.

The boy looked like last week's washing with hair. The peaked hat was of the type which might be worn – and quite possibly had been – by someone who has come about the drains. The shirt billowed free like the snapping sails of an ocean-going clipper and the shorts went on for ever.

In the midst of this milling mass of superfluous material, there flashed from time to time an earring. It could have been Blackbeard the Pirate coming home from a Halloween party. The point is, though, that no-one among the crowd or the officials, fell about laughing.

His opponent, whoever he was, didn't laugh either, but then I wouldn't have expected him to. They're so self-centred and po-faced in that game these days he probably didn't notice the apparition at the other side of the net. As far as most of them are concerned, Goofy could be preparing to receive on the baseline and they'd just grunt like shunting engines and go ahead and serve.

In fact, to take a positive line, the general acceptance of Agassi and his abundance of millinery may point to a more tolerant attitude in society generally and that is surely a good thing. After all, there was a day when somebody in his state would have been escorted from the place and directed to the nearest Salvation Army hostel.

The antidote to the tennis was immediately to hand in the form of the World Cup, which, as you'd expect, was being expertly analysed by expert analysts. As John Motson, covering Ireland's game with Norway put it: "Here goes David Kelly for his first activity," which was probably true, but quaint.

Kelly was later reported to be "hovering for Ireland", which is quite a trick and, indeed, made me wonder whether perhaps I'd picked it up wrongly and that, in fact, Kelly had been hoovering for Ireland, which would have been at once intriguing and commendable in this environmentally-conscious age.

Liam Brady then chipped in to say what a disgrace Norway were and how much better off we'd all be without them. "It would be a tragedy if Norway went through," he said, "they've done nothing for this tournament."

High moral tone having been set, Liam then spoiled things somewhat by congratulating Gary Kelly for a dirty foul. "It was a cynical foul, but a good one," chirped Liam. "It was a good break and the lad did well to bring him down." Who knows, Norway might have played better if people hadn't kept tripping them up every time they made a good break.

Anyway, Ireland went through, Norway went out. The way was clear for Motson to adapt the famous spiel once delivered by a Norwegian commentator at England's expense and yell: "Gro Brunteland, King Harald, Edward Grieg, Thor Heyerdahl, Henrik Ibsen – your boys have taken a hell of a beating." Sadly, he didn't.

Tricolours, tartan and tipples: a universal language

RUTH WISHART

4 July 1994

Rosie O'Grady's was queued round the door, and Paddy O'Reilly's ten thirsty blocks further down town. But sure and wasn't there Houlihan's bar right around the next corner where a Scottish soccer fan, with the misfortune not to have located an Irish granny as yet, could still find a welcome in the parlour.

Every TV set in the place, and there seemed to be one for every dozen customers, was replaying the match that ensured the Emerald Isle a Fourth of July party back in Orlando today.

Martin Kelly is clutching a Guinness and a girlfriend and watching Jack's lads all over again not sure whether to laugh or cry. The grand news is his team are staying in America after all. The bad news is he came here on a ten-day special and will be flying home before the kick-off.

One of his mates has solved the problem by going home and coming back again. Seems he thought it cheaper to spend two days in the air than in Florida and he may just be right.

Still, at least Martin has seen one match in Orlando. Just his luck it was the Mexican game rather than the day the Irish had the waiters weeping in New York's Little Italy.

Still and all, hadn't there been the bonus of meeting his long lost sister, Margaret Kelly Gergan, now based in Boston, but driving to the matches in what had once been a yellow school bus.

Now tastefully resprayed in green, white and gold, it serves as a kind of mobile tricolour. Margaret had called her little brother just before he left home 40 miles from Dublin. Where was he staying in Florida, she needed to know. Somehow that part of the game plan didn't seem to have been filled in. Not to worry, she told him. Meet me in Mulvaney's bar. And, somehow or other, he did.

The Irish bars have served as party HQ, social club, source of unsolicited tactical advice to the team, and general magnet for both native and visiting fans. By midnight, Houlihan's had acquired a Dundonian piper, whose credentials as the cabaret for the evening, while not impeccable, were much enhanced by the announcement that he'd married a Kerry girl.

By the time they'd finished their first-round ties, Jack's army had underscored what a cosmopolitan lot they could be in the matter of international sartorial relations. Here a viking helmet, there a sombrero, and a few flags from vanquished nations draped across shoulders like the spoils of war.

For those of us cheerfully permitted to transfer in from the tartan army, the experience of the last week has deviated markedly from the advance script.

On the coach to the decisive Norwegian game I reflected aloud how remarkable it was to be travelling to a World Cup tie without that familiar gut-wrenching suspicion that the team would again contrive to unravel in spectacularly embarrassing fashion.

It didn't quite work like that. Scotland being out keeps the central nervous system in check only until you get to the stadium and see the Irish fans partying in the car park.

Seeing those banners, watching those faces, hearing those chants and all trace of supposed neutrality vanishes.

And you're not alone, Lads from Glasgow, Clydebank, Shetland, and exiled scots from Toronto, are to be found among the new conscripts in my small corner of the stadium. One or two of them clearly in mid-identity crisis since they're wearing Ireland team shirts but waving lion rampants. Know how you feel boys.

Julie from Chicago sat next to me that game. Julie from Chicago is supposedly a sports writer, but at odd moments you wonder if she's entirely au fait with events down below. When can he come on again, she asks brightly when Aldridge is subbed. Isn't it nice, she says, that so many people she's met from Britain have adopted

Ireland as their team. Especially with England not qualifying. It must, says Julie, have been so disappointing that England wasn't able to make the trip.

I contemplate trying to explain to Julie how effortless it has proved to keep disappointment at bay, but it would have taken too long. Besides, why spoil her illusions about the Scots loving all their neighbours with equal fervour. The other team enjoying my support, since you ask, is the USA. Not because their skills are comparable to the South Americans, or because their organisation rivals the Germans.

But with all the major sports still dominating the headlines here – they were even still playing ice hockey this month – it's been tough to wean local sports fans from their regular brews.

Now the Americans who have stayed faithful to the dream of making soccer a high profile addition to the sporting calendar, the stalwarts who are trying for a second time to launch a professional soccer league, have finally got their reward.

Today's Independence Day match against Brazil at Stanford University near San Francisco is a glamorous encounter for Team USA in anyone's language. I'll be there. But even in San Francisco . . . I've left my heart in Orlando.

233

South African Cricket

MIKE AITKEN

11 July 1994

It was 43 years ago that South Africa last played cricket in Glasgow. Much may have changed on the political front since 1951, but the Scottish weather remains a constant. When South Africa visited Hamilton Crescent that summer there was no play on the first day until after lunch and the final day was washed out. It rained at Titwood yesterday and when it didn't rain it poured.

Such is the enthusiasm of the South Africans, who rejoined

the international cricketing family in 1992, they were actually prepared to bat for 50 overs on a sodden pitch that was demonstrably unplayable. Faced with similar conditions, I don't think an English county side would have ventured off the coach.

"We want to play cricket" acknowledged Fritz Being, South Africa's manager, who sent Andrew Hudson and Gary Kirsten out to bat in a drizzle at 10:45am prompt. The pair lasted for three overs, made six runs, and then the covers came out just before 11am. The tourists wanted to come back out at 2:30 pm and provide some entertainment for the stalwarts in the crowd as well as gaining some much needed batting practice. South Africa have played one rain-free match only against Sussex, in the past fortnight and with the first Test at Lord's set for a week on Thursday, they'd like to take off their waterproofs. The players did come out at 2:50 and batted for a further ten minutes, adding a single run. In all, 5.1 overs were bowled before common sense prevailed and play was abandoned at 3pm. It was the shortest one-day international in Scottish cricket history.

Around 1,000 enthusiastic fans had huddled under multi-coloured umbrellas and were entertained by youngsters playing quick-cricket, the junior game which substitutes plastic bats and balls for the real thing. It would have been interesting to see how briskly Allan Donald, the fastest white bowler in the world, might have fared with a bit of plastic. To be fair, Donald Duck would probably have struggled to survive the deluge at Titwood.

The elements denied Scottish fans the opportunity to see in action Allan Donald, the world's fastest white bowler, who can toss the ball through the air at a chilling 85mph. Not that the 27-year-old, who plays for Warwickshire and has earned a ferocious reputation in 14 Test matches, thinks that power is everything. "That speed was clocked at the World Cup in Christchurch, but it means nothing," he said. "A lot of people have asked me where I get my speed from and I usually say that if I analyse it then the pace comes from rhythm and timing."

"Speak to any bowling coach about Malcolm Marshall (the West Indian fast bowler) and none would describe his action as quick, but he was strong and had a natural rhythm. "To be a fast bowler today you need to be athletic and you need timing." While the weather in Britain doesn't provide the ideal conditions to nurture seam bowlers, Donald reckons that the sheer volume of cricket played in England works against the emergence of a genuine speed merchant. "In the last six to eight years you've not seen any fast English bowlers because they play far too much cricket," he argued. "People get burned out and there is too much chopping and changing in the England team. No-one gets a chance to be moulded into an England side or to become a consistent member. "It's so sad to see so many different players coming and going. I don't think you can build a Test team that way."

As far as the county scene is concerned, even a player of Brian Lara's undisputed talent is beginning to find life a bit of a struggle. Donald had spoken to Lara the other day and reported: "He's finding it really tough. He now knows how demanding county cricket is. When we chatted, he said: 'I can't believe you've played county cricket for seven years. I really admire you for that'.

"The native of Bloemfontein at one point thought about throwing in his hat with England, but was persuaded to bide his time with the promise of change around the corner. Ali Bacher, the managing-director of the United South African cricket-board, told him to be patient. "I didn't believe that so much change could come so quickly, but I made the right choice and I'm very happy about it."

Donald shares the pride in achievement of all South African sportsmen and as one who spends a lot of time coaching black youngsters he reckons that within the next five years a multi-racial South African team will send shock-waves through the test cricket scene. By that time, Allan Donald may have found a Scottish great-granny in his ancestry and we might persuade him in the twilight of his career to play for us. A kindly South African had asked Fritz Bing if any of the team had Scottish relations. When he replied "no", the journalist said that the manager himself must have a Scottish connection. "After all," he grinned, "you never buy a drink . . ."

235
•

Ferguson defends foreign influence

HUGH KEEVINS

21 October 1994

The cosmopolitan approach to football embraced by Manchester
United's manager is under threat from the game's legislators.

Manchester United's spectacular 2-2 draw with Barcelona on
Wednesday restored the spectator's belief in the game and confirmed, if confirmation was needed, that the Old Trafford side are
at the forefront of English football's regeneration.

From a Scottish perspective, the distressing thought is that
there is not one Premier Division player who would get a game
with United on a weekly basis. That is perhaps the most chilling
comparison that can be made between their football and our own.

Of course, it's a Scot, Alex Ferguson, who is running the show
at Old Trafford, and judging by his casual dress and the obvious
omission to brush his hair before he arrived at the Cliff, United's
training ground, the manager had spent a fitful night reliving a
European Champions League tie that had fired his imagination.

Hotel arrangements for Sunday's Premiership game with
Blackburn Rovers were made as he spoke – "Get me Roy Evans
on the phone. He was there with Liverpool last week". Breakfast
was consumed at the same time.

With no break in his momentum – "If the crowd reacted like
that every week, we'd win ten league titles," he told the local
evening paper – Ferguson proceeded to address everything from
the reasons for renaissance to the absence of Scots in his team.

"Strikers have given the Premiership a higher profile," he
began. "Jurgen Klinsmann's at Spurs; Newcastle have Andy
Cole and Peter Beardsley; Chris Sutton and Alan Shearer are at
Blackburn. And we have our two."

Our two happen to be Eric Cantona and Mark Hughes, a Frenchman and a Welshman who will, if the game's legislators have their way, be gradually driven out of the game in England over a three-year period.

Ferguson takes seriously the moves from the Professional Footballers' Association to seek to limit club sides to three foreign players, which is now the maximum allowed by UEFA in European ties.

"Unless they are careful, and the FA has to bear its share of the responsibility for supporting this idea as well, this plan could bring about the death of English football and with it the aspirations of youngsters from Ireland and Wales, too.

"The Irish, north and south, have no professional leagues of their own and the Welsh dabble in the English League.

"What the legislators forget, too, is the contribution that has been made to the good of the game by foreign players for two decades, starting with Ossie Ardiles and coming up to the present day with our own Andrei Kanchelskis and Cantona. They have brought people out to games."

There was no mention of Scots, young or old, for the simple reason that legislation of another type precludes the possibility of a compatriot for Ferguson, unless he is bought from another club for a substantial fee.

"Scottish clubs work hard at fixing up the best youngsters on 'S' forms when they are about 13 years old," he says.

"The rules state that I, or any other English manager, must wait until they have left school before we can make an approach to anyone.

"It's a pity because the game with Barcelona showed the peak that any player would want to reach in his career."

It was also 90 minutes' worth of proof that the Premiership is capable of producing sides able to live with the best on the continent, and explains the growth in attendances at domestic matches.

"The standard has improved significantly over the seven years I have been here. When I came down from Aberdeen, Leeds United, Blackburn and Newcastle weren't even in the top division.

"Europe, though, is *the* platform on which to play. Wednesday night was about technical excellence; quickness of thought and control.

"It is now possible to play really well and lose a game in the

Champions League and that is why Manchester United's ambitions as far as the cup is concerned come down to the level of application we achieve in the Nou Camp Stadium on 2 November.

"The ability is there. That much is unquestionable. Now I need a superb defensive performance and luck given the injuries to the Englishmen."

It is regrettable that the club who last won the European Cup when they had a Scot in charge (Matt Busby) could find room only for Denis Law and Paddy Crerand in radio and television commentary boxes on Wednesday, but none on the pitch for players.

An even bigger regret is that Ferguson probably could not think of one he would buy from a Premier Division club.

Hopefully, for the greater good of the game in Scotland, it is only a temporary condition.

High time to settle some old scores

NORMAN MAIR

24 October 1994

It took the octogenarian Stewart Crerar, a former Edinburgh University scrum-half, no time at all to point out something which had escaped the combined savvy of the members of the International Rugby football board. Namely, that the coming of the five-point try, with its corollary of the seven-point goal, would be ruinous in all too much of the rugby of the younger fry.

He was rapidly proved right as scores mounted astronomically and so many games had to be cut short out of mercy that in some schools it became something of an event for one to go the distance.

As Crerar had forecast, some lads were so discouraged they did not want to play the following week. A team who, early on, found themselves trailing by three goals in a rugby match were after all 21-0 down and were apt to be feeling thrice as sorry for themselves as the side on the neighbouring soccer pitch who were similarly three goals to the bad.

For long an inveterate watcher of school and club rugby, Crerar eventually had his point acknowledged. The scoring in the age-group rugby of S2 and below was changed.

Now it is three points for a try and only one point for any form of successful kick. The latter is a very relevant consideration because, as Merchiston's Frank Hadden was remarking just last week, so often in the more lopsided junior games the try-scorer ends up running round behind the posts.

Nor has the five-point try been without its critics at senior level. As Gavin Hastings stresses in his autobiography, it has meant "that teams have deliberately and cynically conceded the penalty rather than risk having seven points scored against them, a matter which the All Blacks exploited in the UK in 1993.

"To combat that," continues Hastings, "Scotland, in their experimental law changes at the end of the 1993–94 season, changed the try from five points to three points, with one point for the conversion, so that a goaled try became four points and the penalty three in order that the differential would not be as great."

The so-called professional foul, by that or any other name, was not really an issue in bygone days, but not just because standards of sportsmanship were supposedly higher. Simply that, with the penalty goal worth the same as a try – three points apiece – there was scant incentive, save perhaps when the conversion of a try would make the difference.

For my own part, I should much rather have seen the old scoring values for a try retained, but with the scope of the differential penalty greatly extended. Above all, nothing has happened in recent years – in fact very much the reverse – to alter a long-held conviction that there should be a penalty spot bang in front of the posts for foul play *anywhere on the field*. Why, with their recent problems with dirty play, and the barrage of harmful publicity it has detonated, the IRFB have not tried such a penalty spot, beats me.

As noted so often before, the culprit, instead of being seen, as he so often is, as a bit of a hero, a hard man, very macho, would be spotlighted as, say, "the bloody idiot who cost us three points when we were in their 22 and looking like scoring".

What is more, that is no longer mere surmise. The SRU's Iain Goodall, the only man I know who has actually refereed a match with such a penalty spot in operation, will tell you that that is precisely what was being said as the offender's side trooped back . . .

There is, of course, a moratorium on law changes until after the World Cup, but the IRFB, following their meeting in Vancouver, announced a further amendment to the already vastly-improved experimental ruck/maul law.

Now, when the ball becomes unplayable at a ruck, the put-in at the ensuing scrum will no longer necessarily go to the team moving forward immediately prior to the ruck, but to the side going forward at the time of the stoppage.

The thinking, obviously, is to tempt players, who might other-wise hang off, thereby further populating the defence, to come in and hit the ruck so hard that even if possession is stillborn, they will have been the side going forward when the whistle blew.

If you fancy you can detect the hand of Scotland and, more specifically, of their director of rugby, Jim Telfer, in this latest amendment, you may give yourself ten out of ten.